grzimek's
Student Animal Life Resource

● ● ● ●

grzimek's
Student Animal Life Resource

• • • •

Reptiles
volume 1

Turtles to Wormlizards

Leslie A. Mertz, PhD, author

Madeline S. Harris, project editor
Neil Schlager and Jayne Weisblatt, editors

THOMSON

GALE

Detroit • New York • San Francisco • San Diego • New Haven, Conn. • Waterville, Maine • London • Munich

Grzimek's Student Animal Life Resource: Reptiles

Leslie A. Mertz, PhD

Project Editor
Madeline S. Harris

Editorial
Kathleen J. Edgar, Melissa Hill, Heather Price

Indexing Services
Synapse, the Knowledge Link Corporation

Rights and Acquisitions
Sheila Spencer, Mari Masalin-Cooper

Imaging and Multimedia
Randy Bassett, Michael Logusz, Dan Newell, Chris O'Bryan, Robyn Young

Product Design
Tracey Rowens, Jennifer Wahi

Composition
Evi Seoud, Mary Beth Trimper

Manufacturing
Wendy Blurton, Dorothy Maki

LIBRARY OF CONGRESS CATALOGING-IN-PUBLICATION DATA

Mertz, Leslie A.
Grzimek's student animal life resource. Reptiles / Leslie A. Mertz ; edited by Neil Schlager and Jayne Weisblatt.
    p. cm.
Includes bibliographical references and index.
ISBN 0-7876-9404-5 (hardcover set : alk. paper) — ISBN 0-7876-9405-3 (volume 1) — ISBN 0-7876-9406-1 (volume 2)
1. Reptiles—Juvenile literature. I. Schlager, Neil, 1966- II. Weisblatt, Jayne. III. Title.
QL644.2.M427 2005
597.9—dc22   2005000033

ISBN 0-7876-9402-9 (21-vol set), ISBN 0-7876-9404-5 (2-vol set), ISBN 0-7876-9405-3 (vol 1), ISBN 0-7876-9406-1 (vol 2)

This title is also available as an e-book
Contact your Thomson Gale sales representative for ordering information.

Printed in Canada
10 9 8 7 6 5 4 3 2 1

Contents

Reader's Guide

Grzimek's Student Animal Life Resource: Reptiles offers readers comprehensive and easy-to-use information on Earth's reptiles. Order entries provide an overview of a group of families, and family entries provide an overview of a particular family. Entries are arranged by taxonomy, the science through which living things are classified into related groups. Each entry includes sections on physical characteristics; geographic range; habitat; diet; behavior and reproduction; animals and people; and conservation status. All entries are followed by one or more species accounts with the same information as well as a range map and photo or illustration for each species. Entries conclude with a list of books, periodicals, and Web sites that may be used for further research.

ADDITIONAL FEATURES

Each volume of *Grzimek's Student Animal Life Resource: Reptiles* includes a pronunciation guide for scientific names, a glossary, an overview of Reptiles, a list of species in the set by biome, a list of species by geographic range, and an index. The set has 180 full-color maps, photos, and illustrations to enliven the text, and sidebars provide additional facts and related information.

NOTE

Grzimek's Student Animal Life Resource: Reptiles has standardized information in the Conservation Status section. The IUCN Red List provides the world's most comprehensive inventory of the global conservation status of plants and animals. Using a set of criteria to evaluate extinction risk, the IUCN recognizes the following categories: Extinct, Extinct in the Wild, Critically Endangered, Endangered, Vulnerable, Conservation Dependent, Near Threatened, Least Concern, and Data Deficient. These terms are defined where they are used in the text, but for a complete explanation of each category, visit the IUCN web page at http://www.iucn.org/themes/ssc/redlists/RLcats2001booklet.html.

ACKNOWLEDGEMENTS

Gale would like to thank several individuals for their assistance with this set. Leslie Mertz wrote the vast majority of the text; Linda Patricia Kite also wrote a few articles. At Schlager Group Inc., Neil Schlager and Jayne Weisblatt coordinated the writing and editing of the set, while Marcia Merryman Means and Leah Tieger also provided valuable assistance.

Special thanks are also due for the invaluable comments and suggestions provided by the *Grzimek's Student Animal Life Resource: Reptiles* advisors:

- Mary Alice Anderson, Media Specialist, Winona Middle School, Winona, Minnesota
- Thane Johnson, Librarian, Oklahoma City Zoo, Oklahoma City, Oklahoma
- Debra Kachel, Media Specialist, Ephrata Senior High School, Ephrata, Pennsylvania
- Nina Levine, Media Specialist, Blue Mountain Middle School, Courtlandt Manor, New York
- Ruth Mormon, Media Specialist, The Meadows School, Las Vegas, Nevada

COMMENTS AND SUGGESTIONS

We welcome your comments on *Grzimek's Student Animal Life Resource: Reptiles* and suggestions for future editions of this work. Please write: Editors, *Grzimek's Student Animal Life Resource: Reptiles*, U•X•L, 27500 Drake Rd., Farmington Hills, Michigan 48331-3535; call toll free: 1-800-877-4253; fax: 248-699-8097; or send e-mail via www.gale.com.

Pronunciation Guide for Scientific Names

Acanthophis antarcticus uh-KAN-thuh-fuhs ant-ARK-tih-kuhs

Acrochordidae AK-ruh-KOR-duh-dee

Acrochordus granulatus AK-ruh-KOR-duhs GRAN-yoo-LAH-tuhs

Agama hispida uh-GAM-uh HIH-spih-duh

Agamidae uh-GAM-uh-dee

Agamodon anguliceps uh-GAM-uh-don AN-guh-LIH-seps

Agkistrodon piscivorus ag-KIS-truh-DON PIH-sih-VER-uhs

Alligator mississippiensis AL-uh-GAY-der MIS-uh-SIP-ee-EN-suhs

Alligatoridae AL-uh-guh-TOR-uh-dee

Amphisbaena alba AM-fus-BEE-nuh AL-buh

Amphisbaenidae AM-fus-BEE-nuh-dee

Anguidae ANG-gwuh-dee

Aniliidae AN-uh-LY-uh-dee

Anilius scytale AN-uh-LY-uhs SY-tuh-lee

Anolis carolinensis uh-NOH-luhs kar-uh-LINE-en-sis

Anomalepididae uh-NOM-uh-luh-PID-uh-dee

Anomochilidae AN-uh-moh-KIL-uh-dee

Anomochilus leonardi AN-uh-moh-KIL-uhs LEE-oh-nar-DY

Apalone spinifera uh-PAL-uh-nee SPIH-nih-FER-uh

Aspidites melanocephalus a-SPID-uh-teez MEL-uh-noh-SEF-uh-luhs

Atractaspididae at-TRAK-tuh-SPID-uh-dee

Atractaspis bibronii at-TRAK-tuh-spuhs bib-ROH-nee-EYE

Bachia bresslaui buh-KEE-uh BREZ-lou-eye

Bipedidae by-PED-uh-dee

Bipes biporus BY-peez by-POR-uhs

Boa constrictor constrictor BOH-uh kun-STRIK-ter kun-STRIK-ter

Boidae BOH-uh-dee

Bolyeriidae boh-LY-uh-REE-uh-dee

Brookesia perarmata broo-KEEZ-ee-uh per-ARM-uh-tuh

Caiman crocodilus KAY-mun KRAH-kuh-DIL-uhs

Cape ctenosaura hemilopha KAYP STEN-uh-SOR-uh heh-MIL-uh-fuh

Caretta caretta kuh-RED-uh kuh-RED-uh

Carettochelyidae kuh-RED-oh-kuh-LY-uh-dee

Carettochelys insculpta kuh-RED-oh-KUH-leez in-SKULP-tuh

Casarea dussumieri KAY-suh-REE-uh duh-SOO-mee-AIR-eye

Cerastes cerastes suh-ROS-teez suh-ROS-teez

Chamaeleo chamaeleon kuh-MEE-lee-OH kuh-MEE-lee-ON

Chamaeleo jacksonii kuh-MEE-lee-OH JAK-suh-NEE-eye

Chamaeleonidae kuh-MEE-lee-ON-uh-dee

Chelidae KEL-uh-dee

Chelonia mydas kuh-LON-ee-uh MY-duhs

Cheloniidae KEL-uh-NY-uh-dee

Chelus fimbriatus KEL-uhs fim-bree-AH-tuhs

Chelydra serpentina kuh-LIH-druh ser-pen-TEE-nuh

Chelydridae kuh-LIH-druh-dee

Chlamydosaurus kingii kluh-MID-uh-SOR-uhs KIN-jee-eye

Chrysemys picta KRY-suh-meez PIK-tuh

Cistoclemmys flavomarginata sis-TOK-luh-meez FLAV-uh-MAR-gih-NAH-tuh

Cnemidophorus sexlineatus snuh-MID-uh-FOR-uhs SEKS-lih-NEE-ah-tuhs

Coleonyx variegates KOH-lee-ON-iks VAIR-ee-uh-GAH-teez

Colubridae kuh-LOO-bruh-dee

Corallus caninus koh-RAL-is kay-NINE-uhs

Cordylidae kor-DIL-uh-dee

Curucia zebrata kuh-ROO-shee-uh zee-BRAH-tuh

Crocodilians KRAH-kuh-DIL-ee-unz

Crocodilurus lacertinus KRAH-kuh-DIL-oor-uhs luh-SER-duh-nuhs

Crocodylidae KRAH-kuh-DIL-uh-dee

Crocodylus acutus KRAH-kuh-DIL-uhs uh-KYOO-tuhs

Crocodylus niloticus KRAH-kuh-DIL-uhs NY-lah-TIH-kuhs

Crotalus horridus KROH-tuh-luhs hoh-RID-uhs

Cylindrophiidae suh-LIN-druh-FEE-uh-dee

Cylindrophis rufus suh-LIN-druh-FIS ROO-fuhs

Dermatemydidae DER-muh-tuh-MID-uh-DEE

Dermatemys mawii der-muh-TEH-mis muh-WEE-eye

Dermochelyidae DER-muh-kuh-LY-uh-dee

Dermochelys coriacea DER-muh-KEL-eez KOH-ree-ah-SEE-uh

Dibamidae dy-BAH-muh-dee

Dibamus bourreti dy-BAH-muhs BOOR-uh-ty

Dispholidus typus DIS-fuh-LEE-duhs TY-puhs

Draco volans DRAY-koh VOH-lunz

Drymarchon corais DRIH-mar-kun KOR-ray

Elapidae uh-LOP-uh-dee

Emydidae uh-MID-uh-dee

Eumeces laticeps YOO-muh-seez LAD-ih-seps

Eunectes murinus yoo-NEK-teez myoo-REE-nuhs

Gavialidae GAY-vee-AL-uh-dee

Gavialis gangeticus GAY-vee-AL-is gan-JET-uh-kuhs

Gekkonidae geh-KON-uh-dee

Geochelone nigra JEE-oh-KEL-uh-nee NIG-ruh

Geoemydidae JEE-oh-uh-MID-uh-dee

Gerrhonotus liocephalus JER-uh-NOH-duhs LEE-oh-SEF-uh-luhs

Gopherus agassizii go-FER-uhs AG-uh-SEE-zee-eye

Gymnophthalmidae JIM-noh-THAL-muh-dee

Heloderma suspectum HEE-loh-DER-muh suh-SPEK-tum

Helodermatidae HEE-loh-der-MAD-uh-dee

Hemidactylus frenatus HEM-uh-DAK-tih-luhs FREH-nah-tuhs

Heterodon platyrhinos HED-uh-ROH-don PLAD-ih-RY-nohs

Iguanidae ih-GWON-uh-dee

Kinosternidae KIH-nuh-STER-nuh-dee

Lacerta agilis luh-SER-duh uh-JIL-uhs

Lacertidae luh-SER-duh-dee

Lachesis melanocephala luh-KEE-suhs MEL-uh-noh-SEF-uh-luh

Lampropeltis triangulum LAMP-roh-PEL-tuhs TRY-ang-YOO-lum

Laticauda colubrina luh-TIK-oh-duh kuh-LOO-bree-nuh

Leptotyphlopidae LEP-toh-ty-FLOP-uh-dee

Leptotyphlops dulcis LEP-toh-TY-flops DUL-sis

Liotyphlops ternetzii LEE-uh-TY-flops ter-NET-zee-EYE

Loxocemidae LOK-suh-SEM-uh-dee

Loxocemus bicolor LOK-suh-SEM-uhs BY-kuh-ler

Micrurus fulvius my-KRER-uhs ful-VEE-uhs

Morelia viridis moh-REEL-ee-uh vih-RID-is

Naja nigricollis NAH-juh NIH-grih-KOHL-luhs

Ophiophagus hannah ah-FEE-ah-fuh-guhs HAN-nuh

Pelomedusa subrufa puh-LOM-uh-DOO-suh SUB-ruh-fuh

Pelomedusidae puh-LOM-uh-DOO-suh-dee

Platysaurus capensis PLAT-ih-SOR-uhs KAY-pen-sis

Platysternidae PLAT-ih-STER-nuh-dee

Platysternon megacephalum PLAT-ih-STER-nun MEG-uh-SEF-uh-lum

Plectrurus perrotetii plek-TRER-uhs PAIR-uh-TET-ee-eye

Podocnemididae poh-DOK-nuh-MID-uh-dee

Podocnemis expansa poh-DOK-nuh-MIS ek-SPAN-suh

Python reticulatus PY-thon ruh-TIK-yoo-LAH-tuhs

Pythonidae PY-thon-uh-dee

Ramphotyphlops nigrescens RAM-fuh-TY-flops nih-GRES-unz

Rhineura floridana ry-NYOOR-uh floh-RID-uh-nuh

Rhineuridae ry-NYOOR-uh-dee

Sauromalus obesus soh-ROM-uh-luhs oh-BEE-suhs

Scincidae SKIN-kuh-DEE

Scincus scincus SKIN-kuhs SKIN-kuhs

Sphenodon punctatus SFEN-uh-don PUNK-tah-tuhs

Sphenodontidae SFEN-uh-DON-tuh-dee

Squamata skwuh-MOD-uh

Sternotherus odoratus STER-nah-THUH-ruhs OH-duh-RAH-tuhs

Teiidae TEE-uh-dee

Terrapene carolina ter-ROP-uh-nee KAR-uh-LINE-uh

Testudines tes-TYOO-duh-neez

Testudinidae TES-tyoo-DIN-uh-dee

Thamnophis sirtalis THAM-nuh-FIS ser-TAL-is

Trionychidae TRY-un-NIK-uh-dee

Trogonophidae TROG-uh-NOH-fuh-dee

Tropidophiidae TROP-uh-doh-FEE-uh-dee

Typhlopidae ty-FLOP-uh-dee

Ungaliophis panamensis un-GALL-ee-OH-fis PAN-uh-MEN-sis

Uropeltidae YOOR-uh-PEL-tuh-dee
Varanidae vuh-RAN-uh-dee
Varanus salvadorii vuh-RAN-uhs SAL-vuh-DOR-ee-EYE
Viperidae VY-per-uh-dee
Xantusia vigilis ZAN-tuh-SEE-uh vih-JUH-lis
Xantusiidae ZAN-tuh-SEE-uh-dee
Xenopeltidae ZEE-noh-PELT-uh-dee
Xenopeltis unicolor ZEE-noh-PELT-uhs YOO-nih-KUH-ler
Xenosauridae ZEE-noh-SOR-uh-dee
Xenosaurus grandis ZEE-noh-SOR-uhs GRAN-duhs

Words to Know

A

Algae: Tiny plantlike growths that live in water and have no true roots, stems, or leaves.

Ambush: A method of hunting in which the animal finds a hiding place from which it can spring out to attack unsuspecting meal animals that wander past.

Amphibian: An animal with a skeleton inside the body and that spends part of its life in the water and part on land.

Amphisbaenians: A small group of reptiles that look somewhat like long earthworms, but with scales.

Annuli: Rings, such as those seen around the length of an earthworm and some wormlizards.

Antibodies: Substances that fight bacteria, which can cause health problems in humans.

Antivenin: An antidote, or remedy, that neutralizes, or makes ineffective, the poison from the bite of a venomous animal.

Arboreal: Describing an animal living in trees.

Arid: Describing areas with very little water, such as a desert area.

Autohemorrhaging: Bleeding that starts on its own and not because of an injury.

B

Barbel: A bit of flesh that dangles from the chins of some turtles.

Bask: To warm up the body, especially by lying in the sun; basking is seen in such animals as turtles and snakes.

Bay: A part of the sea that cuts into the coastline.

Billabong: An Australian word for a dried-up streambed.

Blunt: Not pointed.

Brittle: Easily broken.

Bromeliad: A plant that often grows high above the ground on the sides of trees.

Burrow: A tunnel or hole in the ground made by an animal for shelter.

C

Caecilians: Salamanderlike animals that live underground.

Camouflage: A way of hiding or disguising something by making it look like its surroundings.

Carapace: The upper shell of a turtle.

Carnivore: An animal that eats meat.

Carnivorous: Meat-eating.

Carrion: Dead animal flesh.

Caruncle: The toothlike part a hatchling reptile uses to break out of its egg.

Centipede: An animal with a segmented, wormlike body and many legs.

Clone: An exact duplicate, seen in a mother and her babies of parthenogenic species.

Cloud forest: A wet, tropical, mountain forest.

Clutch: A nest of eggs.

Cold-blooded: Having a body temperature that changes with the temperature of the surrounding environment.

Concave: Hollowed or curved inward.

Coniferous forest: A forest with trees that have seeds inside cones, such as pines; also called evergreen forest.

Constriction: A method snakes use to kill their prey, by wrapping their bodies around the prey animal and squeezing until it cannot breathe.

Constrictor: A snake that squeezes animals, usually to death, before eating them.

Continent: A large mass of land on planet Earth, such as Africa or South America.

Continental shelf: A shallow plain in the sea that forms the border of a continent, usually with a steep slope to the ocean floor.

Courtship: An animal's activities that are meant to attract a mate.

Crest: A ridge on an animal's body.

Crepuscular: Describing an animal active at twilight, that is, at dusk and dawn.

Crevice: A narrow opening or a crack.

Critically Endangered: Facing an extremely high risk of extinction in the wild in the near future.

Crustacean: An animal that lives in water and has a soft, segmented body covered by a hard shell, such as lobsters and shrimp.

D

Decayed: Rotting.

Deciduous forest: A forest with trees, such as maples, that lose their leaves in dry or cold weather.

Deflate: To cause to collapse by letting out the air.

Deforestation: Clearing land of trees to use the timber or make room for human settlement or farming.

Depression: A hollow or a hole.

Dew: Small drops of water that collect on cool surfaces, especially at night.

Dewlap: The flap of skin that lies under the chin.

Diameter: The width of a circle, measured as a straight line through the center.

Diurnal: Describing an animal active during the day.

Drought: A dry spell.

Dune: A hill of sand piled up by wind or water.

E

Ectothermic: Describing an animal whose body temperature changes when the outside air warms up or cools down; often referred to as "cold-blooded."

Eggs: The reproductive cells that are made by female animals and that are fertilized by sperm, or reproductive cells of male animals.

Embryo: A developing baby that is not yet born.

Endangered: Facing a very high risk of extinction in the wild in the near future.

Endothermic: Describing an animal that uses its own energy to maintain a constant body temperature; often referred to as "warm-blooded."

Equator: The imaginary circle around Earth midway between the North Pole and the South Pole, the points on Earth's surface that are farthest north and south, respectively.

Erosion: The wearing away of earth by wind or water.

Estivation: A period of inactivity during dry spells or during the summer.

Estuary: The wide part at the lower end of a river, where the river meets the sea.

Evolution: The process of change and development that an animal undergoes over time to adapt to its surroundings.

Extinct: No longer alive.

Extinction: Elimination or death, especially of an entire species of animal.

F

Fangs: Long, pointed teeth.

Flexible: Movable or bendable.

Forage: A style of hunting in which an animal wanders about looking for food.

Fossil: The remains, or parts, of animals that lived long ago, usually found set into rock or earth.

Fossorial species: Those that live underground.

Frill: Pleated or ruffled neck folds.

Fused: Firmly joined together.

G

Genus: Defined by scientists, a group of similar species. A group of similar genera (the plural of genus) make up a family.

Granular: Grainy like sand.

Grub: A wormlike young insect.

H

Habitat: The natural environment, or living area, of an animal.

Hatchling: A newly hatched young animal.

Herbivore: An animal that eats only plants.

Hibernate: Become inactive during the winter.

Hibernation: A period of inactivity during the winter.

Humus: A material made up of decayed, or rotting, plants and leaves that feeds soil and holds in water.

Hybrid: Young born to parents from two different species.

Hydrozoan: An ocean-living animal that has tentacles, or long thin body parts used for feeling or holding on to things.

Hyoid: A bone that supports the tongue.

I

Incubation: The period of time after eggs are laid and before they hatch, during which they develop.

Inflate: To make larger or expand.

Infrared vision: The ability to detect, or to "see," heat.

Invertebrate: An animal, such as an insect, spider, or earthworm, that lacks a backbone.

Iridescent: Having the ability to turn light into many colors, much as rain can bend the sunlight into a rainbow; reflecting different colors depending on the light.

Iridescent scale: Seen in a few snakes, scales that shine different colors depending on how the light hits them.

J

Jacobson's organ: Common in reptiles, an organ that connects to the roof of the mouth by a small opening, called a duct, and helps the animal to smell chemical odors picked up by the tongue.

Juvenile: A young animal.

K

Keel: A ridge on the upper shell of a turtle.

Keeled scale: On a snake, a scale with a ridge down the middle.

L

Lagoon: A shallow body of saltwater near the sea.

Larva: In many insects, such as beetles and butterflies, the life stage after the egg and before the pupa.

Ligament: Tough but flexible tissue that connects bones.

Limbs: Legs.

Lineage: A group of animals that connect species through time to their ancestors.

Live-bearing species: A species, or kind, of animal in which the females give birth to babies rather than laying eggs.

M

Mangrove: A tropical tree or shrub that forms thick growths along coastlines.

Marine: Having to do with the sea.

Migrate: To move from one area or climate to another to breed or feed.

Migration: Movement from one region or climate to another, usually for breeding or feeding.

Mimicry: Resemblance of one usually dangerous species by another usually harmless one.

Mollusk: An animal with a soft, unsegmented body usually covered by a shell, such as a snail or a clam.

Molt: As seen in snakes, the shedding of the outer skin.

Murky: Dim or dark.

Musky: Smelling earthy and sometimes stinky, like the spray of a skunk.

N

Native: Natural to a country, that is, produced by nature and not produced or brought in by humans.

Near Threatened: At risk of becoming threatened with extinction in the future.

Nocturnal: Describing an animal active at night.

Nostrils: Nose holes.

O

Omnivore: An animal that eats both plants and meat.

Omnivorous: Describing an animal that eats both plants and meat.

Opportunistic: Taking advantage of what is available, as in feeding on whatever food can be found.

Opportunistic hunters: Animals that will eat almost anything they happen upon if they are hungry.

Oscillation: In spade-headed wormlizards, the back-and-forth swiveling motion of the head that digs through the soil and forms the smooth sides of the tunnel.

Osteoderms: Bony plates that lie under the surface of the scaly skin in some reptiles, including crocodilians.

Oviparous: Describing an animal that produces and lays shelled eggs that later hatch into young.

Ovoviviparous: Describing a female that produces eggs that hatch inside her body just before she gives birth to the young.

P

Palate: A bony plate on the roof of the mouth.

Parthenogenesis: A type of reproduction where a female can have babies by herself without a male.

Parthenogenic species: An all-female species in which a female can become pregnant and have young by herself and without a male.

Pectoral: Relating to the chest area.

Plastron: The lower shell of a turtle.

Pollution: Poison, waste, or other material that makes the environment dirty and harmful to the health of living things.

Predator: An animal that hunts and kills other animals for food.

Prey: An animal hunted and caught for food.

Protrude: To stick out.

Pupa: In many insects, such as beetles and butterflies, the life stage after the larva and before the adult.

Pupil: The part of the eye through which light passes.

R

Rainforest: A tropical woodland area of evergreen trees that has heavy rainfall all year long.

Range: The area where an animal roams and feeds.

Retract: To pull backward.

Rodent: A small animal, such as a mouse, beaver, or hamster, with long front teeth that it uses for gnawing.

S

Sac: A pouch.

Sandbar: A ridge of sand built up by currents, or the flowing movement of water.

Savanna: A flat plain covered with grass and a few trees.

Scale: A clear, thin film or coating over the eyes or a flat, rigid plate that acts as part of a body covering.

Scent: The particular smell of an animal, which can be left on the surface over which it travels.

School: A large number of fish or other water-dwelling animals that swim together.

Scrub: A flat, dry area of land with small bushes.

Scrubland: Land covered with small bushes.

Scute: A bony or horny scale or plate.

Seasonal: Happening as part of the changes at the different times of the year.

Serpentine locomotion: Seen in snakes and legless lizards, the way they slither in an S-shaped motion.

Setae: Tiny hairs or hairlike projections.

Silt: Fine, tiny specks of earth that settle out of water or fall to the bottom.

Snout: Nose area, usually long and pointed.

Sockets: Hollow openings, usually where one body part fits into another.

Species: A group of animals that share many traits and can mate and produce young with one another.

Spectacle: A see-through scale that covers the eye; seen in snakes and some lizards that do not have blinking eyelids.

Sperm: The reproductive cells that are made by male animals and that fertilize the eggs of female animals.

Specimen: A single example that is considered typical of a group.

Squamates: The group of animals that includes the lizards, snakes, and wormlizards.

Stalking: A type of hunting in which the predator sneaks up on the prey before attacking.

Stratum corneum: The outer skin that snakes lose when they shed.

Subspecies: A smaller group within a species that typically lives in a particular area and usually has a slightly different look from the rest of the animals in the species.

Subtropical: Relating to regions that border on the tropics.

Swamp: A wetland that is only partly or now and then covered by water.

T

Tail: In snakes, the part of the body that occurs after the vent.

Temperate climate: Describing areas that have distinct seasons, including cold winters.

Tentacles: Long thin body parts used for feeling or for holding on to things.

Terrestrial: Describing an animal that lives on land.

Territorial: Describing an animal that is protective of a living or breeding area.

Territory: An animal's preferred living area, which is considered off-limits to other animals of the same species.

Toxic: Poisonous.

Trek: A journey, typically one that is long and difficult.

Trunk: In a snake, the portion of the body between the head and the tail.

Tubercles: The cone-shaped bumps on a snake's tail.

V

Venom: Poison, usually injected by snakes, bees, or scorpions by biting or stinging.

Venomous: Poisonous.

Vent: On a snake, a crosswise opening on the belly side and toward the rear of the animal.

Ventrals: In snakes, the scales on the underside of the animal, usually much larger than the scales on the snake's back and sides.

Vertebrate: An animal that has a backbone.

Vertical: Positioned straight up and down.

Vibrate: To move back and forth rapidly.

Viviparous: Describing a female that makes no eggs, but rather provides all of the food for her young through direct connections inside her body and gives birth to live babies.

Vocal: Making sounds.

Vocal cord: Body part used to produce sound.

Vulnerable: Facing a high risk of extinction in the wild.

W

Wetland: Land that is covered with shallow water or that has very wet soil.

Getting to Know Reptiles

Snakes, crocodiles and alligators, lizards, and turtles might not look alike at first glance, but they all share certain features. These animals, plus the tuataras that resemble a cross between a prehistoric dinosaur and a present-day lizard, are reptiles. In all, the world holds 285 species of turtles, 23 crocodiles and alligators, two tuataras, 4,450 lizards, and 2,900 snakes. Scientists suspect that hundreds of other reptile species have yet to be discovered.

Scales

Almost all reptiles have thick tough skin with scales or scutes. Alligators have large heavy rectangular scales covering their bodies, while snakes often have thinner overlapping scales. Most snakes have larger and wider belly scales, which are known as scutes. Even turtles have noticeable scales on the legs and head. These scales and scutes can help protect the reptile from scraping its skin on the ground or from dangerous attacks by other animals that want to eat it. For land-living reptiles, the scales can also keep the body from drying out too quickly. Besides the scales on their legs, turtles also have a different type of scutes. The tops of the upper and lower shell are divided into large pieces, which are also known as scutes.

Reptiles come in many different sizes and colors. Some snakes grow to less than 12 inches (30.5 centimeters) long as adults, while others can reach 25 feet (7.7 meters). Likewise, a whole range of sizes separate the smallest of turtles at just a

People often see reptiles sunbathing, or basking, in the sun. (John M. Burnley, Photo Researchers, Inc. Reproduced by permission.)

few inches (centimeters) long from the largest, which have shells that can reach 8 feet (2.4 meters) in length. Many reptiles have dull drab colors that help them blend into their surroundings, but others are very brightly colored and patterned.

Body temperature

Reptiles are often called cold-blooded animals, but this description is only correct sometimes. A reptile actually changes its body temperature, becoming hotter when the outside temperature is warm, and colder when the outside temperature is cool. In other words, a reptile is only "cold-blooded" on cold days. This changing body temperature is called ectothermy (EK-toe-ther-mee): ecto means outside and thermy refers to the temperature. Reptiles, then, are ectothermic animals. In "warm-blooded" animals, such as human beings, the body has to stay about the same temperature all the time. If a person's body temperature rises or falls more than just a few degrees, he or she can die. For the ectothermic reptiles, however, their body temperatures can swing 20 to 30° F (7 to 13° C)—and sometimes more—in a single day without causing any harm. Because they are ectothermic, reptiles do not have to use their energy to stay warm. Instead, they can simply let the sun warm them up by sunbathing, or basking, on a forest path or the shore of a river or lake. Ectothermy can also have a downside. Reptiles are slower on cooler days or in the cool morning or evening air, which can make them easy prey for attackers. Most reptiles, however, hide themselves away when their bodies start to chill.

Venom

Not all reptiles are venomous, but many snakes and a few lizards are. Venom is a type of toxin, or poison. Venomous snakes generally have two fangs in their upper jaw—sometimes in the front of the mouth and sometimes in back. These fangs usually have grooves that send the venom down the tooth and into the prey. Unlike the snakes, the two venomous lizards, the Gila monster and the Mexican beaded lizard, store their venom in the lower jaw and deliver it through grooves in numerous teeth.

HOW DO REPTILES MOVE?

Walking

Although not all reptiles have legs, many of them do. Crocodiles and alligators, turtles, most lizards, and tuataras can walk on their four legs. Each leg ends in a foot with five or fewer claws. Usually they walk with their legs held out from the body, rather like a human would hold up his or her body when doing a push-up. Many of the smaller lizards, in particular, are very speedy, zipping across the ground at speeds that make their capture difficult. The exceptionally large lizards, known as Komodo dragons, usually walk very slowly, as do crocodiles, which often slide their bellies along the ground while walking. If necessary, however, both can run surprisingly fast. A few reptiles, such as the Nile crocodile and American crocodile, can even do a fast rabbitlike hop, called a gallop, to cover ground quickly. Some lizards can run on just their two hind legs, and the basilisk lizard is even able to run across the surface of a pond without sinking.

Slithering

Snakes slither, usually twisting and bending their bodies in an S-shaped pattern along the ground. This type of movement is called serpentine (SER-pen-teen) locomotion. Like the snakes, some lizards also have no legs. They move much the

FLYING REPTILES?

No reptiles can actually fly, but several can glide through the air much like a paper airplane. The flying tree snake, which is common in Singapore, flattens out its body to soar from one tree branch to a lower one. The common gliding lizard, also known as the common flying dragon, can likewise glide through the air, but it does so by stretching out a large flap of skin, as if opening a fan, on each side of the body. The flying geckos of Southeast Asia have numerous little flaps on their body, tail, legs, and head that help them to glide.

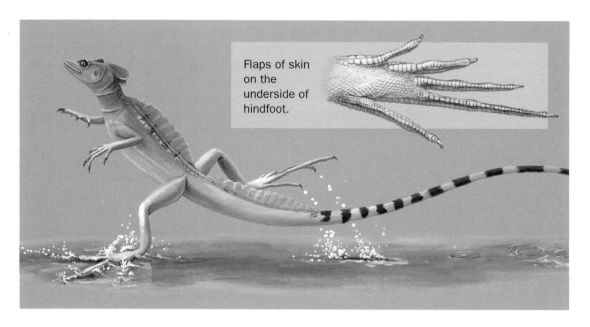

Flaps of skin on the underside of hindfoot.

The green basilisk lizard is able to run across water aided by the flaps of skin on the underside of its hindfeet. (Illustration by Emily Damstra. Reproduced by permission.)

same way as snakes do. Occasionally, some lizards that have legs will slither instead of run. When they are in thick grass that makes running very difficult, some will lie down, hold the legs against the body, and begin to slither.

Swimming

Many turtles, alligators, and crocodiles spend most of their lives in the water. Turtles often have wide feet that they use to push them through the water. A few, like the seaturtles, even

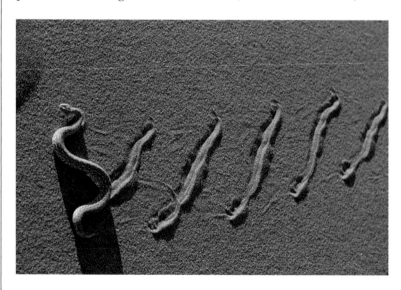

Snakes slither, usually twisting and bending their bodies in an S-shaped pattern along the ground. (David Hughes/Bruce Coleman, Inc. Reproduced by permission.)

have feet that are shaped like paddles. Alligators and crocodiles have very powerful and long tails that propel and steer their bodies through the water. Many snakes are also excellent swimmers, moving through lakes and streams with the same serpentine locomotion they use to slither on land.

WHAT DO REPTILES EAT?

Carnivores

Many reptiles are meat-eaters, or carnivores (KAR-nih-vores). Some of them, especially the smaller lizards and snakes, eat mainly insects, spiders, worms, and other invertebrates (in-VER-teh-brehts), which are animals without backbones. Larger snakes often eat mammals, amphibians, other reptiles, fishes, and birds. A number of snakes and lizards also eat eggs. Snakes usually will only eat living animals, but other species, including snapping turtles, will eat dead, even rotting animals that they find.

Plant eaters

A few reptiles, especially some of the turtle species and a few lizards, eat plants. Animals that eat plants are called herbivores (ER-bih-vores). A few animals will eat both meat and plants. These are called omnivores (OM-nih-vores). Some turtles, including the commonly seen painted turtles, will switch from a mostly meat diet to one that is mostly plants when animal prey are hard to find.

REPTILES AS PREDATORS AND PREY

As predators

Predators (PREH-duh-ters) are animals that hunt and kill other animals for food. Many reptiles hunt by ambush, which means that they find a good hiding spot or lie very still and wait for a prey animal to happen by. Then they lunge out and grab their prey. Other reptiles hunt by foraging, when they crawl, slither, or swim about looking for something to eat. Many

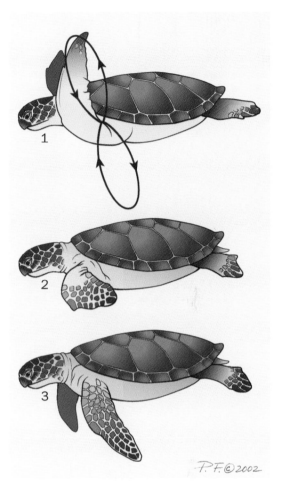

Seaturtle swimming strokes.
(Illustration by Patricia Ferrer.
Reproduced by permission.)

An Amazon tree boa eating a bird. (Joe McDonald, Bruce Coleman Inc. Reproduced by permission.)

reptiles, including lizards and turtles, simply snap their mouths around the prey and swallow it. Crocodiles and alligators clamp their jaws around larger prey, such as deer, drag them underwater to drown, and then tear off hunks of flesh. Snakes usually swallow their meals whole, often by unhinging their jaws. Many snakes are venomous, which allows them to inject a toxin into the prey to either kill it or knock it out.

Some reptiles, especially the lizards, mainly use their eyes to spot their prey. Snakes have an excellent sense of smell and are able to pick up scents from the air and from the ground with the tongue, which they flick again and again while looking for food. Some snakes, including the pit vipers, have small holes on the front of the face. These holes, or pits, are covered with a thin sheet of detectors that can pick up the heat given off by a prey animal. Snakes are also able to sense ground vibrations through the jaw bone, which connects to the ear. They can not only feel the ground move, but they can also hear it.

As prey

Prey are those animals that are hunted by other animals for food. Eagles, hawks, other large birds, along with some mammals, eat snakes and lizards. In fact, some snakes and lizards eat other snakes and lizards. One of the biggest threats to turtles come from mammals that dig up their nests and eat their eggs.

WHERE REPTILES LIVE

Underground reptiles

The tuataras, many lizards, and some snakes, including the blind snakes, spend most of their time underground in burrows, or beneath rocks, logs, or other ground covers. Some of them stay underground all day and only come out at night. Others stay underground all night and sneak out during the day. Some burrowing reptiles dig their own burrows, but many others simply move into the burrow of another animal.

Freshwater reptiles

Alligators and crocodiles, many turtles, some snakes, and a few lizards live in freshwater lakes, ponds, rivers, and streams. Depending on the species, they may spend a good deal of time every day on shore basking in a sunny spot. Some will even do some hunting on land. Crocodiles, for instance, may grab a prey animal on shore but will then drag it into the water to drown it.

Sea reptiles

Among the reptiles, the seaturtles are most known for their association with the oceans. With their paddlelike front legs, they can glide easily through the water and cover very long distances, often migrating hundreds of miles (kilometers) between their nesting beaches in warm climates and their feeding areas in cooler climates. The leatherback seaturtle migrates the farthest, taking trips of up to 3,100 miles (5,000 kilometers) from its nesting place to a feeding site. Some snakes also live in the ocean. The seasnakes make their home in coral reefs, where they eat eels and fishes.

Tree reptiles

Animals that live in trees are said to be arboreal (pronounced ar-BOR-ee-ul). Some reptiles are arboreal. These include many snakes, even large ones like the emerald tree boa that can grow to 7.3 feet (2.2 meters) in length. Many lizards are also excellent climbers and slither through trees looking for insects or bird eggs to eat.

NEW REPTILES

Scientists believe that many more reptiles live on Earth than those they know about. In fact, they are continuing to find new reptiles today.

Sometimes, they discover new species inside old ones. In other words, they decide that a snake or lizard that they always thought was one species is actually two similar-looking species. In 2003, for example, Wolfgang Waster of the School of Biological Sciences at the University of Wales and keepers from the London Zoo received a group of strangely colored spitting cobras. After taking a closer look, they discovered that the snakes were actually a completely different and previously unknown species, which they called the Nubian cobra. Similarly, zoologist Frank Burbrink studied American corn snakes and found that one was so different from the others that it should be its own

species. He named the snake Slowinski's corn snake in honor of snake researcher Joseph Slowinski, who died in 2001 when he was bitten by venomous snake.

Besides finding new species in old ones, scientists are also discovering new never-before-seen species in remote places where few humans have ever traveled. In 2001, for example, scientists Blair Hedges of Pennsylvania State University and Richard Thomas of the University of Puerto Rico discovered a tiny lizard that is smaller than any other known lizard. This little reptile, which measures barely more than one-half inch (16 millimeters) long, is a little gecko that lives on the island of Beata in the Dominican Republic. This species is one of more than four dozen new reptiles and amphibians that Hedges and Thomas have discovered in hard-to-reach spots in the Caribbean.

REPRODUCTION

Most female reptiles lay eggs, but some give birth to babies. Some of the newborn babies may have actually hatched from eggs while they were still inside the mother. Female reptiles all lay their eggs or give birth to their babies on land. Even those that live in the water for the rest of the year crawl onto shore to have their young. Tuataras lay eggs in their burrows. Some female turtles and crocodiles bury their eggs on shore or farther inland. A few turtle species lay their eggs in leaf piles. After laying the eggs, a female turtle leaves the nest, and the young are on their own. Crocodiles care for their young, bringing the new hatchlings from the nest site to the water. Snakes and

Egg laying strategies.
1. Peninsula cooter turtle;
2. American alligator;
3. Python; 4. Copperhead.
(Illustration by Dan Erickson.
Reproduced by permission.)

lizards may lay eggs or have babies. In some species, the female may remain with the eggs and/or the young, although scientists are unsure how much real protection or care many of the mother snakes actually provide.

REPTILES AND PEOPLE

Many people keep reptiles as pets. This can be a problem if the animal bites, if it grows too large, or if it lives too long. Some snakes, for example, can grow to be 6 feet (1.8 meters) long or more, and some turtles can live to be 100 years old. In the wild, most people only see reptiles when the animals are warming themselves in the sun. Usually, the reptile will leave the area as the person draws near. If the animal is surprised, however, some reptiles may bite. Not all snakes are venomous, but some are. A bite from a venomous snake can be dangerous and even deadly and requires an immediate visit to the hospital.

ENDANGERED REPTILES

Reptiles in danger

Many, many species of reptiles may disappear from the Earth soon, if they do not receive some protection. Two-

Reptilian visual displays:
1. Cottonmouth uses gaping mouth as a defensive warning;
2. Frilled lizard looks larger as a defensive display; 3. A ringneck snake draws attention away from its head and shows its coloration as a defense; 4. The alligator snapping turtle uses a food lure to attract its prey;
5. and 6. Territorial or mating displays for green anole (5) and tuatara (6). (Illustration by Dan Erickson. Reproduced by permission.)

thirds of all turtle species, for example, are now listed by the World Conservation Union (IUCN) as being at risk. Overall, the IUCN counts 453 species of reptiles, or more than one in every six species, as being at some risk. Moreover, scientists know so little about many species that others may be at risk, too.

The decline in reptile populations is commonly a result of habitat destruction or of overhunting for their meat or skin or for the pet trade. For turtles, much of the danger comes from the growing number of predator animals that dig up turtle nests and eat the eggs. Scientists estimate, for instance, that 75 to 90

A KwaZulu-Natal Nature Conservation Service staff member cuts notches into the carapace of a loggerhead turtle hatchling as part of a research project. (©Roger De La Harpe: Gallo Images/CORBIS. Reproduced by permission.)

percent of the eggs from some species of North American turtles are lost each year to such predators.

Saving endangered reptiles

In some cases, scientists, government agencies, and/or other concerned groups are protecting the land where the animals live and setting up laws that prevent overhunting. Many zoos are also helping by trying to breed their own captive reptiles. This is especially important for those species that are already very rare.

Too late to save

According to the IUCN, twenty-one species of reptiles are extinct. This includes three snakes, eleven lizards, and seven turtles.

FOR MORE INFORMATION

Books:

Badger, David. *Lizards.* Stillwater, MN: Voyageur Press, 2002.

Behler, John. *Simon and Schuster's Guide to Reptiles and Amphibians of the World.* New York: Simon and Schuster Inc., 1989, 1997.

Cleaver, Andrew. *Snakes and Reptiles: A Portrait of the Animal World*. Wigston, Leicester, England: Magna Books, 1994.

Irwin, Steve, and Terri Irwin. *The Crocodile Hunter*. New York: Penguin Putnam, 1997.

Ivy, Bill. *Nature's Children: Lizards*. Danbury, CT: Grolier, 1990.

Lamar, William. *The World's Most Spectacular Reptiles and Amphibians*. Tampa, FL: World Publications, 1997.

Lockwood, C. C. *The Alligator Book*. Baton Rouge: Louisiana State University Press, 2002.

Mattison, Chris. *Lizards of the World*. New York: Facts on File, 1989.

Mattison, Chris. *The Encyclopedia of Snakes*. New York: DK Publishing Inc., 1997.

McCarthy, Colin. *Eyewitness: Reptile*. New York: DK Publishing, 2000.

Montgomery, Sy. *The Snake Scientist (Scientists in the Field)*. Boston, MA: Houghton Mifflin, 2001.

O'Shea, Mark, and Tim Halliday. *Smithsonian Handbooks: Reptiles and Amphibians*. New York: DK Publishing, 2002.

Rue, Leonard Lee. *Alligators and Crocodiles*. Wigston, Leicester, England: Magna Books, 1994.

Tesar, Jenny. *What on Earth is a Tuatara?* Woodbridge, CT: Blackbirch Press, 1994.

Periodicals:

Barr, Brady, and Margaret Zackowitz. "The Big Squeeze. (The Icky Adventure of Brady Barr)." *National Geographic Kids*. May 2003, page 40.

Calvert, Pam. "Out of Control!: The Brown Tree Snake." *Odyssey*. April 2000, page 23.

Chiang, Mona. "The Plight of the Turtle." *Science World*. May 9, 2003, page 8.

Gill, Paul G., Jr. "Red on Yellow, Kill a Fellow! Get Snake-smart before Heading into the Wild." *Boys' Life*. April 2004, page 26.

Mealy, Nora Steiner. "Creatures from Komodo." *Ranger Rick*. August 2001, page 18.

Murphy, Thomas J. "Swamp Wars." *Boys' Life.* November 2000, page 10.

Myers, Jack. "Flicking tongues." *Highlights for Children.* September 1997, page 32.

O'Meara, Stephen. "Creature from the Black Lagoon." *Odyssey.* March 1999, page 42.

Scheid, Darrin. "It's a Bird! It's a Plane! It's a Snake." *Boys' Life.* January 2003, page 11.

Swarts, Candice. "The Tortoise and the Pair." *National Geographic Kids.* October 2003, page 14.

Thompson, Sharon. "Attention, Lizard Parents." *National Geographic World.* May 2002, page 6.

Web sites:

"All About Turtles." Gulf of Maine Aquarium. http://octopus .gma.org/turtles/ (accessed on November 1, 2004).

"How fast can a crocodile run?" Crocodilian Biology Database, Florida Museum of Natural History. http://www.flmnh.ufl .edu/natsci/herpetology/brittoncrocs/cbd-faq-q4.htm (accessed on November 1, 2004).

"Reptiles." Environmental Education for Kids. http://www.dnr .state.wi.us/org/caer/ce/eek/critter/reptile/index.htm (accessed on November 1, 2004).

"Reptiles." San Diego Natural History Museum. http://www.sdnhm .org/exhibits/reptiles/index.html (accessed on November 1, 2004).

"Snakes." Defenders of Wildlife. http://www.kidsplanet.org/ factsheets/snakes.html (accessed on November 1, 2004).

Sohn, Emily. "The Cool Side of Snake Pits." *Science News for Kids.* http://www.sciencenewsforkids.org/articles/20030625/ Note2.asp (accessed on November 1, 2004).

Sohn, Emily. "Delivering a Little Snake Venom." *Science News for Kids.* http://www.sciencenewsforkids.org/articles/20030903/ Feature1.asp (accessed on November 1, 2004).

Trivedi, Bigal P. "Smallest Known Lizard Found in Caribbean." *National Geographic.* http://news.nationalgeographic.com/ news/2001/12/1203_TVtinylizard.html (accessed on November 1, 2004).

order

CHAPTER

PHYSICAL CHARACTERISTICS

The dinosaurs are a large group of reptiles that lived from 230 to 65 million years ago. Some, such as the well-known *Tyrannosaurus rex*, were enormous meat-eating animals. Others, however, were small and timid creatures that nibbled on plants.

Scientists divide the dinosaurs into two orders. One order is Saurischia, which includes the theropods (THAIR-oh-pods) that walked on their two hind legs and were mostly meat-eating dinosaurs and the sauropods (SAWR-oh-pods) that walked on all fours and ate plants. The theropods had more primitive features, including jagged teeth, and some, such as the *Ceratosaurus*, had hornlike knobs jutting out of their skulls. *Tyrannosaurus rex* was a theropod. Although it was quite large at 40 to 50 feet (12.2 to 15.2 meters) long, its ancestors only grew to about 10 feet (3 meters) long.

The sauropods looked much different than the theropods. They had very long necks and tiny heads. Some of them were able to lift their front legs off the ground and grab leaves or other things with their hands. Other species, including *Brachiosaurus*, had longer front legs than hind legs, similar to the arrangement in current-day giraffes. Their tall front legs, combined with their overly long necks, helped them easily reach food even at the tops of most trees.

The other order within the dinosaurs is Ornithischia, which included those dinosaurs that ate plants and had hip bones that looked like those found in present-day birds. Many of them had crests, beaks, horns, or helmets, and some had armor-like plates, called scutes, covering their bodies and occasionally spikes. Stegosaurs are an example of an Orinithischian. These dinosaurs had armor-like spines down the middle of the back and spiked tails. The Ornithischia also includes the duckbill dinosaurs with their wide snouts.

Within these two orders of dinosaurs, the animals are further split into several hundred smaller groups, called genera (jen-AIR-uh). One or more species is grouped into each genus (JEAN-us), which is the singular of genera.

Although the name dinosaur actually means "terrible lizards," dinosaurs are not lizards and are different from all other groups of reptiles. One of the major differences between dinosaurs and other reptiles is in the way they moved. Lizards and crocodiles walk with their legs held out to the side, in the same type of position a person's arms take when doing pushups. A few dinosaurs sprawled their front legs like a lizard, but the vast majority of them walked like a dog or cat—with the legs directly below the hips and shoulders.

Many scientists also now suspect that at least some of the dinosaurs were warm-blooded, instead of cold-blooded like other reptiles. A warm-blooded animal, more properly called an endothermic (EN-doe-THER-mik) animal, uses its own energy to keep its body at a constant temperature. Cold-blooded, or ectothermic (EK-toe-THER-mik), animals get their body heat from an outside source, like the warmth of the sun.

Dinosaurs came in many shapes and sizes. The *Seismosaurus*, or "earth-shaking dinosaur," may have been the longest at 120 to 150 feet (36.6 to 45.7 meters) long. The heaviest may have been the *Argentinosaurus*, which grew to 100 to 130 feet (30.5 to 39.6 meters) long and weighed 110 tons (99,800 kilograms). Other enormous dinosaurs include the *Supersaurus* at 100 feet (30.5 meters) long and about 50 tons (45,000 kilograms) and the *Brachiosaurus* at 85 feet (25.9 meters) long and about 75 tons (68,000 kilograms). The *Tyrannosaurus rex*, a name that is often shortened to *T. rex*, was considerably smaller at 40 to 50 feet (12.2 to 15.2 meters) long and 6 tons (5,400 kilograms) in weight. Since *T. rex* stood on its hind legs rather than on all fours, it towered over most other dinosaurs. Other similarly sized meat-eating dinosaurs were the *Gigantosaurus*, *Spinosaurus*, and *Carcharodontosaurus*. All dinosaurs were not giants, however. Some, such as the *Saltopus* and *Lesothosaurus*, were only 24 to 36 inches (61 to 91 centimeters) long, and the tiny *Microraptor*'s full-grown size may have been only about 16 inches (41 centimeters) long.

GEOGRAPHIC RANGE

The Earth that the early dinosaurs knew looked much different than the Earth does today. The planet had a single, huge land mass, called Pangaea, and the dinosaurs lived over much of this area, particularly in the warmer climates. About 180 million years ago—50 million years after the dinosaurs first evolved—Pangaea began to split up and eventually formed the continents seen on Earth today. Given such huge changes, a fossil found nowadays in Germany, for example, says nothing about the location of the dinosaur that left it 220 million years ago.

HABITAT

Because scientists are studying fossils from many millions of years ago, rather than living animals, they usually cannot tell much about the dinosaur's habitat. They do, however, suspect that none of them lived in the water. Although a few dinosaurs may have been able to keep their bodies afloat for brief periods, or could wade to catch fish, none were full-time swimmers. Some scientists believe that sauropod dinosaurs may have been able to float and, based on footprints left behind, think they pushed themselves along by bouncing their front feet on the bottom of the pond or lake.

DIET

About two-thirds of all genera contain dinosaurs that were plant eaters, and a third of the genera include meat-eating dinosaurs. Scientists can determine whether a dinosaur ate meat or plants by looking at its teeth. The teeth of meat-eaters, also known as carnivores (KAR-nih-voars), are pointed for tearing flesh. The teeth of a plant-eater, or herbivore (ER-bih-voar), are flatter for grinding grasses and leaves. Studies of other dinosaur bones can also reveal information about their diet. One study, for instance, showed that some dinosaurs were cannibals. By looking at teeth marks on the bones of certain dinosaurs and comparing the marks to the teeth of the same species, the scientists figured out that the reptile was eating its own kind. This particular species, a theropod called *Majungatholus atopus*, grew to 29.5 feet (9 meters) long.

BEHAVIOR AND REPRODUCTION

With almost nothing but fossils to study, scientists can only guess at most dinosaur behavior. For example, although *T. rex* is often described as a ferocious predator, scientists only know that it had a skeleton that likely supported a strong body, and it had the jaws and teeth necessary to eat large prey animals. It is possible, however, that *T. rex* never even attacked live animals, but instead ate only animals that were already dead. Recently, scientists think they may have found evidence that some dinosaurs were social animals, which means that they spent time together in groups. They based this idea on a fossil find in Patagonia, where the bones of six, large, carnivorous dinosaurs were found huddled together in one area. The scientists think the dinosaurs, a new species that measures 40 feet (12.2 meters) long and had sharp and bladelike teeth, may have hunted together so they could attack and kill sauropods that grew to at least twice their size. Scientists believe some dinosaurs were social because their bones suggest that they were able to make loud noises. The lambeosaurs, for instance, had sound-producing tubes inside the skull, and scientists suspect that the animals communicated with one another.

Scientists sometimes find dinosaur footprints that have been preserved over time. From these, they can learn how the animal moved. Footprints of ornithomimids, which were ostrich-like dinosaurs, show that they could run at least 25 miles (40 kilometers) an hour, while those of a 3-foot-long (9 meter) meat eater called a *Megalosaurus* could zip along on its hind legs at speeds of 29 miles (48 kilometers) an hour. By looking at the bones of dinosaurs, scientists can also guess their fastest running speed. A recent study of *T. rex* bones shows that it probably could run no faster than the much smaller ornithomomids.

Scientists have recently found many dinosaur eggs, some of them with young still inside. A group of *Allosaurus* eggs found in Portugal provided some clues to the way they were born. The egg shells were covered with tiny holes, called pores, and looked very much like the pore-covered eggs of current-day crocodilians. The pores allow air to flow into the eggs, so the growing babies can breathe. Based on these findings, scientists believe the female dinosaurs of this species laid their eggs in mounds of vegetation or buried them, just as the now-living crocodilians do.

One of the best places in the world to find dinosaur fossils is Mongolia. In 1993, scientists learned that it was also an excellent place to find eggs with developing babies, called embryos (EM-bree-ohs), still inside. Here, they discovered a nest containing the first embryo ever found of a meat-eating dinosaur. It was a theropod, called an oviraptorid, that looked much like an ostrich, and the embryo dated back 70 to 80 million years ago. Interestingly, they also found the skulls of two small velociraptors in the nest. Were the velociraptors there to eat the eggs, or had the mother oviraptorid brought the velociraptors to feed her babies? Scientists do not know for sure. Some even guess that the mother velociraptor may have laid her eggs in the oviraptorid nest. If the oviraptorid mother did not notice the intruders, she would raise them as her own.

DINOSAURS AND PEOPLE

Despite the pictures in some cartoons and science fiction movies that show cave people living at the same time as the dinosaurs, scientists know that this is not true. By dating dinosaur fossils, they can definitely state that dinosaurs lived between 230 to 65 million years ago. Humans did not evolve until about one million years ago. Nonetheless, people nowadays are very interested in these reptiles from the planet's past. Television programs, films, books, web sites, and entire museum wings are devoted to the description or study of these animals.

CONSERVATION STATUS

The dinosaurs became extinct 65 million years ago. Their deaths likely resulted from a huge asteroid, a rock from outer space, that slammed into the Earth, probably near the Yucatan Peninsula of Mexico. The impact from the 4 to 9 mile-wide (6 to 15 kilometer) asteroid sent up a thick plume of dust and caused a chain reaction that resulted in a severe change in the planet's climate. For years afterward, the sun was unable to penetrate the dark curtain of dust. Temperatures around the world began to drop. Without sunlight, plants died, and with fewer plants to eat, many herbivores also perished. With fewer and

BRING BACK THE DINOS!

Movies and TV shows sometimes pretend that humans today can bring the extinct dinosaurs back to life by growing them from bits of their DNA found in fossils. In one such film, called "Jurassic Park," a scientist found dinosaur blood in the stomachs of prehistoric blood-sucking insects that had been preserved through the ages in tree sap. The blood contained DNA, which is found in each of a body's cells and holds the instructions for making the animal. In the film, he was able to create a dinosaur from that DNA. Although scientists do sometimes find prehistoric insects, they have yet to find any blood inside, whether from a dinosaur or not. Even if they did, any DNA in the ancient blood would most likely be in such bad shape that it would be useless.

fewer herbivores to eat, the carnivores may have begun to eat each other, until they also disappeared. Scientists believe that one group of dinosaurs survived the great extinction, however. These were the dromaeosaurids that eventually evolved into the birds. For this reason, some books refer to birds as modern-day dinosaurs.

FOR MORE INFORMATION

Books:

Farlow, James O., and M. K. Brett-Surman, eds. *The Complete Dinosaur.* Bloomington and Indianapolis: Indiana University Press, 1997.

Haines, Tim. *Walking with Dinosaurs: A Natural History.* New York: Dorling Kindersley, 2000.

Holta, Thomas R., Michael Brett-Surman, and Robert Walters. *Jurassic Park Institute (TM) Dinosaur Field Guide.* New York: Random House Books for Young Readers, 2001.

Lambert, David, and Steve Hutt. *DK Guide to Dinosaurs.* New York: Dorling Kindersley, 2000.

Paul, Gregory S., ed. *The Scientific American Book of Dinosaurs.* New York: St. Martin's Press, 2000.

Weishampel, David B., Peter Dodson, and Halszka Osmólska, eds. *The Dinosauria.* Berkeley: University of California Press, 1990.

Periodicals:

Adams, Judith. "Footsteps in Time." *Faces: People, Places, and Cultures.* April 2003, vol. 19: 30.

Hesman, Tina. "Dinosaurs, party of six, meat eating." *Science News.* April 1, 2000, vol. 157: 223.

Mandel, Peter. "Dino Might! 10 Recent Discoveries That Have Rocked the Dinosaur World." *National Geographic Kids.* March 2003: 14.

Davy, Emma. "Crash Test: What Wiped Out the Dinosaurs? Scientists Studying an Enormous Crater in Mexico Hope to Find the Answer." *Current Science.* September 27, 2002, vol. 88: 6.

Perkins, Sid. "Bob, Bob, Bobbin' Along: Dinosaur Buoyancy May Explain Odd Tracks." *Science News.* October 25, 2003, vol. 164: 262.

Web sites:

"Dinosaur embryo." American Museum of Natural History. http://www.amnh.org/exhibitions/expeditions/treasure_fossil/Treasures/Dinosaur_Embryo/embryo.html?dinos (accessed on December 22, 2004).

"Dinosaurs." BBC. http://www.bbc.co.uk/dinosaurs/ (accessed on December 22, 2004).

"Dinosaurs." EnchantedLearning.com. http://www.enchantedlearning.com/subjects/dinosaurs/ (accessed on December 22, 2004).

"Dinosaurs." KidSites.com. http://www.kidsites.com/sites-edu/dinosaurs.htm (accessed on December 22, 2004).

"Dinosaurs." Scholastic. http://teacher.scholastic.com/researchtools/articlearchives/dinos/general.htm (accessed on December 22, 2004).

"The Science of 'Jurassic Park': Frequently Asked Questions." San Diego Natural History Museum. http://www.sdnhm.org/research/paleontology/jp_qanda.html (accessed on December 22, 2004).

"What is a Dinosaur?" San Diego Natural History Museum. http://www.sdnhm.org/kids/dinosaur/dino.html (accessed on December 22, 2004).

order

phylum

class

subclass

● **order**

monotypic order

suborder

family

PHYSICAL CHARACTERISTICS

Turtles and tortoises, which are in the order Testudines, have bony upper and lower shells that surround much of the body. The upper shell, or carapace (KARE-a-pays), can be tall and rounded, can be flat, or can be some shape in between. The lower shell, or plastron (PLAS-trun), can cover most or just a portion of the bottom of the animal, depending on the species. In most cases, the upper shell connects to the lower shell by way of a bony bridge. In some species, the bridge is made of more flexible tissue called ligament (LIH-guh-ment). The hard shell often is covered with large scales called scutes (SCOOTS). In some species, new scutes grow under the old ones, and the old ones pile up. A person can count the number of scutes in the pile to tell how old the turtle is. Softshell turtles have no scutes. They do have small bony shells, but the bones are covered with leathery or rubbery skin.

Besides shells, another feature of turtles and tortoises is that they have no teeth. Instead they have hard, flat surfaces on their jaws that allow them to grip and tear off bits of plants or animals for feeding. Sometimes these surfaces come to a sharp point in front and look much like the hook on the end of a hawk's or eagle's beak. Turtles with such pointed upper jaws are often said to have horny beaks.

Turtles and tortoises, like birds, dogs, humans, and other animals, are vertebrates (VER-teh-brehts), which means they have a backbone. Turtles and tortoises are unlike all other vertebrates in that their hip and shoulder bones are inside the rib cage instead of outside because the ribs are attached to the upper and lower shells. If the shoulder and hip bones were outside the rib cage, they would have to be outside the shell.

Many turtles and tortoises have long necks, which they can pull back or stretch out. Because some species can pull their necks straight back and others can only pull them sideways, scientists often describe them as being in the hidden-necked group, called Cryptodira, or in the side-necked group, called Pleurodira. A hidden-necked turtle can pull its neck straight back and usually tuck its whole neck and head inside the shell. A side-necked turtle pulls its neck back sideways, often tucking the neck and head along the side of the body and against the bridge between the upper and lower shells.

Turtles come in many sizes. The largest living species is the leatherback sea turtle, which can weigh up to 1,191 pounds (540 kilograms), or more than half a ton. The upper shell can become 8 feet (2.4 meters) long. Some of the smallest of the Testudines are the speckled cape tortoise, flattened musk turtle, and bog turtle. The carapace on each of these three animals barely reaches 4.7 inches (12 centimeters) long.

GEOGRAPHIC RANGE

Turtles and tortoises live on all continents except Antarctica.

HABITAT

Depending on the species, turtles and tortoises can live on land, in fresh water, in the ocean, and along the coast. They live on many of the larger islands of the oceans and on every continent of the world except Antarctica.

DIET

Some species of turtles and tortoises are almost completely vegetarian, some eat almost nothing but meat, and still others eat a mix of meat and plants. Many turtles are opportunistic (ah-per-too-NIS-tik) feeders, meaning that they eat just about anything they can find, from fruits and leaves to live tadpoles and bits of dead fish. In some species, baby turtles eat mostly insects and other meat but switch to mostly plants as they get older.

BEHAVIOR AND REPRODUCTION

One of the most commonly known behaviors of turtles and tortoises is their ability to pull their legs, tail, neck, and head inside the shell. Many of them hide from attackers this way, but not all of them are able to do it. Side-necked turtles, for example, can pull in the tail and legs but can only tuck their necks along the bridge. Other species, like the big-headed turtle, are hidden-necked but their heads are too large to fit inside the shell. Other turtles have hinges in the lower shell that allow them to draw the lower and upper shells tight against one another once the head, neck, legs, and tail are inside. A few species even have hinges on the upper shell. Attacking animals, or predators (PREH-duh-ters), find it very difficult to get at the turtle's soft body inside such a tightly closed shell, and the turtle usually survives without harm. Besides protecting the turtle from attackers, the shells protect the turtle from drying out too much on hot, dry days. Hinges in the back of the plastron also allow the shell to open wide enough for some female turtles to lay large eggs.

Many water-living turtles are excellent swimmers. Some, such as leatherback turtles, have paddle-like front legs that help them swim hundreds of miles in a year. Others, such as softshell turtles, have webbing between their toes that helps them sweep through the water. Some species of water-living turtles, however, are poor swimmers. American mud and musk turtles, for example, are small to medium-sized turtles that move slowly through the water by walking across the bottom rather than swimming. Land-living turtles and tortoises can get around quite well on the ground, although their shells do not allow enough leg movement for fast running.

Turtles and tortoises are able to protect themselves from predators by hiding inside their shells and in other ways. Many turtles have musk glands, which are small sacs that ooze a substance with a strong odor. This odor may be enough to make a predator stop its attack and leave the area. Some turtles fight back with strong bites. Snapping turtles, for example, are vicious and quickly fling out their long necks to bite at anything or anyone coming too close. Besides having a hard bite, snapping turtles have sharp claws that can badly scratch anyone who picks up the turtle from behind. Other species that are quick to bite include softshell and musk turtles.

During mating season, or courtship, the males of many species of turtles and tortoises try to attract females by methods that can range from head bobbing and gentle rubbing against the female to biting her legs or ramming his shell into hers. Some species, on the other hand, have no such courtship behaviors. Species that live in warmer areas may mate and nest at various times of the year, but those that live in cooler areas usually mate in the fall or spring and nest in the spring or summer. In many species, the female can mate once and lay eggs from that mating for several years.

Most female turtles and tortoises nest by finding a spot on dry land, digging a hole, dropping the eggs inside, and burying them. A few species skip making a hole and simply lay their eggs among leaves on the surface of the ground. Most turtles and tortoises provide no further care for their eggs or young. The Asian giant tortoise is an exception. The female of this species lays her eggs and stays with the nest for a few days to keep away predators. Most of the smaller species of turtles and tortoises lay one to four eggs at a time, but larger species can lay fifty or more. For most turtles and tortoises, the temperature of the nest controls whether the eggs hatch into males or females. A very warm nest usually produces females, and a cooler nest produces males. In some species, an extremely cold nest temperature produces females too. In a few species, the nests have about equal numbers of males and females, no matter what the temperature of the nest. Newly hatched turtles and tortoises, or hatchlings, have a small, hard, tooth-like part on the upper jaw called a caruncle (KAR-un-kul), which helps them break out of the egg. Hatchlings usually head straight for the water or for a hiding spot on land, but a few species that hatch during cold winter months stay underground until spring. Adults of many species that live in colder climates enter a state of deep sleep, or hibernation (high-bur-NAY-shun), during the winter months. Many species that live in hotter areas survive dry weather by entering a state of deep sleep known as estivation (est-ih-VAY-shun).

HOW TURTLES AND TORTOISES USE THEIR SHELLS

A turtle's shell can be important in several ways. It can help the turtle protect itself from attacking animals. The shells of some turtles are so thick and strong that they can even resist the bite of a large crocodile. Other turtles, such as Asian river turtles, often dive very deeply, where the water pressure would be severe enough to crush their lungs if they were not protected by the shell. In turtles that live in very dry places, the shell provides a shield from the sun and helps the turtle keep from drying out too much. Tortoises, which live only on land, use their shells for yet another purpose. They collect rain in the crevices of their upper shells and then tip their bodies forward so the water runs down the sides and into their mouths.

TURTLES, TORTOISES, AND PEOPLE

Many people hunt turtles for food or to use in making traditional medicines. Humans also collect many kinds of turtles and tortoises for the pet trade.

CONSERVATION STATUS

According to the World Conservation Union (IUCN), nearly half of all living species of turtles and tortoises are at risk of becoming extinct. The U.S. Fish and Wildlife Service lists thirteen U.S. species and twenty-four foreign species as Endangered. Many species are at risk because of overhunting and overcollecting or because their habitat is disappearing. Efforts are under way to protect many species.

FOR MORE INFORMATION

Books:

Behler, John L., and F. Wayne King. *The Audubon Society Field Guide to North American Reptiles and Amphibians.* New York: Knopf, 1979.

Burnie, David, and Don E. Wilson, eds. *Animal: The Definitive Visual Guide to the World's Wildlife.* London: Dorling Kindersley, 2001.

Conant, Roger, and Joseph T. Collins. *A Field Guide to Reptiles and Amphibians of Eastern and Central North America.* 3rd ed. Boston: Houghton Mifflin, 1998.

Ernst, C. H., and R. W. Barbour. *Turtles of the World.* Washington, DC: Smithsonian Institution Press, 1989.

Ernst, C. H., J. E. Lovich, and R. W. Barbour. *Turtles of the United States and Canada.* Washington, DC: Smithsonian Institution Press, 1994.

Harding, J. H., and J. A. Holman. *Michigan Turtles and Lizards.* East Lansing: Michigan State University, 1990.

Pough, F. H., R. M. Andrews, J. E. Cadle, M. L. Crump, A. H. Savitzky, and K. D. Wells. *Herpetology.* Upper Saddle River, NJ: Prentice Hall, 1998.

Stebbins, Robert C. *A Field Guide to Western Reptiles and Amphibians.* 3rd ed. Boston: Houghton Mifflin, 2003.

Zug, G. R., L. J. Vitt, and J. P. Caldwell. *Herpetology: An Introductory Biology of Amphibians and Reptiles.* San Diego, CA: Academic Press, 2001.

PIG-NOSE TURTLE

Carettochelyidae

Class: Reptilia

Order: Testudines

Family: Carettochelyidae

One species: Pig-nose turtle (*Carettochekys insculpta*)

PHYSICAL CHARACTERISTICS

This family has only one member: the pig-nose turtle. This is quite a large freshwater turtle, with an upper shell that can reach 22 inches (56 centimeters) in length and 14 inches (35.6 centimeters) in width. It may weigh up to 50 pounds (22.7 kilograms). It often swims with just its long snout sticking out of the water. That long snout is one of its most notable features. A fleshy, tube-shaped structure, it is similar in appearance to the snout of a pig. The shell of the pig-nose turtle is also different from that of most other turtles. The shells of most turtles are covered in bony plates, called "scutes" (SCOOTS). The pig-nose turtle, on the other hand, has a hard shell with a leathery covering.

This turtle also has long front legs that can stretch to a length almost half as long as the carapace (KARE-a-pays), or upper shell. The legs are flat and wide, like paddles or flippers. In fact, the limbs, or legs, more nearly look like the front legs of marine turtles, or turtles that live in the sea, than those of other freshwater turtles. Each front limb is tipped with two claws. In color, the turtle is mostly olive or gray on the tops of its limbs and high-domed upper shell and is whitish or yellowish on its bottom shell, or plastron (PLAS-trun), and on its chin, lower neck, and the undersides of its limbs. Males and females look very much alike, except for the male's larger tail. Besides their smaller size, juveniles (JOO-vuh-nuhls), or young turtles, differ from adults in the smoothness of the carapace. The juvenile carapace has a lumpy ridge, called a "keel," down the middle and is jagged along the edge, whereas the adult carapace does

phylum

class

subclass

order

monotypic order

suborder

▲ **family**

not have a keel anywhere except toward the back, and it is rounded at the edge.

At one time scientists believed that these turtles should be included with the side-necked turtles, a group known as the Pleurodira, rather than the hidden-necked turtles, or the Cryptodira. The better-known hidden-necked turtles pull their heads and necks straight back into their shells, whereas side-necked turtles fold their necks sideways. Scientists based their decision mostly on the location of the first turtle discovered back in the late 1800s. The original specimen (SPEH-suh-muhn), or example, was not whole; it was missing the part of its backbone that would have shown scientists whether it was a side-necked or a hidden-necked turtle. Because it was found in New Guinea and all of the other turtles known from New Guinea or from Australia at that time were of the side-necked variety, the scientific community assumed that the pig-nose turtle must be a side-necked turtle too. As more of these turtles turned up, however, scientists were able to take a closer look at the backbone, and they discovered that this species should be considered a hidden-necked turtle.

GEOGRAPHIC RANGE

This turtle is found in southern New Guinea and northern Australia.

HABITAT

The pig-nose turtle usually lives in freshwater rivers, lakes, swamps, and other water bodies with shady shorelines. Sometimes it makes its home in saltier estuaries (EHS-chew-air-eez), or the wide parts at the lower end of rivers that link these water bodies to the ocean. They tend to prefer slower-moving and even unmoving waters that have soft bottoms of silt, or loose earth, on top of sand or gravel. The pig-nose turtle is sometimes also called Fly River turtle, because it is found in the Fly River in Papua, New Guinea. Scientists once thought the turtle lived only in New Guinea, but ten of the turtles were discovered in Australia's Daly

River in 1970. They later were also found in the Alligator River system of Australia about 240 miles (386 kilometers) from the Daly River site, as well as other places in northern Australia.

DIET

Pig-nose turtles will eat just about anything they can find. They seem to prefer plants; they especially like figs and other fruits that drop from trees along the shoreline, but they will eat leaves, flowers, underwater plants, and the tiny plantlike growths called algae (AL-jee). They will also eat hard cones that require a solid bite to break open. They are not strict plant eaters, however. If the turtles find the wormlike young form of an insect, called a "grub"; a beetle; or an ant, they will eat those too. They will even partake of freshwater snails or other mollusks, crustaceans (krus-TAY-shuns) such as shrimp, or even dead mammals or birds.

BEHAVIOR AND REPRODUCTION

Unlike most other water-living turtles, the pig-nose turtle swims by paddling its large front legs, rather than using mainly its hind legs. It uses the hind limbs, which have webbing, to help them paddle and steer. They do not bask, or sun themselves, but they do warm their bodies by swimming to areas of the water with higher temperatures, such as small thermal springs, or hot springs. There, they lie on the river bottom, above the outpouring of hot water, and heat up their "cold-blooded" bodies. Like other animals that are cold-blooded, their body temperatures vary, depending on the outside temperature: In cool water, they are cool; in warm water, they are warm.

These turtles spend much of the day eating. Several of them will sometimes group together and share a good food source when they find one. Otherwise, the turtles spread out, with males and females ranging over a fairly large area: males are known to travel over a 5-mile (8-kilometer) area of river and females over a 2-mile (3.2-kilometer) area.

Males and females come together once a year or possibly once every two years to mate. Scientists know little about their courtship or other mating activities, but the turtles have been seen nesting in the evening and at night toward the end of the dry season, and some females have more than one set of young in a single year. The female makes her nest in a dry spot, often on a high beach. She scrapes out a shallow hole with her

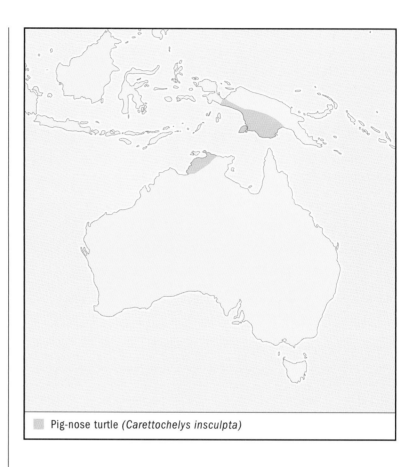

Pig-nose turtle (*Carettochelys insculpta*)

hind legs and drops in seven to thirty-nine round, brittle (BRIH-tuhl), or easily broken, eggs that measure 1.5–2.1 inches (3.8–5.3 centimeters) around and weigh 1.1–1.6 ounces (32–46 grams). The white eggs begin developing into young turtles immediately and are ready to hatch in sixty-four to seventy-four days, but the hatching time can be delayed temporarily until the rainy season starts. Because of this delay, the time from egg laying to hatching can be as little as eighty-six days or as much as 102 days. As with many other turtles, the outside temperature during the time before the eggs hatch can affect the number of male and female hatchlings. In this species, a warm spell about halfway through incubation produces females, and a cool spell produces males.

PIG-NOSE TURTLES AND PEOPLE

Pig-nose turtle eggs often fall victim to local people in New Guinea, who find the turtle's beach nests and collect the eggs for food. In both New Guinea and Australia, local people trap, net, spear, fish, and simply collect the turtles by hand for their meat. The turtle also is popular in the international pet trade, although it is protected in Australia.

CONSERVATION STATUS

Collection of the pig-nose turtle for food and as pets, combined with loss or destruction of their habitat, or preferred living areas, have all threatened this turtle. The World Conservation Union (IUCN) has given its status as Vulnerable, meaning that it faces a high risk of extinction, or dying out, in the wild. Logging and farming can destroy waterside plants and drastically increase erosion (ih-ROH-zhen), or wearing away of the land, both of which can affect the turtles. In addition, the passage of water buffalo on their way to watering holes may also hurt the turtles' chances of survival. The buffalos crush the plants that the turtles eat, and they also trample across the beaches used by the turtles to lay their eggs. Heavy foot traffic can destroy the nests and the eggs inside.

Pig-nose turtles often swim with just their long snouts sticking out of the water. (Illustration by Barbara Duperron. Reproduced by permission.)

FOR MORE INFORMATION

Books:

Cann, John. *Australian Freshwater Turtles.* Singapore: Beaumont Publishing, 1998.

Periodicals:

Bargeron, Michael. "The Pig-nosed Turtle, *Carettochelys insculpta.*" *Tortuga Gazette* 33, no. 3 (March 1997): 1–2.

Web sites:

"Carettochelyidae." Herpetology: Reptiles and Amphibians. http://www .nafcon.dircon.co.uk/Carettochelyidae.htm (accessed on August 19, 2004).

"The Pig-nosed Turtle." University of Canberra Australia Applied Ecology Research Group. http://aerg.canberra.edu.au/pub/aerg/herps/fncchely .htm (accessed on August 2, 2004).

AUSTRALO-AMERICAN SIDE-NECKED TURTLES

Chelidae

Class: Reptilia

Order: Testudines

Family: Chelidae

Number of species: 50 species

phylum

class

subclass

order

monotypic order

suborder

▲ **family**

PHYSICAL CHARACTERISTICS

Australo-American side-necked turtles are a varied group of medium-sized to rather large turtles with necks that fold sideways under their shells, rather than retracting, or pulling backward, into the shell. In some cases, the neck can be as long as the upper shell, or carapace (KARE-a-pays) or even longer. A few side-necked turtles, however, have very short necks. Depending on the species, the upper shell of adults can range in length from 6 to 19 inches (15–48 centimeters). Most turtles have dark upper shells, and a few have brightly colored lower shells, or plastrons (PLAS-truns); heads; necks; legs; or tails. These parts of the body may be red, orange, or yellow. Often, the juveniles (JOO-vuh-nuhls), or young turtles, are the most brightly colored; the color fades as they age. Some of these turtles have glands, or special organs, that give off a bad smell, which wards off predators, or other animals that hunt and kill the turtles. Males and females look quite similar, although the females in most species are larger than the males. In a few cases, the males have especially long tails that they may use in mating with females.

GEOGRAPHIC RANGE

These turtles range across New Guinea, Australia, Indonesia, and South America.

HABITAT

The Australo-American side-necked turtle typically lives in freshwater lakes, ponds, rivers, and streams that are always filled with water, but they spend part of their time in wetlands or flooded forests that are wet for just a short period of time each year. Only one species, the New Guinea snake-necked turtle, can be found in estuaries (EHS-chew-air-eez), or that part of a river where it meets the sea, and other areas of partially salty water.

DIET

Most members of this family eat meat or both meat and plants. The adult northern Australian snapping turtle may live only on vegetation, including algae (AL-jee), which are tiny plantlike growths that live in water, and the leaves and fruits of waterside trees they find during the dry season. The meat eaters may feed on worms, insects, fishes, and frogs. Some also eat mollusks, such as clams; crustaceans (krus-TAY-shuns), such as shrimp; or dead animal matter. Many of the mollusk eaters have large, broad jaws that they use to crush their prey's shell. Other species, particularly those that dine on fishes, have long necks that burst through the water when they are going after prey. As the turtle opens its mouth, both water and prey rush in. The turtle then spits out the water and swallows the animal.

OUT OF ANTARCTICA?

Australo-American side-necked turtles, both living animals and fossils (FAH-suhls), or remains of animals that lived long ago, are found in Australia and South America, but nowhere else. The large gap in their geographic range makes scientists believe that the South American and Australian species are related through a common ancestor that lived long ago in Earth's history, when the two continents were still linked together by what is now Antarctica. This common ancestor, which spread across Antarctica, could have migrated, or traveled, into the areas that eventually split off to become South America and Australia.

BEHAVIOR AND REPRODUCTION

Many Australo-American side-necked turtles feed mainly at night and spend their days basking, or warming themselves, in the sun. When a dry spell strikes, some species bury themselves in the mud and become inactive until the rains come. Steindachner's turtle is one example. This turtle can survive droughts (DROWTS), or dry spells, as long as two years by living off water that it stores inside its body in sacs, or pouches, called "accessory bladders." In cooler climates, some also hibernate, or become inactive, during the winter months. Most hibernate alone, but the common snake-necked turtle of Australia hibernates in groups. Other turtles, like the Argentine side-necked turtle, will take occasional breaks from hibernation (high-bur-NAY-shun) on warm days, when they venture out to a sunny spot and stretch out in the sun.

Except for the most tropical of species, which may breed all year, side-necked turtles mate in the early spring. Depending on the species, the female lays one to twenty-eight round or oblong eggs in a shallow depression, or hollow, under leaves; in an underground nook, or sheltered space; or in some other nest. The female of one species, the northern snake-necked turtle, lays her eggs underwater in the muddy bottom of a temporary pond. The eggs develop only after the pond dries up, and the young hatch before the next rainy season arrives. For those eggs laid in underground nests, the young hatch out of the eggs but stay in the nest until the rains come to soften the soil above them. Then they claw their way to the surface and take their first steps aboveground. The outdoor temperature has no effect on whether the eggs hatch into males or females, as it does with many other turtles.

AUSTRALO-AMERICAN SIDE-NECKED TURTLES AND PEOPLE

Some people hunt and kill these turtles for their meat, which they use as food. Although certain species are kept as pets, the pet trade does not harm their survival.

CONSERVATION STATUS

The World Conservation Union (IUCN) lists three species as Critically Endangered, or facing an extremely high risk of extinction, or death, in the wild, and four as Endangered, or facing a very high risk of extinction. Six are Vulnerable, meaning that they face a high risk of extinction, and eight are Near Threatened, meaning that they face the risk of becoming extinct in the near future. One of the Critically Endangered turtles is the western swamp turtle, of which fewer than four hundred individuals survived in 2003, and all live in a few small areas of Brazil. Another turtle, called Hoge's side-necked turtle, is also very rare, existing in just a few spots in the same country. The U.S. Fish and Wildlife Service lists two species as Endangered. The main reason for concern about these species is loss of their habitat, through either damage or complete destruction. Efforts are under way to save these threatened species from extinction by removing them from the wild and breeding them in captivity, possibly for future release back into the wild.

Matamata (*Chelus fimbriatus*)

MATAMATA
Chelus fimbriatus

Physical characteristics: The matamata is one of the larger side-necked turtles as well as one of the biggest freshwater turtles; its dark upper shell can reach up to 18 inches (46 centimeters) in length, and it can grow to a weight of 27 pounds (12 kilograms). It has a flat, lumpy, triangular head, with a rough fringe, or edging. The head sticks out from a flat, knobby shell. Two tiny eyes dot the head. The turtle's upper shell is mostly dark brown. Juveniles have a pinkish-orange lower shell. Often, only the turtle's head is visible in the water, and

sometimes just its tube-shaped nose breaks the water's surface as the turtle moves about underwater. Females usually are larger than males.

Geographic range: The matamata lives in northern South America.

Habitat: These turtles prefer still or slow-moving freshwater habitats, or areas in which to live, but some are able to live in saltier waters. Although matamatas sometimes live in swift-moving rivers, they stay out of the current and move beneath underwater banks or logs.

Diet: The matamata is mainly a fish-eating species; it ambushes, or attacks, its prey by settling on the bottom and waiting for a fish to approach. Water currents brush the turtle's head fringes back and forth, and many scientists think that this movement attracts fishes. When the prey is close enough, the turtle darts out its head while enlarging its neck and mouth, and sucks in a great gulp of water along with the prey. The turtle then releases the water from its mouth and eats the fish. Some turtle experts believe that the skin flaps, or fringes, on the head may also help the turtle sense water movement and know when prey species are swimming through the murky, or dark, water of muddy ponds.

Behavior and reproduction: Rarely seen, this side-necked turtle often travels through the water by walking along the bottom and only occasionally takes an awkward swim. Juveniles are known to bask, but adults do not. Once a year, the females make nests, sometimes in riverbanks, where they lay eight to twenty-eight round eggs that measure 1.4–1.6 inches (3.6–4 centimeters) in diameter, or width. The eggs hatch more than six months later. Little is known about courtship, mating, or other activities of these turtles in the wild.

Matamatas and people: Matamatas are quite popular in the pet trade, probably because of their unusual fringed heads.

Conservation status: This turtle is not threatened. ■

FOR MORE INFORMATION

Books:

Burnie, David, and Don E. Wilson, eds. *Animal: The Definitive Visual Guide to the World's Wildlife.* London: Dorling Kindersley, 2001.

Cann, John. *Australian Freshwater Turtles.* Singapore: Beaumont Publishing, 1998.

Pritchard, Peter C. H., and Pedro Trebbau. *The Turtles of Venezuela.* Athens, OH: Society for the Study of Amphibians and Reptiles, 1984.

SEATURTLES

Cheloniidae

Class: Reptilia
Order: Testudines
Family: Cheloniidae
Number of species: 6 species

phylum
class
subclass
order
monotypic order
suborder
▲ **family**

PHYSICAL CHARACTERISTICS

The seaturtles are large animals that live in the ocean. Their upper shell, or carapace (KARE-a-pays), is quite flat rather than highly rounded. The lower shell, or plastron (PLAS-trun), is a bit smaller than in most turtles and attaches to the upper shell by tough but flexible tissues called ligaments (LIH-guh-ments), rather than the bony bridge common to land turtles. Seaturtles are excellent swimmers, gliding through the water with sweeps of their large, broad, and powerful front limbs, which look like flippers or paddles. Unlike many other turtles, they cannot retract, or pull back, their limbs or heads into their shells. The largest members of the family, the leatherback seaturtles, tip the scales at half a ton (454 kilograms) or more. The leatherbacks have a carapace that measures 6 to 7 feet (1.8–2.1 meters) in length.

GEOGRAPHIC RANGE

Seaturtles inhabit all the oceans of the world and the Mediterranean Sea.

HABITAT

These turtles live in saltwater from the tropics to areas with mild climates well north and south of the equator, the imaginary circle around Earth that is midway between the poles. They are more common close to shore than far out to sea, and they feed and nest at sites along the coastlines on continental shelves, or shallow plains forming the borders of continents.

DIET

Most seaturtles are primarily meat eaters. Their diets are made up of a variety of marine, or sea, animals, including fishes; snails and other mollusks (MAH-lusks), or animals with a soft, unsegmented body covered by a shell; barnacles and other crustaceans (krus-TAY-shuns), or animals with a soft, segmented body covered by a shell; and certain sponges and sea urchins. The green seaturtle is the only member of the family that is known to prefer eating plants. Sea grasses make up the majority of its diet.

BEHAVIOR AND REPRODUCTION

Perhaps the most famous behavior of seaturtles is migration (my-GRAY-shun). An individual seaturtle may travel hundreds of miles to go from its feeding area to its nesting site and back. Usually, the feeding grounds are in temperate waters, which are neither very warm nor very cold; the nesting areas, on the other hand, are in tropical waters, which are very warm. The distance between the two places can result in a trek, or journey, of 190 miles (306 kilometers) or more, one way. When the winter months arrive, many turtles migrate (MY-grayt) to warmer tropical waters, but some drop down to the muddy bottoms of coastal waters and bury themselves there to survive the coldest temperatures.

Female seaturtles typically produce several clutches, or nests, of eggs in a season—sometimes seven or more—but they do so only once every two or three years. Rarely, a seaturtle will nest every year. In some cases, the female turtles will gather offshore in groups. Members of these groups clamber onto shore to make nests near one another. The females of almost all species wait until nightfall to dig their nests and lay their eggs. The round eggs are leathery and range from about 1 to 2 inches (2.5–5 centimeters) in diameter, or width across each egg. A single clutch may contain up to 250 eggs, but 90–130 is more com-

TRAWLING AND TURTLES

Trawling is a type of fishing business that many scientists believe is dangerous to marine life, including seaturtles. In this kind of fishing, a device scrapes the seafloor and collects animals that live on the bottom. For turtles, the danger is not in accidentally collecting them but rather in disturbing them as they move from feeding grounds to nesting sites. One study of olive ridley seaturtles found that trawling delayed the arrival of the female turtles at their nesting sites, and the females laid their eggs later in the year, when temperatures were warmer. The warmer temperature meant that the young ridleys were mostly females. Scientists believe that if this shift in the numbers of males and females continues, it could have an effect on the survival of this endangered species.

mon. The eggs hatch in forty to seventy days. As with most turtles, the outdoor temperature during their incubation (ing-kyuh-BAY-shun), or the period of time before the eggs hatch, determines whether the egg will become a male or female upon hatching. When the weather is warm, more females hatch; males usually hatch when the weather is cooler.

SEA TURTLES AND PEOPLE

Humans have long sought seaturtles and seaturtle eggs as food. Some people make the eggshells into trinkets. Adult leatherback seaturtles are also prized for their skins.

CONSERVATION STATUS

The World Conservation Union (IUCN) lists the olive ridley, loggerhead, and green seaturtles as Endangered, meaning that they face a very high risk of extinction in the wild in the near future. The hawksbill and Atlantic ridley seaturtles are Critically Endangered, meaning that they face an extremely high risk of extinction in the wild in the near future. Hunting and egg collecting, along with dangers that come from shrimping and fishing practices, are responsible for much of the decline in turtle numbers. The U.S. Fish and Wildlife Service lists the olive ridley seaturtle as Threatened, meaning that it is likely to face the danger of extinction in the near future in the United States. Certain populations of green seaturtle are Endangered, and others are Threatened. The hawksbill and Kemp's ridley are Endangered, and the loggerhead is Threatened.

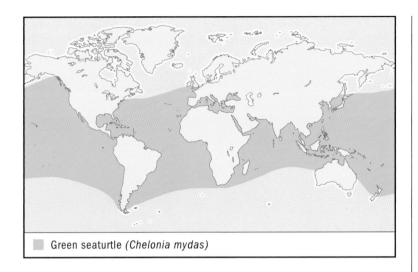

Green seaturtle (*Chelonia mydas*)

GREEN SEATURTLE
Chelonia mydas

Physical characteristics: The green seaturtle is dark brown to black, with a whitish underside. This turtle gets its name from the color of its body fat, which is green from their diet of algae (AL-jee), or tiny, plantlike growths that live in water. The upper shell of this large turtle can measure 5 feet (1.5 meters) in length, and the turtle itself can weigh as much as 750 pounds (340 kilograms). It has large, flipper-like front legs, with which it swims, and a fairly flat upper shell, to slice more easily through the water. Compared with females, males have a long claw on the front flipper and a lengthier tail and narrower upper shell.

Geographic range: The green seaturtle lives in tropical and temperate seas around the world.

Habitat: Although they sometimes can be found in temperate salt-water areas or far out at sea, green seaturtles are much more common in shallow, sea-grass-covered coastlines and in the warmer waters of the tropics.

Diet: Adult green seaturtles spend much of the daylight hours munching on sea grasses and algae, which are the main items of their diet. Only rarely do they eat a bit of meat, such as a sponge or jellyfish. Some

The upper shell of the green seaturtle can measure 5 feet (1.5 meters) in length, and the turtle itself can weigh as much as 750 pounds (340 kilograms). (©Dr. Paula A. Zahl/Photo Researchers, Inc. Reproduced by permission.)

scientists believe that the young may eat much more meat, but there is no evidence that they do.

Behavior and reproduction: As a cold-blooded animal, or one that gets its body warmth from the surrounding environment, the seaturtle does different things to maintain a healthy body temperature, such as rising to the sunshine-drenched top of the water column. Unlike other saltwater-living turtles, this species will even crawl up on the shoreline to bask, or rest, in the sun. When winter cold arrives, some species hibernate (HIGH-bur-nayt), or become inactive, by dropping down to the bottom of the water and burying themselves in the mud. In the breeding season, when they reproduce, males and females may migrate more than 1,900 miles (3,058 kilometers) from their feeding grounds to their nesting sites. There, males try to attract the females by giving them little nips, nudges, and sniffs; the turtles mate in the water. A single female may mate with several males, and so the young in a female's clutch may have different fathers, some from matings that happened several years earlier. When she is ready to lay her eggs, the female will crawl up onto a dry coastline, dig a hole, and drop in fewer than a dozen to nearly 240 eggs, although 108 to 120 per nest is typical. She may lay two to five nests, and sometimes as many as seven, in a single season. The leathery, round eggs hatch in one to three months.

Green seaturtles and people: For centuries, humans have hunted green seaturtles for their meat and their eggs, which they eat for food.

Conservation status: The IUCN lists this species as Endangered. The U.S. Fish and Wildlife Service lists the breeding populations in Florida and the Pacific coast of Mexico as Endangered and all other populations as Threatened. Besides hunting and collecting, these turtles are in danger from the development of their nesting grounds into seafront resorts, from fishing nets that entangle them and often lead to their deaths by drowning, and from boaters who unknowingly run over them with their motor propellers. ■

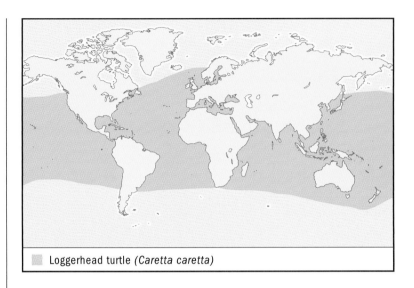

Loggerhead turtle (*Caretta caretta*)

LOGGERHEAD TURTLE
Caretta caretta

Physical characteristics: The loggerhead turtle has a short head that is wide at the rear and rounded at the front. It is the largest seaturtle, with a carapace up to 7 feet (2.1 meters) long and a weight of half a ton (454 kilograms). It has a hard shell with a keel, or upper ridge, down the middle and large, flipper-like front limbs. The upper shell is reddish brown to greenish, and the lower shell is whitish to yellowish.

Geographic range: The loggerhead lives in tropical and temperate oceans of the world, as well as the Mediterranean Sea.

Habitat: For the breeding season, this saltwater turtle prefers tropical waters in protected areas, such as bays, or parts of the sea that cut into a coastline, and estuaries (EHS-chew-air-eez), or the wide parts at the lower ends of rivers, where the river meets the sea. The turtle travels well into temperate regions during the remainder of the year.

Diet: Meat is the primary food of both young and adult loggerheads. Hatchlings, or newly hatched turtles, will also eat pieces of the algae mats among which they float, and adults will munch on underwater

plants and algae. Favored food items for adults include snails and other mollusks, sponges, squid, and fishes.

Behavior and reproduction: Females sometimes migrate every year, but usually every two to three years, from feeding areas to nesting sites, which may be 1,300 to 1,700 miles (2,092–2,736 kilometers) away. While migrating, the males court the females with little bites, and the two turtles mate while floating in the water. After mating with one or more males, the female arrives at the nesting site, waits until nightfall to crawl onshore, digs a hole, and typically lays 96 to 120 round eggs. She may lay up to seven clutches in a single season. In about two months the eggs hatch. The young from a single female—even young from the same clutch—may have more than one father. The incubation temperature determines the sex of turtles, with higher temperatures producing females and lower temperatures producing males.

Loggerhead turtles and people: Some people still hunt this turtle and collect its eggs for food.

Conservation status: The IUCN lists the loggerhead as Endangered, and the U.S. Fish and Wildlife Service describes them as Threatened. Development of coastal properties seems to be destroying their nesting areas, which has led to their decline. ◼

FOR MORE INFORMATION

Books:

Bjorndal, Karen A. *Biology and Conservation of Sea Turtles.* Washington, DC: Smithsonian Institution Press, 1995.

Dunbier, Sally. *Sea Turtles.* Hauppauge, NY: Barron's Educational Service Series, 2000.

Kalman, Bobbie. *The Life Cycle of a Sea Turtle.* New York: Crabtree Publishing, 2002.

Laskey, Kathryn. *Interrupted Journey: Saving Endangered Sea Turtles.* Cambridge, MA: Candlewick Press, 2001.

Lutz, Peter L., and John A. Musick, eds. *The Biology of Sea Turtles.* 2 volumes. Boca Raton, FL: CRC Press, 1996–2003.

O'Keefe, M. Timothy. *Sea Turtles: The Watcher's Guide.* Lakeland, FL: Larsen's Outdoor Publishing, 1995.

Web sites:

"Animal Bytes: Sea Turtles." Animals. http://www.seaworld.org/animal info/animalbytes/animalia/eumetazoa/coelomates/deuterostomes/ chordates/craniata/reptilia/testudines/sea-turtles.htm (accessed on September 7, 2004).

"Sea Turtles for Kids." Kidz Korner. http://www.turtles.org/kids.htm (accessed on September 7, 2004).

"Turtles in Trouble." *National Geographic Kids.* http://www.nationalgeo graphic.com/ngkids/9911/turtle (accessed on September 7, 2004).

SNAPPING TURTLES

Chelydridae

Class: Reptilia

Order: Testudines

Family: Chelydridae

Number of species: 4 species

PHYSICAL CHARACTERISTICS

Snapping turtles are large, unfriendly turtles that have strong, clawed legs; a powerful bite; and a long neck. With its long neck, the snapping turtle can quickly swing its large head far forward as well as sideways and back over the upper shell. These turtles also have a long, strong tail with a row of ridges. The upper shell, or carapace (KARE-a-pays), has three keels, or ridges, but older turtles usually lose the keels and have smooth shells. The lower shell, or plastron (PLAS-trun), is quite small, which allows the turtle to move its legs easily. The length of an adult's upper shell ranges from 7.1 to 31.5 inches (18 to 80 centimeters), and the lower shell may be only about one-fourth that size. Females weigh about 4.4 to 5.5 pounds (2 to 2.5 kilograms). Males generally are larger than females and can weigh as much as 249 pounds (113 kilograms).

GEOGRAPHIC RANGE

Snapping turtles live in North America, Central America, and South America, from southern Canada to Ecuador.

HABITAT

These turtles mainly live in permanent water bodies, ones that are filled with water all year long. Some are able to survive in somewhat salty waters, but they typically prefer freshwater. Although they spend the majority of their time in the water, they will travel quite a distance over land to nest, and one species makes overland trips from one watering hole to another.

phylum

class

subclass

order

monotypic order

suborder

▲ **family**

THE LURE OF THE TURTLE

Besides being the biggest member of the snapping turtle family, the alligator snapping turtle has another interesting feature. It uses a bit of flesh on its tongue to draw in hungry fishes. This "lure" not only looks like a pink worm but also wiggles like a worm. When a fish approaches to nab an easy lunch, the turtle quickly lashes out and clamps its strong jaws around the unsuspecting fish. Besides fishes, this turtle's diet includes snails, clams, plant roots, other turtles, birds, and even small alligators.

DIET

Snapping turtles are primarily meat eaters, dining on almost anything they can find, whether it is alive or dead. The diet includes worms, insects, snails, and larger items, such as other turtles, ducklings, and small mammals. Although it is not common, some turtles can live on an all-plant diet.

BEHAVIOR AND REPRODUCTION

Most people know snapping turtles for their unfriendly personality. The turtles can quickly strike out with their long necks and powerful jaws and snap at any passing animals, whether it is a fish or other prey they want to eat or a person who comes too close. Instead of teeth, they have a hook at the front of the upper jaw that helps in grasping and then tearing apart prey. Snapping turtles occasionally sunbathe, or "bask," on land, but more typically they float just below the water's surface and soak up the warmth there. Snapping turtles that live in warmer climates are active day and night all year long, but those that live in cooler areas usually are active only during the day and typically spend the cold winter months buried in the muddy bottom of a waterhole.

During the breeding season, the female digs a hole on land, sometimes near the water and at other times quite far away, in dry areas. There, she lays up to 109 round eggs and buries them. Snapping turtles provide no care for the eggs or the young that hatch from the eggs. The outdoor temperature controls the number of males and females in each batch of eggs.

SNAPPING TURTLES AND PEOPLE

Although snapping turtles are not especially friendly, they are of little threat to humans who do not bother them. Humans hunt the turtles for food and occasionally for the pet trade.

CONSERVATION STATUS

The World Conservation Union (IUCN) lists the alligator snapping turtle as Vulnerable, which means that there is a high threat of their extinction: they could die out entirely. There are many sources for these threats, including too much hunting of them and the loss of good habitat.

Snapping turtle (*Chelydra serpentina*)

SNAPPING TURTLE
Chelydra serpentina

Physical characteristics: The snapping turtle, or snapper, is a fairly large member of this family. The upper shell is up to 19.3 inches (49 centimeters) in length. The shell is dark, usually black to greenish-brown, and frequently covered with green, slimy algae (AL-jee), or plantlike growths. The upper shell and the long tail have a series of ridges. The shell ridges become less and less noticeable as the animal ages. Snapping turtles have large heads with a hook on the upper jaw.

Geographic range: Snapping turtles live in North America, Central America, and South America, from southern Canada to Ecuador.

During the breeding season, the female snapping turtle digs a hole on land. There, she lays up to 109 round eggs and buries them. The outdoor temperature controls the number of males and females in each batch of eggs. (E. R. Degginger/Bruce Coleman, Inc. Reproduced by permission.)

Habitat: These turtles typically live in plant-filled, shallow, calm waters with mucky bottoms. Most make their homes in freshwater areas, but some live quite well in somewhat salty waters.

Diet: Like most members of this family, the snapping turtle eats mostly meat. It is not a picky eater. Snapping turtles will eat earthworms and leeches; clams; insects and spiders; frog eggs, tadpoles, and adult frogs; reptiles, including other turtles; ducklings and other small birds; small mammals; and almost any dead animal they come across. Plants are not uncommon, and some populations of turtles even live by eating only plants.

Behavior and reproduction: Despite its usually slow walking speed on land, this turtle is amazingly swift when it comes to striking out with its powerful jaws to grab a passing animal as a meal or to defend itself against a large attacking animal or a person who is just a bit too curious. With its long neck, this turtle can swing its head forward, sideways, and backward almost half as far as it is long, and its powerful jaws can deliver a nasty bite to a person's hand or fingers.

For the most part, the snapping turtle stays in the water, where it spends most of its time sunbathing or hunting for food. To sunbathe, or "bask," the turtles float in warm water near or at the surface. Rarely, a snapper will bask on shore on a log or rock. They often hunt by hiding in the muddy bottom to wait for a tasty treat, like a fish or tadpole, to swim by. They also hunt by slowly walking along the water bottom and looking for their next meal. Turtles living in warmer climates are active day and night and all year long. Those living in cooler, northern areas are mostly active early and late in the day and spend the colder months buried underwater in the mucky bottom.

Mating season runs from spring to fall. Some males may sway their heads in front of females to attract them, but usually the males skip courtship altogether. Females lay one batch of eggs a year. Sometimes they make their nests, which are just holes they dig in the ground, close to the water, but they also may travel great distances, in some cases nearly 10 miles (16 kilometers). Females can lay six to 109 round, white eggs; they typically lay about thirty-two eggs per nest. The eggs hatch in about seventy-five to ninety-five days, but sometimes they hatch in as little as two months or as much as six months.

Nest temperature controls the sex of the newly hatched young turtles. High and low temperatures produce females, and moderate temperatures produce males. Because a female can lay so many eggs at a time and the nest is so large, some parts of the nest may be warmer or cooler than others. This often means that females will hatch from one part of the nest and males from another.

Snapping turtles and people: Humans hunt snapping turtles for their meat. Many turtles also die each year from being hit by cars as they cross roads to move from a water hole to a nesting site and back.

Conservation status: These turtles are not threatened, although many snapping turtle eggs are destroyed each year when raccoons and other mammals dig up the freshly laid nests and eat the eggs. ■

FOR MORE INFORMATION

Books:

Behler, John L., and F. Wayne King. *The Audubon Society Field Guide to North American Reptiles and Amphibians.* New York: Knopf, 1979.

Burnie, David, and Don E. Wilson, eds. *Animal: The Definitive Visual Guide to the World's Wildlife.* London: Dorling Kindersley, 2001.

Conant, Roger, and Joseph T. Collins. *A Field Guide to Reptiles and Amphibians: Eastern and Central North America.* Boston: Houghton Mifflin, 1998.

Harding, J., and J. Holman. *Michigan Turtles and Lizards: A Field Guide and Pocket Reference.* East Lansing: Michigan State University Museum, 1990.

Hickman, Pamela. *Turtle Rescue: Changing the Future for Endangered Wildlife.* Richmond Hill, Ontario, Canada: Firefly Books, 2004.

O'Keefe, M. Timothy. *Sea Turtles: The Watcher's Guide.* Lakeland, FL: Larsen's Outdoor Publishing, 1995.

Pritchard, P. C. H. *The Alligator Snapping Turtle: Biology and Conservation.* Milwaukee, WI: Milwaukee Public Museum, 1989.

Stebbins, Robert C. *A Field Guide to Western Reptiles and Amphibians.* Boston: Houghton Mifflin, 2003.

Web sites:

"Common Snapping Turtle." Chesapeake Bay Program. http://www.chesapeakebay.net/info/snapping_turtle.cfm (accessed on September 14, 2004).

Dillon, C. Dee. "The Common Snapping Turtle" *Tortuga Gazette* 34, no. 3 (March 1998): 1–4. http://www.tortoise.org/archives/snapping.html (accessed on September 14, 2004).

LeClere, Jeff. "Snapping Turtle: *Chelydra serpentine.*" Iowa Herpetology. http://www.herpnet.net/IowaHerpetology/reptiles/turtles/snapping_turtle .html (accessed on September 14, 2004).

family
C H A P T E R

PHYSICAL CHARACTERISTICS

The only living Central American river turtle, which has the scientific name *Dermatemys mawii*, is a large animal with a small head and a pointy snout. It has a dark-colored, somewhat flat upper shell, or carapace (KARE-a-pays). The carapace of adults is thick, heavy, and smooth. It is so smooth that is almost looks like it is made of leather. The yellow- or cream-colored lower shell, or plastron (PLAS-trun), is large, as is the bony bridge that connects the upper and lower shells. The feet are webbed. Females and males look similar, but females are generally larger. In addition, the upper surface of a male's head has a large yellowish gold patch, while females as well as juveniles (JOO-vuh-nuhl), or the young, have gray on the top of the head. The biggest Central American river turtles can weigh as much as 49 pounds (22 kilograms) and have a carapace as long as 26 inches (66 centimeters).

GEOGRAPHIC RANGE

Central American river turtles live in Mexico, Guatemala, and Belize.

HABITAT

Although some of them may wander into somewhat salty water, Central American river turtles live mainly in freshwater, such as rivers and large lakes. The turtles live in the lowlands of southern Mexico near the Gulf of Mexico. They also live in Belize and northern Guatemala, and possibly in Honduras.

phylum

class

subclass

order

monotypic order

suborder

▲ **family**

THE TURTLE OF MANY NAMES

Besides Central American river turtle, this animal has other common names, including hickety in Belize; jicotea, tortuga plana, and tortuga aplanada in Mexico; and tortuga blanca in Mexico and Guatemala. The word "blanca" means "white" in Spanish and refers either to the white underside of the turtle or to the color of its meat. Some people refer to this turtle as the Mesoamerican (MEH-soh-American) river turtle. Mesoamerican is the word used to describe the culture of Mexico and northern Central America before the Spanish explorers arrived.

DIET

Central American river turtles eat mostly plants. They prefer figs and other fruits as well as leaves that fall into the water from the trees lining the shoreline. They also eat plants that grow in the water and sometimes an insect, fish, or mollusk (MAH-lusk). Mollusks are soft-bodied animals covered by a shell, such as snails and clams.

BEHAVIOR AND REPRODUCTION

Central American river turtles spend most of their lives in the water. Turtles have lungs and breathe air, but the Central American river turtle is able to stay underwater for long periods of time. In the rare instances when the turtles do leave the water, they are very slow, awkward walkers. They sometimes float in the surface waters on sunny days to soak up some heat, but they do not leave the water, as many other turtles do, to sunbathe, or bask. Besides floating near the surface on warm days, the turtles do little during the day. They become active at night, when they do most of their feeding.

Central American river turtles mate anytime from March to September. For the most part, the only time the turtles leave the water is during the nesting season, which starts in September, when the rainy season is in full force. The turtles nest any time from September to December, but some females start as early as late August or wait until March or April. When she is ready to lay her eggs, the female walks a few feet onto the shore, usually no more than 10 feet (3 meters), and digs a hole. She lays two to twenty brittle-shelled eggs that are about 2.1–2.8 inches (53–71 millimeters) long and 1.2–2 inches (30–51 millimeters) wide and weigh about 1.2–2.5 ounces (34–71 grams) each. A typical nest has eight to fourteen eggs. The female buries the eggs under mud and bits of rotting, nearby plants. The mother turtles usually produce two nests a year, but some have only one nest, and others may make three or four nests each season. Usually the largest females lay the most eggs in a year, and the smallest females lay the fewest. Because female Central American river turtles lay their eggs so close to the water,

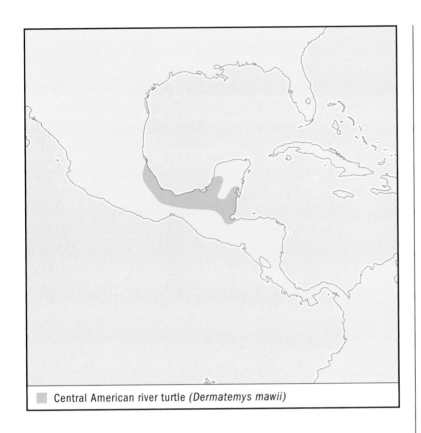

Central American river turtle (*Dermatemys mawii*)

during the rainy season the lake or river can overflow onto the shore and flood the nests. The good news is that the eggs can survive being underwater for up to one month. The eggs need about seven to ten months to hatch, and most hatch anytime from late May to July, just when the rainy season starts up. As happens with many other kinds of turtles, warmer nest temperatures turn most Central American river turtle eggs into female hatchlings, or newly hatched young, and cooler temperatures produce males. The warm or cool weather has to occur when the eggs are about halfway along in their development.

CENTRAL AMERICAN RIVER TURTLES AND PEOPLE

Many local people in southern Mexico, northern Guatemala, and Belize consider the meat of Central American river turtle a delicacy and also collect the eggs. Even though these turtles are protected in some areas, hunting continues and threatens the survival of the species.

The Central American river turtle usually remains in the water because it is a slow, awkward walker. (©Jean-Gerard Sidaner/Photo Researchers, Inc. Reproduced by permission.)

CONSERVATION STATUS

Both the World Conservation Union (IUCN) and the U.S. Fish and Wildlife Service label the Central American river turtle as Endangered, or facing a very high risk of extinction in the wild or throughout all or a significant portion of its range. Some governments have protected these turtles, which makes hunting or collecting them illegal.

FOR MORE INFORMATION

Books:

Burnie, David, and Don E. Wilson, eds. *Animal: The Definitive Visual Guide to the World's Wildlife.* United Kingdom: Dorling Kindersley, 2001.

Lee, Julian C. *The Amphibians and Reptiles of the Yucatán Peninsula.* Ithaca, NY: Comstock, 1996.

Web sites:

"Family Dermatemydidae (Mesoamerican River Turtles)." http://www.embl-heidelberg.de/uetz/families/Dermatemydidae.html (accessed on August 7, 2004).

Lowry, H. 2001. "*Dermatemys mawii.*" Animal Diversity Web. http://animaldiversity.ummz.umich.edu/site/accounts/information/Dermatemys_mawii.html (accessed on August 7, 2004).

"Mexico Coalition Launches Strategy to Stop Destruction of Country's Richest Forest." Conservation International. http://www.conservation.org/xp/news/press_releases/2003/062603.xml (accessed on August 7, 2004.

"Turtle, Central American River." U.S. Fish and Wildlife Service. http://ecos.fws.gov/species_profile/SpeciesProfile?spcode=C04H (accessed on August 7, 2004).

family

CHAPTER

phylum

class

subclass

order

monotypic order

suborder

▲ **family**

PHYSICAL CHARACTERISTICS

The leatherback seaturtle, which is the only member of its family, is extremely large. The carapace (KARE-a-pays), or upper shell, measures up to 8 feet (2.4 meters) long, and the turtle itself weighs just under a ton, at 1,911 pounds (867 kilograms). Most seaturtles have a hard and bony upper shell, but this turtle's carapace has a smooth, leathery skin. It also has an unusual outline. The upper shell is wide at the front but then narrows to a point at the back, giving it a teardrop shape. In addition, seven very noticeable ridges run from the front of the carapace to the back. This shell is usually black with a few white or yellow spots—almost as if someone had shaken a paintbrush over the back of the turtle. The plastron (PLAS-trun), or bottom shell, has coloring that is the opposite of the carapace coloring. Instead of black with light spots, it is white with dark spots. Leatherback turtles also have large front legs, which do not have separate toes and claws but instead look like paddles or fins.

GEOGRAPHIC RANGE

This species lives in oceans around the world.

HABITAT

The leatherback seaturtle is found over more of the world than perhaps any other species of reptile. It can live quite well in the warm ocean waters of the tropics and in cooler ocean waters as far north of the equator as Alaska and Iceland and as far south as New Zealand and the Cape of Good Hope at the southern tip of Africa. It rarely comes into shallow, shoreline waters, staying instead in deeper water for most of its life.

DIET

The diet of the leatherback seaturtle is mostly jellyfish. It also eats many other ocean-living animals, including snails, octopuses, squids, crabs, small fishes, and hydrozoans (hy-druh-ZOH-uhns). Hydrozoans and jellyfish are both sea-dwelling animals without a backbone that have tentacles (TEN-tih-kuhls), or long, thin body parts used for feeling or for holding on to things. These two types of animals look somewhat alike. Seaturtles sometimes think that floating balloons and plastic bags look much like these creatures too, and they eat them by mistake. This can kill the turtle. The turtles also eat plants, such as sea grasses and kelp, which is a type of seaweed.

BEHAVIOR AND REPRODUCTION

Like other turtles, the leatherback seaturtle is cold-blooded, meaning that its body temperature gets cooler when the outside temperature drops and warmer when the outside temperature rises. In most turtles, body temperature very closely matches the outdoor temperature. The seaturtles are a little different. Because they are so large and their muscles heat up when they swim, they can stay warm much longer than a smaller turtle can. They also have oily skin that acts like a jacket, to help keep the body warm. For these reasons, they are able to travel to much colder waters, like those off Alaska or Iceland. These turtles take advantage of this ability to travel to warm and cold waters. They often swim very long distances in what are called migrations (my-GRAY-shuns), moving from one region or climate to another to find food and to lay their eggs. Scientists have tracked some turtles that have swum as far as 3,100 miles (4,989 kilometers) one way to go from a nesting site to a feeding site. On average, these turtles swim about 19 miles (30.5 kilometers) a day for weeks at a time.

SAVING LEATHERBACKS

Leatherback seaturtles have survived on Earth for at least 100 million years. They have even outlasted the great dinosaurs, yet they are now facing extinction. The number of female leatherbacks worldwide dropped from 115,000 in 1982 to fewer than 25,000 two decades later, and the turtles living in the Pacific Ocean suffered the biggest decline in numbers. Many conservation groups, as well as country governments, are worried about the future of this turtle and are trying to do away with hunting and egg collecting. They are also preserving their nesting beaches and protecting adult turtles from fishing and other activities at sea that accidentally harm the turtles.

Many leatherback seaturtles may join together at a particularly good feeding site, like a school, or group, of jellyfish. They also hunt for food alone. Seaturtles are excellent divers, and they can swim down to more than 3,300 feet (1,006 meters) to find deep-water animals to eat. Turtles do most of their diving at night, but they are active both day and night.

Scientists know very little about courtship or mating in leatherback turtles. The turtles may mate before or during the long migration from a feeding area to a nesting area or just off-shore from the nesting site. Females make their nests about once every three or four years on tropical beaches. Those that live in the Atlantic Ocean nest from April to November. Pacific Ocean leatherbacks nest at different times of the year, depending on the beach they choose. A small group of females usually nests together on one beach.

The females climb up onto shore, usually at night, and find a spot on dry land. They typically pick a nesting site that is just beyond the highest point that water reaches. Like the upper shell, the lower shell of leatherbacks is softer than that of most turtles, so the females choose sandy rather than rocky beaches to crawl over and dig their nests. They use both their front and back legs to dig a wide hole that can fit the entire body. Then they continue to dig a smaller, deeper pit with just the rear legs. Each female lays 47 to 263 eggs in the pit. Only some of the eggs hatch. From the time she lays them, 1 to 103 eggs have no yolks and so cannot develop into turtles. The rest are normal eggs. Eggs are round and range in diameter, or width, from 1.9 to 2.6 inches (4.8 to 6.6 centimeters) in diameter. Each egg weighs 2.5 to 3.2 ounces (71 to 91 grams).

Usually, the biggest females lay the most eggs and the largest eggs. In addition, turtles of the Atlantic typically lay more eggs than those of the Pacific, and nests made during the middle of the nesting season often contain more eggs than nests made earlier or later. Females may make up to eleven nests a year, although five or six is more common. Once she lays the eggs, the female uses her hind legs to cover them with sand and then continues with her front and rear legs to bury the larger body hole. She then leaves the area and provides no care for the eggs or the newly hatched young.

The eggs hatch in sixty to sixty-eight days, although some may hatch in as little as fifty days or as much as seventy-eight

days. If the beach, and therefore the nest, is especially warm about halfway through the eggs' development, most of the eggs hatch into females. If the nest is particularly cool, most of the eggs will hatch into males. The hatchlings wait until nightfall to climb out of the nest and onto the surface of the beach. They then head to the area that is most open to the sky and is the most brightly lit—usually the ocean. The young turtles continue to grow at sea, and when the reach the age of thirteen to fourteen years, they are ready to become parents themselves.

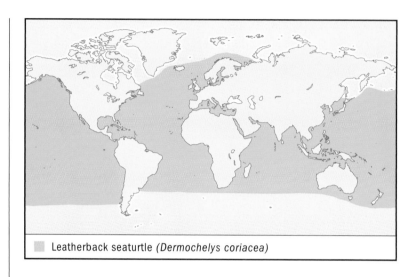

Leatherback seaturtle (*Dermochelys coriacea*)

LEATHERBACK SEATURTLES AND PEOPLE

Because this turtle is found in so many areas of the world, it has many names. In Trinidad, for example, people call it caldon, while in the Caribbean and Latin America the turtle is known as canal. This familiarity can pose a problem, however. Although it is illegal in most countries, some people continue to raid the turtles' nests for their eggs or hunt them for their meat or the oil in their shells.

CONSERVATION STATUS

According to the World Conservation Union (IUCN), this species is Critically Endangered, which means it faces an extremely high risk of extinction in the wild. The U.S. Fish and Wildlife Service lists the leatherback turtle as Endangered, meaning that the turtle is in danger of extinction through all or most of its range, or the region over which it roams and feeds. The number of leatherback turtles has dropped rapidly over a very short time, mostly due to hunting of adults and gathering of their eggs. Development of tropical beaches for homes and resorts is also making it more and more difficult for the turtles to find a safe nesting spot. Many countries are now making it illegal to kill adult turtles or take their eggs or else protecting the beaches where they lay their eggs.

FOR MORE INFORMATION

Books:

Burnie, David, and Don E. Wilson, eds. *Animal: The Definitive Visual Guide to the World's Wildlife.* New York: DK Publishing, Inc., 2001.

Hickman, Pamela. *Turtle Rescue: Changing the Future for Endangered Wildlife.* Richmond Hill, Canada: Firefly Books, 2004.

O'Keefe, M. Timothy. *Sea Turtles: The Watcher's Guide.* Lakeland, FL: Larsen's Outdoor Publishing, 1995.

Pritchard, Peter C. H., and Pedro Trebbau. *The Turtles of Venezuela.* Athens, OH: Society for the Study of Amphibians and Reptiles, 1984.

Watt, E. Melanie. *Leatherback Turtles.* Austin, TX: Raintree Steck-Vaughn Publishers, 2002.

Web sites:

"Leatherback Sea Turtle." In the Wild: Oceans. http://www.bagheera .com/inthewild/van_anim_turtle.htm (accessed on September 10, 2004).

"The Leatherback Turtle." Oceanic Resource Foundation. http://www .orf.org/turtles_leatherback.html (accessed on September 10, 2004).

"The Leatherback Turtle (*Dermochelys coriacea*)." Turtle Trax.

http://www.turtles.org/leatherd.htm (accessed on September 10, 2004).

NEW WORLD POND TURTLES

Emydidae

Class: Reptilia

Order: Testudines

Family: Emydidae

Number of species: 35 species

phylum

class

subclass

order

monotypic order

suborder

▲ **family**

PHYSICAL CHARACTERISTICS

The New World pond turtles come in many shapes and sizes. Adult small bog turtles have upper shells, or carapaces (KARE-a-pays), that grow to about 5 inches (12.7 centimeters) in length, while the carapaces of the large Gray's sliders can reach a length of 2 feet (61 centimeters) or more. Most pond turtles have a least a little webbing between their toes. The males and females look very much alike, though sometimes the females are larger. In some species, the male is more colorful and has long, thin front claws.

GEOGRAPHIC RANGE

Members of this family live in North and South America, Europe, western Asia, and northern Africa.

HABITAT

New World pond turtles may live in tropical areas, where it feels like summer all year, or in cooler areas that have all four seasons, including winter. These cooler areas are known as "temperate climates." Many turtles spend almost their entire lives in or near ponds, lakes, and other freshwater areas, though some can live quite well in saltier waters. Other species live their lives mainly on land.

DIET

Depending on the species, New World pond turtles may eat meat, plants, or a combination of meat and plants. Sometimes, baby turtles begin their lives as meat eaters but start to munch plants as they grow older. The meat eaters may dine on such animals as fishes, tadpoles, insects, worms, and slugs. Turtles that eat plants prefer grasses, flowers, and berries. They also eat algae (AL-jee), or tiny plantlike growths that live in water.

BEHAVIOR AND REPRODUCTION

Many people have seen these turtles, because most of the animals in this family like to sunbathe, or "bask." Turtles that live in the water typically climb up onto a rock or log sticking up above the water's surface and soak in the sunshine. Often, many turtles will climb onto the same rock or log and may stack up on one another. Turtles that live on land simply find a sunny spot and bask there. Many of these turtles are active all year, but those that live in temperate climates sink underwater and bury themselves in the muddy bottom or bury themselves in shallow holes or under piles of leaves to wait out the winter. Some that live in areas with long, dry spells also become inactive until the rains come again.

COUNT THE RINGS

In many turtles, including some New World pond turtles, a person can tell how old a turtle is by counting its rings. The rings are on the upper shell, which is split into little sections, called scutes (SCOOTS). Wood turtles, for example, have five scutes down the middle of the shell and another four on each side. Every year the turtle gets a new set of scutes, which grow underneath the old ones; they stack up in a pyramid shape, with older and slightly smaller scutes on top. By counting all of the scutes in one pile, a person can guess the age of the turtle. Sometimes the oldest scutes wear away, so the turtles may actually be a little older than their scutes reveal.

During breeding season, usually in the spring, the males try to attract the females by bobbing their heads or waving their front claws in front of a female's face. After mating, the female finds a dry spot onshore, sometimes up to 0.6 miles (1 kilometer) away from the water, and digs a hole. She lays as few as one egg and as many as two dozen eggs in the hole and then covers them up. Afterward, she provides no care for the eggs or the young. As with most turtles, the temperature of the nest controls whether the egg becomes a male or a female turtle. Warm nest temperatures produce females, and cool temperatures produce males. The eggs hatch in about two to three months.

NEW WORLD POND TURTLES AND PEOPLE

People enjoy seeing turtles in the wild, but the numbers of many New World pond turtles are dropping. People once collected and killed these turtles to eat their meat. While that practice is not as common anymore, turtles still face threats from too much collecting for the pet trade or from car traffic on roads they cross to reach a pond, nesting site, or other area.

CONSERVATION STATUS

According to the World Conservation Union (IUCN), six New World pond turtles are Endangered, meaning that they face a very high risk of extinction in the wild. Seven species are Vulnerable, meaning that there is a high risk that they will become extinct in the wild, and fourteen are Near Threatened, meaning that they are at risk of becoming threatened with extinction in the future. The U.S. Fish and Wildlife Service lists the Alabama red-bellied turtle as Endangered and three other species as Threatened. Pollution, collection for the pet trade, and destruction of habitat, or the areas in which the turtles prefer to live, are major reasons that the numbers of these turtles are low. In addition, raccoons and other animals often dig up nests and eat the turtle eggs.

Painted turtle (*Chrysemys picta*)

PAINTED TURTLE
Chrysemys picta

Physical characteristics: The painted turtle is a medium-sized turtle that is mostly olive or black on the legs, head, neck, and upper shell. Adults can grow to 3.5–10 inches (9–26 centimeters). The head has yellow stripes, and there are both red and yellow stripes on the neck and legs and red striping around the edge of the upper shell, the carapace. The bottom shell, or plastron (PLAS-trun), is yellow or tan, with a long, dark blotch running down the middle. Males and females look very much alike, except that the females are larger and the males have longer and thinner front claws. A large female's carapace can reach almost 10 inches (26 centimeters) in length.

Geographic range: These turtles are found in Canada and the United States.

Painted turtles are mainly freshwater animals, although a few live in saltier waters. They prefer waters with little, if any current. (Illustration by Gillian Harris. Reproduced by permission.)

Habitat: Painted turtles are mainly freshwater animals, although a few live in saltier waters. They prefer waters with little, if any current, or swift-moving water. They live in southern Canada and mostly in the far northern, central, and eastern United States, though a few populations live in the southwestern United States and just over the border in Mexico.

Diet: Painted turtles are not picky eaters. Their meals consist of plants, insects, snails, leeches, tadpoles, and small fishes that they find in the water. They will also eat dead animals. Young turtles are mainly meat eaters and then switch to eating more and more plants as they grow older.

Behavior and reproduction: The painted turtle spends much time sunbathing, or "basking," on logs or rocks that poke up out of the water. During the winter months, which can become quite cold in the northern part of their range (the region where they roam and feed), they bury themselves underwater in the muddy bottom and wait for spring. If the winter day is warm enough, they may crawl through a hole in the ice and bask before returning underwater. Males and females mate in the fall or in the spring. The male attracts the female by tickling the sides of her head with his long claws. The females leave the water from late spring to midsummer to nest on land, usually somewhat near the water. The nest is a hole she digs in the ground. She lays one to twenty eggs in each nest and typically makes one or two nests a year. Nest temperature controls the number of males and females in the clutch. The eggs hatch in seventy-two to eighty days.

Painted turtles and people: Most people know these turtles as the ones they see basking on logs in lakes and rivers. Some people collect the turtles for the pet trade, and a few eat their meat.

Conservation status: Painted turtles are not threatened, but many of them are killed every year by raccoons and other animals that dig up their nests and eat the eggs or by cars that run over the turtles as they attempt to cross roads. ■

Eastern box turtle (*Terrapene carolina*)

EASTERN BOX TURTLE
Terrapene carolina

Physical characteristics: The eastern box turtle is a small- to medium-sized turtle with a rounded upper shell. The adult's lower shell has two hinges. When the turtle is frightened, it can pull its head, legs, and tail into the shell and use the hinges to close up the lower shell. The carapace is black with a pattern of short yellow stripes. Males have red eyes, a longer and thicker tail than that of the females, and a lower shell that is indented rather than flat. Females are larger than males and have carapaces that can reach 9 inches (23 centimeters) in length.

Geographic range: Theses turtles live in the United States and Mexico.

Eastern box turtles live on land, so they cannot swim away from danger, and they are not fast runners. To protect themselves against predators the adults tuck their legs, tails, and heads inside their shells and use the hinges in the upper shells to close up tight. (Illustration by Gillian Harris. Reproduced by permission.)

Habitat: This species lives in much of the eastern half of the United States and parts of Mexico near the Gulf of Mexico. It is a land turtle that roams forests and fields.

Diet: Eastern box turtles eat a variety of plants and animals, including grasses, flowers, and berries as well as insects and earthworms.

Behavior and reproduction: These turtles live on land, so they cannot swim away from danger, and they are not fast runners. To protect themselves against predators (PREH-duh-ters), or animals that might want to eat them, the adults tuck their legs, tails, and heads inside their shells and use the hinges in the upper shells to close up tight. Predators cannot get through the sealed shell. Young turtles, however, do not have hinges. Instead, they release a strong odor that persuades predators to leave them alone. Like other members of this family, eastern box turtles sunbathe to warm up. When the day gets too hot, they hide just barely underground. In the winter months these turtles bury themselves beneath a pile of leaves or just under the soil and wait until spring. Sometimes, if the winter becomes particularly cold for a few days, a turtle will freeze, and its heart will stop beating, but they do not die.

Males and females mate in the spring. The male attracts the female by biting at her shell and sometimes her head and bumping into her. Females lay their eggs from spring to midsummer, sometimes making five nests a year, though most of them make just one or two. The female lays one to eleven eggs in each nest, and the eggs hatch in about two and a half months. The nest temperature controls the number of males and females in each nest. A warmer nest produces all females, and a cooler nest produces all males.

Eastern box turtles and people: This turtle is popular in the pet trade because of its size and friendly behavior. People rarely see them live in the wild, except when the turtles attempt to cross a road—an activity that too often results in death from a passing car.

Conservation status: According to the IUCN the eastern box turtle is Near Threatened, meaning that it is at risk of becoming threatened with extinction in the future. Habitat loss has caused some of the drop in turtle numbers. ■

FOR MORE INFORMATION

Books:

Behler, John L., and F. Wayne King. *The Audubon Society Field Guide to North American Reptiles and Amphibians.* New York: Knopf, 1979.

Burnie, David, and Don E. Wilson, eds. *Animal: The Definitive Visual Guide to the World's Wildlife.* London: Dorling Kindersley, 2001.

Conant, Roger, and Joseph T. Collins. *A Field Guide to Reptiles and Amphibians: Eastern and Central North America.* Boston: Houghton Mifflin, 1998.

Dodd, C. Kenneth, Jr. *North American Box Turtles: A Natural History.* Norman: University of Oklahoma Press, 2001.

Gibbons, J. Whitfield. *Life History and Ecology of the Slider Turtle.* Washington, DC: Smithsonian Institution Press, 1990.

Harding, J. H. *Amphibians and Reptiles of the Great Lakes Region.* Ann Arbor: University of Michigan Press, 1997.

Harding, J. H., and J. A. Holman. *Michigan Turtles and Lizards.* East Lansing: Michigan State University, 1990.

Stebbins, Robert C. *A Field Guide to Western Reptiles and Amphibians.* Boston: Houghton Mifflin, 2003.

family

CHAPTER

phylum

class

subclass

order

monotypic order

suborder

▲ **family**

PHYSICAL CHARACTERISTICS

Eurasian pond and river turtles and neotropical turtles are small to large turtles. The upper shell, or carapace
(KARE-a-pays), is bony. Most of these turtles have webbing between their toes. Some of them have a side-to-side hinge in the
bottom shell, or plastron (PLAS-trun), which allows them to
close up tight if they feel threatened. In some species, the males
and females look quite different from each other. The male Indian tent turtle, for example, grows to only about a third of the
size of the female, which is typically 1 foot (30.5 centimeters)
long. The largest members of this family weigh 110 pounds
(50 kilograms) and have upper shells that can reach 32 inches
(81 centimeters) in length.

GEOGRAPHIC RANGE

These turtles live in Eurasia, North Africa, Mexico, and Central and South America.

HABITAT

The members of this family live in the saltwater of the ocean's
coastline, in inland freshwater areas, or on land in forests. They
typically are found in the tropical areas of many countries, including China and the nations of the East Indies and Europe.
They live from northern Mexico in North America to Ecuador
and Brazil in South America. They also live in regions bordering
the tropics, which are called "subtropical" regions.

DIET

Some Eurasian pond and river turtles and neotropical wood turtles eat only meat, and some eat only plants; others will dine on both meat and plants. In one species, called the Chinese stripe-necked turtle, the juveniles (JOO-vuh-nuhls), or young turtles, and the males eat mainly meat in the form of insects, but the females are primarily vegetarians and eat mostly leaves, seeds, and roots from the shoreline plants.

BEHAVIOR AND REPRODUCTION

Just as the habitat, or the natural living area, differs from species to species in this family, so, too, does their behavior and method of reproduction. Some of them hardly ever leave the water, but others live on land. Many of them are active all year long, but others become inactive during the winter months or during dry spells. Some, such as the Chinese stripe-necked turtle, sunbathe, or "bask," onshore to warm their bodies.

Although scientists know few details about many of these turtles, they have noted that the adult male of some species will bite or bump up against a female to persuade her to mate. Also, the heads and legs of a few species will become more brightly colored during mating season, probably to attract a mate. Male painted terrapins, for example, normally have gray heads, but their heads become white with a red stripe during mating season.

Females of the larger species lay the most eggs—up to thirty-five eggs at a time. The smallest species may lay just a single egg. Female painted terrapins travel as far as 31 miles (50 kilometers) to reach a good nesting site and then lay their eggs at night. They lay eggs about five times a year. In many cases, the temperature of the nest does not affect the sex of the newly hatched young turtles. In other species, however, a particularly warm nest temperature produces all females, and a cool one produces males. In at least one species, the eggs may also become females if the nest temperature is especially cold.

Eggs hatch in sixty to 272 days. In some species, males can become parents when they reach three or four years old, but females must wait until they are five to eight years old. Sometimes two different species of Eurasian pond and river turtles and neotropical wood turtles mate with each other and produce young turtles. This can happen often when two turtles from different species of this family are put together in one aquarium, but it may not happen as often in the wild.

EURASIAN POND AND RIVER TURTLES AND NEOTROPICAL WOOD TURTLES AND PEOPLE

Some people who live near these turtles collect them to eat their meat or to use them in making medicines. They are also popular in the pet trade. The painted terrapin, for example, is especially popular, because some people believe that this turtle brings good luck.

CONSERVATION STATUS

According to the World Conservation Union (IUCN) eleven species are Vulnerable, meaning that there is a high risk that they will become extinct in the wild. Eighteen species are Endangered, or facing a very high risk of extinction, and thirteen are Critically Endangered, or facing an extremely high risk of extinction. One species is Extinct; there is no longer any living turtle in the species. The U.S. Fish and Wildlife Service describes the Indian sawback turtle and river terrapin as Endangered. Turtle declines can be traced to too much collecting and to loss of their habitat. Efforts are under way to breed some of the most threatened species in captivity to increase their numbers.

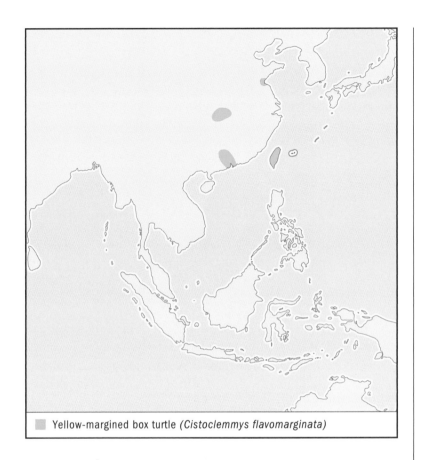

Yellow-margined box turtle (*Cistoclemmys flavomarginata*)

YELLOW-MARGINED BOX TURTLE
Cistoclemmys flavomarginata

Physical characteristics: The yellow-margined box turtle has a bright yellow stripe down its upper shell and another yellow stripe that runs from behind the eye onto the neck. The upper shell is arched and rounded, and the lower shell is large, with a side-to-side hinge that allows the turtle to tightly close it. In this small turtle, the upper shell measures just 7 inches (17.8 centimeters) in length.

Geographic range: This turtle is found in China, Taiwan, and the Ryukyu Islands of Japan.

Habitat: Yellow-margined box turtles mainly live in the warm-weather forests of southern China, Taiwan, and the Ryukyu Islands.

Yellow-margined box turtles mainly live in the warm-weather forests of southern China, Taiwan, and the Ryukyu Islands. (Lief Linder/Bruce Coleman Inc. Reproduced by permisson.)

They sometimes travel into rice paddies and freshwater ponds and streams. Some of them only rarely, if ever, leave the forests.

Diet: Some members of this turtle group eat only plants, some eat only meat, and others eat both plants and meat.

Behavior and reproduction: Since they live on land, the yellow-margined box turtles must be able to defend themselves against animals that might attack and kill them. These predators (PREH-duh-ters) can easily outrun them, but they can protect themselves by tucking in their heads, legs, and tails and then using the hinges on their lower shells to seal shut the shells and keep the predators from reaching their soft flesh. If the weather turns particularly hot, the turtles may also hide inside the sealed shell so they do not dry out. When the cooler winter months arrive, the turtles bury themselves under leaves or hide under a log or inside another animal's underground burrow and wait for warmer weather.

During mating season, the male runs at and bumps against the female to encourage her to mate with him. Depending on where she lives, the female may nest from May or June through July, August, or September. Some nest only every other year, but they may make one to three nests in a single season. The female picks a spot in an open area at the edge of a forest, digs a shallow hole, and lays one to four eggs, ranging in length from 1.6 to 2.1 inches (40–53 millimeters) and in width from 0.9 to 1.1 inches (23–28 millimeters). An egg can weigh 0.4–1.0 ounces (11.3–28.3 grams). The eggs hatch in about two months. The young cannot mate until they are twelve to thirteen years old.

Yellow-margined box turtles and people: Many local people eat this turtle or collect and kill it to make medicines. It is also popular in the pet trade.

Conservation status: According to the World Conservation Union, this species is Endangered. Threats to its survival include too much collection and the destruction of the forests where it lives. ■

FOR MORE INFORMATION

Books:

Burnie, David, and Don E. Wilson, eds. *Animal: The Definitive Visual Guide to the World's Wildlife.* London: Dorling Kindersley, 2001.

Liat, Lim Boo, and Indraneil Das. *Turtles of Borneo and Peninsular Malaysia.* Kota Kinabalu, Malaysia: Natural History Publications (Borneo), 1999.

Zhou, J., and T. Zhou. *Chinese Chelonians Illustrated.* Nanjing, China: Jiangsu Science and Technology Publishing House, 1992.

AMERICAN MUD AND MUSK TURTLES
Kinosternidae

Class: Reptilia

Order: Testudines

Family: Kinosternidae

Number of species: 25 species

PHYSICAL CHARACTERISTICS

American mud and musk turtles have glands, or sacs, along their sides that produce a musky substance that smells like the spray of a skunk. The upper shell, or carapace (KARE-a-pays), is rather tall, giving each turtle the outline of half a flattened ball when viewed from the side. The lower shell, or plastron (PLAS-trun), looks different in separate species. In some species the plastron has one or two hinges reaching from the left to the right side of the shell, but in others the shell has no hinges. The hinges allow the plastron and carapace to pull tight against one another after the turtle pulls its head, neck, legs, and tail into the shell. Some mud and musk turtles have a plastron that covers only part of the lower body, while others have a quite large plastron that almost entirely conceals the undersides.

All of these small to medium-sized turtles have barbels (BAR-buhls), which are small bits of flesh that dangle from the chin. A few have very large heads. Most of the species in this family have a carapace that is less than 8 inches (20 centimeters) long and in some cases grows to just 4 inches (10 centimeters) in length. The largest species, called the Mexican giant musk turtle, has a carapace that reaches 15 inches (38 centimeters) long. Males and females look quite similar. Males, however, usually have thicker and longer tails that are tipped with a spine. Males also have two rough, scaly patches on each hind leg.

GEOGRAPHIC RANGE

Members of the American mud and musk turtle family live in North and South America.

HABITAT

American mud and musk turtles are freshwater species. Most live in still or slow-moving waters and prefer lakes and ponds that are filled with water all year long. A few make their homes in shallow, seasonal ponds, which have water only a few months a year, usually during the spring season. American mud and musk turtles are found mainly in eastern and southern North America and as far south as Argentina in South America.

DIET

American mud and musk turtles are mainly meat eaters. They eat snails, clams, insects, worms, leeches, and sometimes freshly killed fishes they come across. Turtles that have large heads typically prefer snails and clams, which the turtle can easily open with its massive jaws. Turtles in seasonal ponds may also eat a large number of seeds.

BEHAVIOR AND REPRODUCTION

Although most American mud and musk turtles stay in the water for most of their lives, these turtles are only fair swimmers and move rather slowly. In the rainy season, some turtles may crawl onto land and look for food there, but for the most part, most of the trips to land are for nesting. Some turtles are active only during the day, and some only at night. Others may be up and about at any time of day or night. Those that live in warm, wet climates are active all year. In areas with cold winters and in deserts with long stretches of dry weather, the turtles may be active only a few months a year and spend the rest of the year underground, where they wait for better conditions. This period of inactivity in the winter is called hibernation (high-bur-NAY-shun). A period of inactivity in dry summers is called estivation (es-tuh-VAY-shun). In both cases, the turtle enters a state of deep sleep.

During breeding season, males and females have no real courtship, or mating, rituals. They mate in the water. The females scramble onto land to make their nests. Some dig holes,

THE LONG SLEEP

The yellow mud turtle holds the record among turtles for the amount of time it spends in a deep sleep every year. In very dry years this small, yellow-throated reptile buries itself in the ground and waits for the rains to come, even if that means the turtle has to stay underground up to ten months of the year. While underground the turtle enters a deep sleep. Usually this period of inactivity is called estivation if it occurs during the summer and hibernation if it occurs in the winter. Yellow mud turtles, however, are inactive from summer through fall and winter to the following spring. In other words, they both estivate and hibernate. When the spring rains flood the ground, the turtles crawl out of their slumber to mate, eat, and prepare for another long sleep.

lay their eggs at the bottom, and then bury them. Others bury themselves first and then dig a deeper hole for their eggs. Still other species skip the hole and simply lay their eggs among leaves on the surface of the ground. Females usually lay three to six eggs in each clutch, or group of eggs, although some clutches have as few as one egg or as many as twelve eggs. The female may lay up to six clutches a year. The oblong eggs range from 0.9 to 1.7 inches (2.3–4.3 centimeters) long and from 0.6 to 1.0 inches (1.5–2.5 centimeters) wide. The eggs hatch seventy-five days to a year after being laid. The nest temperature controls whether the eggs in most species hatch into males or females. Very warm or very cold temperatures produce females, and medium temperatures produce males. In a few species, such as the Mexican giant musk turtle and Pacific Coast giant musk turtle, the nest temperature has no effect on whether the eggs become males or females.

AMERICAN MUD AND MUSK TURTLES AND PEOPLE

Other than once in a while collecting a turtle for the pet trade or for its meat value, people generally leave mud and musk turtles alone.

CONSERVATION STATUS

Most species of American mud and musk turtles are quite common in their habitats, but according to the World Conservation Union (IUCN), four species are Vulnerable, which means they face a high risk of extinction in the wild. Three of the four live in very small areas, and the fourth lives in a disappearing habitat. The U.S. Fish and Wildlife Service lists one species, the flattened musk turtle, as Threatened, or likely to become endangered in the near future.

Stinkpot *(Sternotherus odoratus)*

STINKPOT
Sternotherus odoratus

Physical characteristics: As its name says, the stinkpot can give off quite an odor. This odor comes from a substance known as musk, which comes from sacs, or glands, on the sides of the turtle's body. The stinkpot is small, has a somewhat rounded upper shell, or carapace, and a small lower shell, or plastron, that covers only the center of its underside. The plastron has one side-to-side hinge near the front. The turtle's head typically has two yellow stripes on each side that run backward from a pointy snout. The stinkpot also has at least two barbels, or bits of hanging flesh, on its chin and neck. Stinkpots, which are also known as common musk turtles, grow to about 5.4 inches (13.7 centimeters) in carapace length, although some adults only reach about 3 inches (7.6 centimeters) long.

The stinkpot is a small freshwater turtle most at home in mud-bottomed, weedy lakes and ponds in southeastern Canada and through much of the eastern half of the United States. (Henri Janssen. Reproduced by permission.)

Geographic range: Stinkpots are found in Canada and the United States.

Habitat: The stinkpot is a small freshwater turtle most at home in mud-bottomed, weedy lakes and ponds in southeastern Canada and through much of the eastern half of the United States.

Diet: Stinkpots eat a variety of animals and plants. Their diet includes worms, snails, clams, crayfish, insects, tadpoles, fishes and their eggs, and even bites of flesh they take from dead animals. Stinkpots are also fond of seeds, tiny aquatic plantlike growths called algae (AL-jee), and pieces of plants that grow in the water.

Behavior and reproduction: Like other members of their family, stinkpots stay in the water much of their lives but are poor swimmers and often simply walk along the water bottom looking for food. Although they are small, stinkpots can put up quite a fight if an animal attacks them or if a human tries to pick one up. Often a turtle that feels threatened ducks its head, legs, and tail as far as possible into the shell. At other times, however, the stinkpot snaps out with its mouth wide open, sometimes taking a firm bite at the attacker.

Stinkpots sometimes sunbathe, or bask, on land. Turtles that live in a warmer area may stay active all year long. Turtles that live in an area that has cold winters may hibernate for a few months.

Most musk turtles mate in the spring or fall, but some mate at other times of the year. The male may try to attract the female by biting at her shell or nudging her, but these turtles often mate without much fuss. The females lay their eggs from spring to midsummer, sometimes as early as February in warmer areas. Some female stinkpots simply drop their eggs among leaves, but others dig a hole, lay the eggs inside, and then bury them. The white, oblong eggs range from 0.9 to 1.2 inches (2.3–3.0 centimeters) long and from 0.5 to 0.7 inches (1.3–1.8 centimeters) wide. The female usually lays a clutch, or group, of two to five eggs at a time but sometimes lay as few as one or as many as nine eggs. The stinkpot may lay one or two clutches a year in colder areas and up to four clutches a year in southern climates. The eggs hatch in about sixty-five to eighty-five days. Very warm and very cool nest temperatures produce females, and temperatures in between produce males.

Stinkpots and people: Some people collect stinkpots for the pet trade, but this practice is not very common.

Conservation status: Neither the World Conservation Union (IUCN) nor the U.S. Fish and Wildlife Service consider the stinkpot threatened. ■

FOR MORE INFORMATION

Books:

Behler, John L., and F. Wayne King. *The Audubon Society Field Guide to North American Reptiles and Amphibians.* New York: Knopf, 1979.

Burnie, David, and Don E. Wilson, eds. *Animal: The Definitive Visual Guide to the World's Wildlife.* London: Dorling Kindersley, 2001.

Conant, Roger, and Joseph T. Collins. *A Field Guide to Reptiles and Amphibians of Eastern and Central North America.* 3rd ed. Boston: Houghton Mifflin, 1998.

Harding, J. H., and J. A. Holman. *Michigan Turtles and Lizards.* East Lansing: Michigan State University, 1990.

AFRICAN SIDE-NECKED TURTLES
Pelomedusidae

Class: Reptilia

Order: Testudines

Family: Pelomedusidae

Number of species: 18 species

PHYSICAL CHARACTERISTICS

African side-necked turtles are small- to medium-sized turtles that fold their necks sideways under their shells, rather than pulling them straight back into the shell, along with their heads. They have five claws on each hind foot. The upper shell, or carapace (KARE-a-pays), of adults usually is less than 1 foot (30.5 centimeters) long, but the length of shells can range from about 4 to 21.6 inches (10–55 centimeters). The turtle has a large lower shell, or plastron (PLAS-trun), that covers much of the chest and belly. Sometimes the plastron has a hinge that allows the animal to pull its lower shell quite tight against the upper shell and offers protection from predators (PREH-duh-ters), or animals that seek these turtles out as a source of food. In addition, the turtles have glands, or special organs, along the sides of their bodies that give off a musky, or earthy, smell to ward off attackers.

GEOGRAPHIC RANGE

African side-necked turtles live in Africa, Madagascar, and the Seychelles Islands, which are northeast of Madagascar.

HABITAT

These turtles often are seen in freshwater lakes and rivers that hold water all year long, but they also are found in temporary freshwater ponds, which lose their water during the dry season. Some side-necked turtles, including those that are called "mud turtles," spend much of their time in soft-bottomed ponds that are filled with water for only a few weeks every year.

DIET

African side-necked turtles are mainly meat eaters, although a few will eat plants. The main items in their diet are worms; clams and other mollusks, or soft-bodied animals covered by shells; shrimp and other crustaceans (krus-TAY-shuns), or animals with a soft, segmented body covered by shells; insects; fish; frogs and other amphibians (am-FIB-ee-uns), or animals that spend part of their lives in water and part on land. These turtles also eat whatever dead animal matter they can find. Those that eat plants prefer water lettuce and grasses that grow in lakes, ponds, and streams and various fruits that drop into the water from overhanging trees.

BEHAVIOR AND REPRODUCTION

Although these side-necked turtles can be quite noticeable in their habitat, scientists know very little about their behavior. The turtles bask, spending warm days sunning themselves near the shoreline. They are especially active during the wet season, when they may roam over land. When the weather turns dry, many side-necked turtles seek shelter underground. Those that live in the cool, mild climate of the far south of Africa may hibernate, or become inactive, on land or under water through the winter months.

These turtles breed during late spring or summer, with the females laying six to four dozen oblong-shaped eggs. Scientists suspect that the turtles may have more than one set of young every year. The outside temperature controls how many eggs in a clutch, or group, will develop into males and how many will develop into females. Scientists call this "temperature-dependent sex determination," or TDSD. If the weather is constantly warm or especially cool, most of the young are females. If the weather is more temperate, or mild, most are males.

AFRICAN SIDE-NECKED TURTLES AND PEOPLE

African side-neced turtles are unpopular as pets and as food, but people occasionally eat them. One reason for their lack of popularity is their smell. The musk glands are very powerful weapons against predators, including humans. Pet owners who

THE TURTLE-RHINO CONNECTION

Although few people would think that turtles get much of their food from rhinoceroses, several African side-necked turtles do rely on the large mammals for some of their food. The turtles do not eat the rhinos but rather wait for them to wade into a water hole and then swim up to nibble off the ticks that cling to their hides. Rhinos are not the only buffet table for the turtles. They will do the same with other large herding animals that stop by for a drink.

keep African side-necked turtles often find that they are un-friendly and can be aggressive; they will bite at other turtles in the same aquarium and will nip at humans who put their hands too close.

CONSERVATION STATUS

In 2003 the World Conservation Union (IUCN) listed one species, the Seychelles mud turtle, as Extinct; none of these turtles is still alive. In addition, it listed the Magdalena river turtle and the Madagascar big-headed turtle as Endangered, meaning that it faces a very high threat of extinction in the wild. Five species are Vulnerable, which means that there is a high threat of their extinction, and one is Near Threatened, meaning that it is at risk of becoming threatened with extinction soon. Many of these species live in very small areas, so even slight disturbances can kill populations and possibly the entire species. For example, the Broadley's mud turtle, which is listed as Vulnerable, is found only in Lake Rudolph (also known as Lake Turkana) in Kenya.

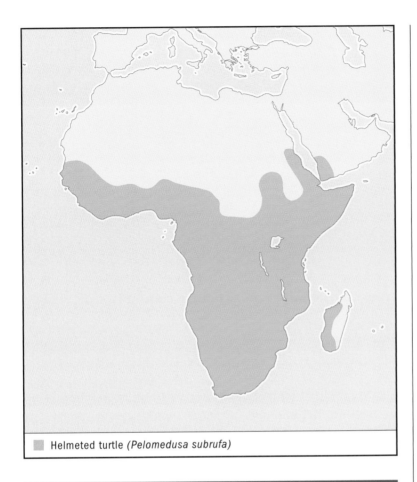

Helmeted turtle (*Pelomedusa subrufa*)

HELMETED TURTLE
Pelomedusa subrufa

Physical characteristics: Adult helmeted turtles have upper shells that reach 13 inches (33 centimeters) in length. The brown to greenish-brown upper shell is fairly flat. The lower shell is usually yellow or cream-colored, sometimes with dark seams or large, dark smudges. The lower neck is also yellow or cream-colored. These turtles have a rather pointed face with a mouth that looks as if it is set in a permanent grin. Males and females look alike, except that males have longer tails and concave, or indented, lower shells. Males may have red spots or white coloration on their heads during mating season.

Helmeted turtles are mostly meat eaters, feeding on worms, snails and clams, insects and other small invertebrates, fishes, frogs, and whatever dead animals they can find. (Illustration by Barbara Duperron. Reproduced by permission.)

Geographic range: Helmeted turtles inhabit Madagascar, southern Saudi Arabia, Yemen, and central to southern Africa.

Habitat: Helmeted turtles can be found in various water bodies, including ponds, marshes, and streams that are filled with water all year long and temporary ponds that dry up from time to time. They move from water site to water site during the year, so they are often seen on land.

Diet: Like other side-necked turtles, helmeted turtles are mostly meat eaters, feeding on worms; snails and clams; insects and other small invertebrates (in-VER-teh-brehts), or animals without backbones; fishes; frogs; and whatever dead animals they can find. They also eat small reptiles and mammals. They are some of the only reptiles that will band together and hunt as a pack to catch, drown, and tear apart birds, mammals, and other reptiles. An occasional piece of fruit or water-living plant rounds out the diet.

Behavior and reproduction: Except those individuals that live in the hottest of climates, these turtles spend much of the day basking near the shoreline. They are also noticeable when they are moving from water body to water body. The young will eat all day long and into the night, but the adults tend to feed only in the early morning or early evening hours. When the weather is too dry, they will bury themselves in the mud until the rains come. This period of inactivity in dry weather, which is called estivation (es-tuh-VAY-shun), can last for months. In the cooler areas where they live, they hibernate by finding a spot under leaves or below ground to wait out the winter.

Mating usually happens in the spring. During courtship, a male will chase a female, touching and sometimes nipping at her back legs and tail; bob his head from side to side; and shoot water out of his nostrils. The females lay one set of thirteen to forty eggs every year (fewer than twenty eggs is typical) in a nest that is sometimes set among rocks. The outside temperature determines the number of male and female young in the clutch. Especially warm or cool temperatures will produce more females, while moderate temperatures yield males.

Helmeted turtles and people: Although people frequently see this common turtle, it does not usually notice or mind their presence, even sometimes entering and making good use of man-made ponds. Some people eat helmeted turtles or drain their blood for folk medicines; a few become pets. These practices have not affected the survival of the species.

Conservation status: The helmeted turtle is not threatened. ■

FOR MORE INFORMATION

Books:

Boycott, R. C., and O. Bourquin. *The Southern African Tortoise Book: A Guide to Southern African Tortoises, Terrapins and Turtles.* KwaZulu-Natal, South Africa: privately printed, 2000.

Branch, B. *Field Guide to the Snakes and Other Reptiles of Southern Africa.* Cape Town, South Africa: Struik Publishers, 1998.

Burnie, David, and Don E. Wilson, eds. *Animal: The Definitive Visual Guide to the World's Wildlife.* London: Dorling Kindersley, 2001.

Spawls, S., K. Howell, R. Drewes, and J. Ashe. *A Field Guide to the Reptiles of East Africa.* San Diego: Academic Press, 2002.

Web sites:

"*Pelomedusa subrufa.*" ETI—Turtles of the World. http://www.eti.uva.nl/Turtles/Turtles3a.html (accessed on July 27, 2004).

family
CHAPTER

PHYSICAL CHARACTERISTICS

The family Platysternidae has only one member, the big-headed turtle, which has the scientific name *Platysternon megacephalum*. This small to medium-sized turtle is most known for its huge head, which is about half as wide as the upper shell. The head is shaped like a triangle and covered with a single, large, hard scale, known as a scute (SCOOT). The upper shell, or carapace (KARE-a-pays), is quite flat and sometimes has a single ridge running down the middle from front to back. The carapace is yellow to dark-brown and may have a pattern on it. A few big-headed turtles have red or pink markings on the carapace. Like that of many other turtles, the lower shell, or plastron (PLAS-trun), of the big-headed turtle is yellow and covers most of the underside. Unlike those of many other turtles, the upper and lower shells of the big-headed turtle are not connected by a bony bridge, but by softer, more flexible tissue, called ligaments (LIH-guh-ments). The upper jaw, also known as the beak, comes to a sharp point in the front. The big-headed turtle has a scaly tail that is nearly as long as the upper shell. The feet have obvious claws and just a bit of webbing between the toes. Turtle size is measured by the length of the carapace. The carapace length of the big-headed turtle reaches about 8 inches (20 centimeters). Males and females are similar, but the males have a more indented plastron.

GEOGRAPHIC RANGE

The big-headed turtle lives in China, Laos, Myanmar, Thailand, and Vietnam.

HABITAT

The big-headed turtle is rare and has been found only in small mountain streams from southern China to Thailand and southern Myanmar. These turtles appear to be very particular about the type of stream, living only in rock-bottomed, cool waters and only in mountainous regions up to 6,600 feet (2,000 meters).

DIET

Because the big-headed turtle is so rare, scientists have been able to learn about its diet only by observing captive, rather than wild, turtles. In captivity, the turtles eat meat, fish, and insects. The big-headed turtle is probably a meat-eater in the wild and may eat no plants at all. The turtle most likely gets most of its meals by gathering insects, mollusks, crustaceans, and other small invertebrates from the stream bottom, but it also may crawl out of the water onto shore and search for food on land. Invertebrates (in-VER-teh-brehts) are animals without backbones. Both mollusks (MAH-lusks) and crustaceans (krus-TAY-shuns) are invertebrates with shells. Mollusks, such as snails and clams, have an unsegmented body, and crustaceans, such as crayfish and shrimp, have a segmented body.

CHANGES IN CLOSEST RELATIVES

Big-headed turtles are the only species in the family Platysternidae. Scientists once believed these turtles were most closely related to New World pond turtles, including the painted turtles that are common in much of North America. That idea has faded, however. Now many people believe the closest relatives are the snapping turtles, which are in the family Chelydridae, or possibly the Eurasian pond and river turtles and neotropical wood turtles of the family Geoemydidae. A few scientists believe the big-headed turtles should be included in the snapping turtle family, but most argue that these turtles are different enough to be in a separate family.

BEHAVIOR AND REPRODUCTION

All turtles fall into one of two groups: the Cryptodira or the Pleurodira. The difference between the two is the way each pulls its neck and head back toward or into the shell. The Cryptodira, also known as hidden-necked turtles, can pull their heads and necks straight back and are usually able to tuck both into the shell. The Pleurodira, also known as side-necked turtles, can only pull their necks sideways rather than straight back, so most tuck their head and neck along the side of the shell. The big-headed turtle is unusual because it is a Cryptodira in that it can pull its neck backward, but it cannot draw its head into the shell because its head is so large.

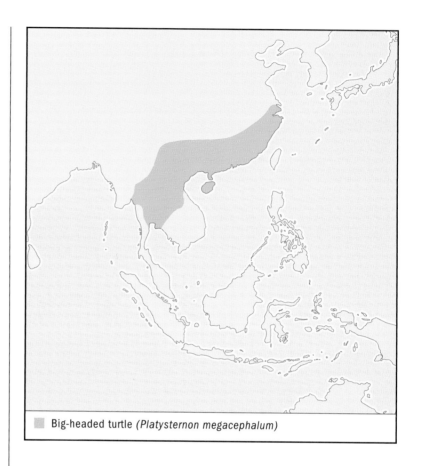

Big-headed turtle (*Platysternon megacephalum*)

Most hidden-necked turtles are shy animals that pull their heads, limbs, and tails into the shell whenever they feel threatened. Attacking animals, called predators (PREH-duh-ters), find it difficult, if not impossible, to get past the shell, and the turtle usually survives with little if any injury. The big-headed turtle cannot hide this way and instead defends itself by drawing its legs and tail into the shell and then ducking down its head so that the chin is on the ground and only the hard top shows. Sometimes the turtle may lash out with a quick bite. It may continue biting, and biting quite hard, until the predator leaves. Captive turtles also squeal when threatened. In addition, this turtle has glands, or sacs, on the sides of the shell that squirt out a bad-smelling musk, which may be used to scare off predators.

The big-headed turtle is a surprisingly good climber and uses its long tail for balance. The turtle may also use its beak to grab vertical surfaces when climbing. When placed in a fenced-in, indoor area, the turtle is able not only to climb over the fence

but also to grab onto window curtains and scramble all the way to the ceiling. In the wild, the turtles likely put this climbing ability to good use for crawling over rocky stream bottoms and against fast current. Some people report seeing the turtles climbing trees and bushes in the wild.

Big-headed turtles appear to be nocturnal (nahk-TER-nuhl) and crepuscular (kreh-PUS-kyuh-lur) in the wild. Nocturnal means they are active at night, and crepuscular means they are active at dusk and dawn. During the day, these turtles take cover and relax underwater beneath logs or rocks and wedged into cracks in boulders. Big-headed turtles that live in colder waters disappear in the winter. Although no one knows where the turtles go, scientists believe they probably hibernate (HIGH-bur-nayt), which means they enter a deep sleep. Some people think the turtles may hibernate in a protected spot on land.

Little is known about the courtship, or mate-attracting activities, of big-headed turtles or about their mating and nesting behaviors. In the wild the females probably nest sometime from May to August. The only egg ever seen hatching did so in captivity, and it hatched in September. In each clutch, or nest of eggs, females lay one or two eggs, sometimes as many as four. The eggs are 1.5–1.7 inches (3.8–4.3 centimeters) long and are about 0.9 inches (2.3 centimeters) wide. The eggs are quite large considering that the turtle's carapace length only reaches 8 inches (20 centimeters). No one knows whether the turtle lays one or more than one clutch a year. In captivity these turtles can live to be as old as twenty-five years.

BIG-HEADED TURTLES AND PEOPLE

Some people consider the meat of the big-headed turtle a delicacy, so the turtles face threats from hunters. Other people collect the turtles for use in folk medicines. Despite their tendency to bite, these turtles are fairly popular pets.

CONSERVATION STATUS

According to the World Conservation Union (IUCN) the big-headed turtle is Endangered because of overcollection. Endangered means that this species is facing a very high risk of extinction in the wild in the near future.

FOR MORE INFORMATION

Books:

Burnie, David, and Don E. Wilson, eds. *Animal: The Definitive Visual Guide to the World's Wildlife*. United Kingdom: Dorling Kindersley, 2001.

Web sites:

Kirkpatrick, David T. "The Big-headed Turtle, *Platysternon megacephalum*." www.unc.edu/dtkirkpa/stuff/bigheads.html (accessed on August 6, 2004).

Class: Reptilia

Order: Testudines

Family: Podocnemididae

Number of species: 8 species

family
CHAPTER

PHYSICAL CHARACTERISTICS

The Afro-American river turtle is described as a "side-necked" turtle because it cannot pull its neck and head straight back into the shell. Instead, it folds its neck sideways under its shell. The largest member of this family has an upper shell, or carapace (KARE-a-pays), that reaches 42 inches (107 centimeters) in length. Afro-American river turtles have only four toes on their hind feet. Some species also have barbells (BAR-buhls), which are bits of flesh that dangle from their chins. Some scientists believe that these turtles should be grouped with similar turtles in the family Pelomedusidae, which live in mainly in Africa.

GEOGRAPHIC RANGE

Afro-American river turtles are found in Madagascar and northern South America.

HABITAT

Many of these freshwater turtles live on riverbanks and in large lakes, but some also live in streams and swamps, wetlands partly covered with water. Sometimes they move into flooded forests. Their range, or the area in which they live and feed, includes Madagascar, which lies off the eastern coast of southern Africa, and northern South America.

DIET

Afro-American river turtles are mainly plant eaters; they are especially fond of fruits that drop off the trees on the shore and fall into the water. They also eat stems, leaves, and grasses.

phylum

class

subclass

order

monotypic order

suborder

▲ **family**

THE LARGEST TURTLE EVER

Afro-American river turtles live only in South America and thousands of miles away in Madagascar, but it was not always that way. Scientists have found fossils (FAH-suhls), or the dead remains, of these turtles on every continent except Australia and Antarctica. Although the river turtles live only in freshwater rivers, ponds, and streams, the fossils show that the turtles once also lived in saltwater and on land. One of the species in this family was the largest turtle that ever lived. This turtle, known as *Stupendemys geographicus,* had an upper shell that measured 7.5 feet (2.3 meters) in length and might have weighed 4,000–5,000 pounds (1,814–2,268 kilograms).

They dine on meat once in a while, and when they do, they eat insects, fishes, or other freshwater animals.

BEHAVIOR AND REPRODUCTION

These turtles' behavior depends on where they live. Some of them hardly ever leave their river homes. In these species, the female often makes the only trips on land. To lay her eggs, she crawls up onto a sandbar, a ridge of sand built up by currents in the water. Besides those turtles that live only in rivers, other species live in calm pockets of water along the river, sometimes in flooded forest pools, and the females lay their eggs on riverbanks. Still other species of these turtles also make their homes in small streams and ponds, and the females make long trips over land to nest. When the dry season empties the stream or pond, they crawl underground, become inactive, and wait for the rains to return. The Madagascan big-headed turtle, for example, spends the dry season buried in the mud. Scientists know few details about the activities of the Afro-American river turtles, including whether the males "court" the females to attract them or how they mate.

Nesting time is tied to the rainy season. As the rainy season ends, the females typically start to sunbathe in the early morning and late afternoon. She then begins her migration to a nesting site, which can take a very long time. Many Afro-American river turtles nest in large groups. Each female of the group digs her own hole, where she lays and buries her eggs. The females of some species are known to use only their hind legs in digging the nest and covering up their eggs. Different species lay varying numbers of eggs in their nests. The smaller river turtles, for instance, lay about five to twenty eggs per nest, while the largest species can lay up to 156 eggs. In all species except the South American river turtle, the eggs are longer than they are wide. The South American river turtle has round eggs. Some species make one nest a year, and others make two or more. Female Madagascan big-headed turtles skip a year between nestings. Nest temperature controls the number of males and females in the nest, with very warm and sometimes particularly cold temperatures producing females, and more moderate, or mild, temperatures producing males. The eggs hatch in forty to 149 days.

AFRO-AMERICAN RIVER TURTLES AND PEOPLE

People hunt these turtles for their meat and their eggs.

CONSERVATION STATUS

According to the World Conservation Union (IUCN), seven of the eight species face some threat of survival. Two species are Endangered, meaning that there is a very high risk that they will become extinct in the wild soon. Four species are Vulnerable, facing a high risk of extinction. One species is listed as Lower Risk: Conservation Dependent, meaning that its survival depends on conservation measures. The U.S. Fish and Wildlife Service lists two species as Endangered. Much of the decline in this family of turtles can be traced to too much hunting of adults and collecting of their eggs. Efforts are under way to protect the turtles' nesting areas, so that the females have a safe place to lay their eggs.

South American river turtle (*Podocnemis expansa*)

SOUTH AMERICAN RIVER TURTLE
Podocnemis expansa

Physical characteristics: Also known as the arrau or tartaruga, the South American river turtle sometimes is described as "giant" because it is so large. The upper shell can measure more than 3.5 feet (1 meter) in length. The carapace is rather flat and a bit wider at the rear than it is at the front. It is typically dark brown, but in spots it may be worn away to a paler, almost orange color in older turtles. The head is dark on top and down the cheeks but pale yellowish-tan on the bottom and on the neck. Two barbels hang from its chin. Young

turtles have a more patterned head with yellow blotches outlined or spotted in black.

Geographic range: These turtles live in northern South America.

Habitat: These freshwater turtles live in large river branches in the Orinoco and Amazon river systems of northern South America. If the water rises high enough and overflows into areas next to the rivers, they may move into these flooded areas, too.

Diet: This species eats plants, insects, and sponges, but it prefers the fruits of riverside trees.

Behavior and reproduction: Nesting begins shortly after the rainy season ends. During the nesting period, which may last ten to sixty days, the female travels upstream or downstream to reach a nesting site, which she shares with other females. Late at night the females climb onto a sandbar, and each one uses both her front and hind legs to dig a hole more than 1 yard (1 meter) around and 1.5 feet (0.5 meters) deep. At the bottom of the hole, the female uses only her hind legs to continue digging another pit, where she lays her eggs. Unlike other members of the family, which lay oblong eggs, the South American river turtle lays round eggs. Most of the eggs are about 1.6 inches (4 centimeters) across, but one or two may have a diameter twice that size. A typical nest holds about eighty eggs, but it contain as few as forty-eight eggs or as many as 156 eggs.

The females make only one nest per year. After laying her eggs, the female covers up at least the bottom hole, containing the eggs, and sometimes also the hole above it. The eggs hatch in about a month and a half; within a couple of days after hatching, the young make their way out of the nest. The sex of the hatchlings, or young turtles, depends on the temperature of the nest: extremely warm or very cool temperatures produce females, whereas temperatures that are more moderate, or mild, produce males. Scientists know few details about other activities of these large turtles.

South American river turtles and people   Although it is now illegal to do so, some people still hunt and kill adults and sometimes even baby turtles for their meat and collect eggs for the oil they contain.

Conservation status   The U.S. Fish and Wildlife Service lists this turtle as Endangered, which means that it is facing a risk of extinction in the wild. The World Conservation Union (IUCN) lists it as Lower Risk/Conservation Dependent, which means that its survival relies on sound conservation efforts. These listings result from the fact that humans have killed adults and destroyed their eggs over many decades. The turtle's range became smaller and smaller as the hunting and collecting continued. Efforts are under way to protect their nesting areas and to prevent further collecting of turtles or their eggs. ■

FOR MORE INFORMATION

Books:

Burnie, David, and Don E. Wilson, eds. *Animal: The Definitive Visual Guide to the World's Wildlife.* London: Dorling Kindersley, 2001.

Web sites:

Pecor, Keith. "Pelomedusidae." Animal Diversity Web. http://animaldiversity.ummz.umich.edu/site/accounts/information/Pelomedusidae.html (accessed on August 6, 2004).

phylum

class

subclass

order

monotypic order

suborder

▲ **family**

PHYSICAL CHARACTERISTICS

Tortoises are small- to large-sized, land-living turtles. Most of them have a tall upper shell, or carapace (KARE-a-pays). Their back legs are thick and somewhat resemble the legs of an elephant. The front legs, on the other hand, are rather flat and covered with large scales. Their toes have no webbing between them, and many species have five claws on each front foot. The largest members of this family can weigh as much as 562 pounds (255 kilograms) and have upper shells that grow to 4 feet 7 inches (1.4 meters) long. Some of them have a hinge in the carapace or in the lower shell, which is called the plastron (PLAS-trun).

GEOGRAPHIC RANGE

Tortoises exist on all large islands and continents, except Australia and Antarctica.

HABITAT

Tortoises live in many habitats, including deserts, grasslands, shrubby areas, and forests. Most live in warmer climates in North and South America, Europe, Asia, and Africa, and many make their homes on large islands in the ocean.

DIET

The tortoises are mainly plant-eaters, eating everything from grasses, flowers, and leaves to fruits and seeds. If they come across them, a few tortoises will also eat insects, worms, or other living or dead animals.

TORTOISES AND BIRDS

Galápagos tortoises have an unusual relationship with small birds, known as Darwin's finches. Ticks and other small biting insects often hitch a ride on a tortoise's skin, but the tortoise frequently cannot reach them to remove them. The birds feed on these same organisms. Darwin's finches and Galápagos tortoises seem to have struck a deal. When the finches fly in, the tortoises stand up as tall as they can and stretch out their necks, so the birds can pick off the insects and mites from every nook and cranny on their skin. Both the birds and the tortoises benefit: The bird gets an easy meal, and the tortoise gets some needed relief.

BEHAVIOR AND REPRODUCTION

Tortoises are known for their slow, lumbering movements on land. The males often fight among themselves, either by ramming their shells against one another or by biting at each other's legs. A male will also do the same things to a female in an attempt to convince her to mate with him. In addition, he will bob his head at her and chase her. Females lay from one to 51 eggs at a time. Each of the round or oblong eggs is about 1 to 2 inches (3 to 6 centimeters) in diameter and is typically quite brittle, or easily broken. Some females may not nest every year, but when they do, they may have more than one clutch, or nest of eggs, per season. Although scientists have not tested all of the species, the eggs in most become males or females based on the temperature of the nest. A particularly warm nest produces mostly females, and an especially cool one produces males. The eggs typically hatch in 100 to 160 days, but one species' eggs hatch only after 18 months. Some species may live 200 years or more.

Many tortoises become inactive in the summer when the weather is very dry. Many simply hide during the day in a shady spot, but some will dig a hole, or burrow, and spend the hottest part of the day there. On cooler days, some of these tortoises will seek out a warm spot and sunbathe, or bask, to increase their body temperature. Those species that live in colder climates may become inactive in the winter months.

TORTOISES AND PEOPLE

People hunt these tortoises for food and traditional medicines and collect them for the pet trade.

CONSERVATION STATUS

According to the World Conservation Union (IUCN), one species is Critically Endangered or facing an extremely high risk of extinction in the wild, seven are Endangered or facing a very high risk of extinction in the wild, and sixteen are Vulnerable or facing a high risk of extinction in the wild. The U.S. Fish and Wildlife Service lists two U.S. species as Threatened or likely to become endangered in the near future and five foreign species as Endangered, or in danger of extinction throughout all or a significant portion of their range. Although most countries make collecting illegal, it still continues. People find these land-living turtles easy to find and collect.

Galápagos tortoise (*Geochelone nigra*)

GALÁPAGOS TORTOISE
Geochelone nigra

Physical characteristics: This large, bulky tortoise usually has a tall and rounded, dark-colored upper shell that may be black, gray, or brown. Sometimes the upper shell, or carapace, is saddle-shaped. The carapace can measure up to 51 inches (130 centimeters) in length.

Geographic range: They only live on the Galápagos Islands.

Habitat: This species lives on the volcanic Galápagos Islands in the Pacific Ocean, west of Ecuador in South America. They make their homes anywhere from rather dry to moist areas.

Diet: The Galápagos tortoise eats almost nothing but plants, including grasses, cacti, fruits, and leaves.

Behavior and reproduction: Active during the day, they spend their nights sleeping among plants or rocks. Males of this species, like the males of some other species, fight one another by ramming their shells together. Males do the same thing to females during mating season, which runs from December to August. During mating, he will make roaring noises. The female lays up to four sets, or clutches, of eggs from late June to December. She digs a hole, drops in two to nineteen eggs, and then buries them. She provides no other care for the eggs or young. The round eggs measure 2.2 to 2.6 inches (56 to 65 millimeters) in diameter. The eggs hatch eighty-five to two hundred days later.

Galápagos tortoises and people: Rarely collected for its food, this tortoise has become a prized tourist attraction on the Galápagos Islands.

Conservation status: According to the World Conservation Union (IUCN), the Galápagos tortoise is Vulnerable, which means it faces a high risk of extinction in the wild. Certain populations of this tortoise have disappeared completely. The U.S. Fish and Wildlife Service lists the tortoise as Endangered, or in danger of extinction throughout all or a significant portion of its range. Many of them die from attacks by cats, rats, dogs, and pigs. ■

Desert tortoise (*Gopherus agassizii*)

DESERT TORTOISE
Gopherus agassizii

Physical characteristics: This medium-sized tortoise has a tall, dome-shaped upper shell, or carapace, and flat front legs. The carapace can reach up to 19 inches (49 centimeters) in length.

Geographic range: Desert tortoises live in the United States and Mexico.

Habitat: Found in the southwestern United States and northwestern Mexico, this species makes its home in cactus deserts and spots with thorny shrubs.

Diet: The desert tortoise eats mostly plants, including grasses, cacti, and flowers.

Behavior and reproduction: The desert tortoise is unusual in that it makes burrows into which it crawls to escape attackers and hot, dry weather. In some cases, the burrow is barely big enough for the tortoise to fit inside, but in others, it can be up to 33 feet (10 meters) long. In especially cold weather, the tortoises will crawl to the deepest part of the burrow and enter a deep sleep, called hibernation (high-bur-NAY-shun). When they are active, desert tortoises notice and interact with one another. When two meet each other, they bob their heads back and forth. During mating season, which runs from spring to fall, a male will try to convince a female to pair with him by biting at her legs, bobbing his head at her, and occasionally by ramming into her shell with his. A male frequently will ram shells with other males, too. He often hisses or grunts while mating with a female. The female lays eggs one to three times a year, usually laying five or six eggs at a time, although she may lay as few as two or as many as fifteen. Sometimes, she skips an entire year. The eggs range from 1.6 to 1.8 inches (4.0 to 4.5 centimeters) long and 1.3 to 1.5 inches (34 to 38 centimeters) wide. They hatch in about three to four months.

Desert tortoises and people: People hunt these tortoises for their meat, which is often shipped to Asian food markets located in the western United States.

Conservation status: According to the World Conservation Union (IUCN), the desert tortoise is Vulnerable, which means that it faces a high risk of extinction in the wild. The U.S. Fish and Wildlife Service lists the tortoise as Threatened, or likely to become endangered in the foreseeable future. The danger to the tortoises comes from both loss of their habitat and a dangerous bacterial infection. ■

FOR MORE INFORMATION

Books

Ballasina, D., ed. *Red Data Book on Mediterranean Chelonians.* Bologna, Italy: Edagricole, 1995.

Burnie, David, and Don E. Wilson, eds. *Animal: The Definitive Visual Guide to the World's Wildlife.* United Kingdom: DK Publishing Inc., 2001.

Pritchard, Peter C. H., and Pedro Trebbau. *The Turtles of Venezuela.* Athens, OH: Society for the Study of Amphibians and Reptiles; Oxford, OH, 1984.

family
CHAPTER

phylum

class

subclass

order

monotypic order

suborder

▲ **family**

PHYSICAL CHARACTERISTICS

From above, softshell turtles look almost like rubber dinner plates swimming through the water. Although the turtles actually have a bony upper shell, it is completely covered by leathery skin, which usually reaches out past the edge of the bone and overlaps the tail and feet. The upper shell, or carapace (KARE-a-pays), is flat and often round. The turtles also have a tube-like snout and a long neck that they can pull in or extend out. Their webbed front feet each have three claws. A few species have flap-like hinges on the lower shell, or plastron (PLAS-trun), below the hind legs. Softshell turtles can be big or small, depending on the species. The smallest has a carapace that only measures up to 5 inches (12 centimeters) long, while the largest has a carapace ten times that length and sometimes more. In addition, most of them have a one-color carapace, but a few have stripes or spots. Sometimes, young turtles are more colorful. Usually, the males have longer tails than the females do. In some species, the males are smaller than the females, and/or more colorful.

GEOGRAPHIC RANGE

Members of this family live in North America, Africa, and Asia.

HABITAT

These water-loving turtles live in all types of year-round fresh water, occasionally in ponds that dry up for part of the year. A few can swim into somewhat salty water for a brief time, but only one species, the Asian giant softshell, actually lives in the

FLAPS FOR PROTECTION

Some species of softshell turtles have flaps near the hind legs that they can use to shield themselves from the glaring sun during dry spells. One species, called the Indian flapshell turtle, buries itself in the mud, pulls its legs inside its shell, covers up the hind legs with the flaps, and stays inside the shell in a state of deep sleep until the rains come. This period of deep sleep, which can last up to 160 days in this turtle, is called estivation (es-tih-VAY-shun). Estivation is similar to the inactive period known as hibernation (high-bur-NAY-shun), but hibernation occurs over the wintertime.

saltier waters of the coast. Overall, members of this family live east of the Rocky Mountains in North America and in mainly warmer climates in northern Africa, southern Asia, and the Indo-Australian archipelago, which is near Australia. They have also been introduced elsewhere, including Hawaii.

DIET

Most of these turtles are almost completely meat-eaters, and they eat anything they happen to come across, whether it is alive or dead. Once in a while, they will eat plants. A few species hunt by ambush, which means that the softshell turtle waits in hiding underwater — usually buried just under the bottom — for a fish or other water-living animal to swim by and then juts out its long neck and quickly grabs it with its mouth.

BEHAVIOR AND REPRODUCTION

For the most part, these turtles remain hidden for much of the day. They fall to the bottom of the lake, pond, or other watering hole where they live and wiggle their bodies back and forth until they are buried. When they move about in the water, they are excellent swimmers. Many species sunbathe, or bask, to warm their bodies. Some spend several hours a day basking on logs that stick up out of the water or on the shoreline, but they typically dash back into the water at even the slightest disturbance. Some prefer to sunbathe by simply floating in the top layer of water. They can breathe through the nose, but they can also get oxygen directly from the water, so they can stay below the surface for long periods of time. Those that live in colder areas enter a state of deep sleep, or hibernation (high-bur-NAY-shun), in the winter. During this period, which may last several months, they bury themselves in the sand or mud at the water bottom to wait for spring and warmer temperatures to come.

Softshell turtles usually mate each spring, although females can actually mate one year and have young from that single mating for several years. In some species, the male attracts the female by rubbing his chin on her carapace and bobbing his head at her. The female lays her round eggs in sandy, dry spots on shore. Depending on the species, a female may lay three to one hundred eggs at a time and have more than one clutch a year. The nests contain both male and female hatchlings, regardless of the nest temperature. In many other turtles, nest temperature controls the number of eggs that become male or female, but this is not known to occur in softshell turtles.

SOFTSHELL TURTLES AND PEOPLE

People hunt softshell turtles for food and to make traditional medicines. While many countries now have laws to protect at least some species, illegal hunting continues.

CONSERVATION STATUS

According to the World Conservation Union (IUCN), more than half of the family's 25 species are at risk. Five species are Critically Endangered, which means that they are facing an extremely high risk of extinction in the wild. In addition, five are Endangered and face a very high risk of extinction in the wild, and six are Vulnerable and at high risk of extinction in the wild. The U.S. Fish and Wildlife Service also lists four non-U.S. species as Endangered, or in danger of extinction throughout all or a significant portion of their range. Softshells are coping with overhunting, polluted waters that can weaken and/or kill the animals, and loss of their habitat.

Spiny softshell *(Apalone spinifera)*

SPINY SOFTSHELL
Apalone spinifera

Physical characteristics: Also known as a gooseneck turtle or leatherback turtle, the spiny softshell is a medium-sized turtle with a long neck and a rubbery upper shell, or carapace, with tiny spines at the front edge. Its flat carapace is mostly brownish green, but it has black spots and circles in both males and young turtles. The plastron is white or yellowish white. The turtles also have webbed feet, greenish legs usually mottled with black, and typically two yellow stripes on each side of the head. The carapace in females, which are about twice as large as the males, can reach up to 18.9 inches (48 centimeters) in length.

Geographic range: They live in Mexico, the United States, and Canada.

The spiny softshell is also known as a gooseneck turtle or leatherback turtle.
(©Steve & Dave Maslowski/Photo Researchers, Inc. Reproduced by permission.)

Habitat: Spiny softshells live in year-round, sandy- or muddy-bottomed bodies of fresh water, such as large lakes and ponds, as well as in shallow rivers and streams. They live in northeastern Mexico, the eastern half of the United States plus a few spots in western states, and into southeastern Canada.

Diet: Spiny softshells mostly eat meat in the form of just about anything they can find, including crayfish, fishes, and insects that live in the water. They will also eat acorns and leaves.

Behavior and reproduction: This turtle will bask on shore, but it quickly retreats at the slightest movement, so people rarely see them. Larger turtles especially also bask in the upper level of water. Usually, however, this turtle spends the majority of its days buried in the muddy or sandy bottom of its watery home. From this well-hidden spot, a turtle can keep an eye out for passing fishes or insects and dart out its long neck to grab the unsuspecting animal with its jaws for a quick meal. Because it can get oxygen directly from the water, the spiny softshell can stay underwater for long periods without drowning. Those that live in colder areas hibernate from fall to spring by burying themselves in the mud or sand beneath the water and remaining inactive.

Spiny softshells mate in the spring in deep waters. Scientists know little about their courtship or mating behaviors. In June and July, the female crawls on shore and then quickly digs a hole, drops the eggs inside, and covers it up. She provides no additional care for the eggs or the young turtles. She may lay two clutches a year. Each clutch contains four to thirty-two round eggs, each of which measures about 1.1 inches (2.8 centimeters) in diameter. They hatch in about fifty-five to eighty-five days. When the males reach four to five years old and the females reach eight to ten years old, they are ready to mate and become parents themselves. They live to be fifty years old or more.

Spiny softshells and people: People hunt this turtle for food, either to eat themselves or to ship overseas to meat markets in Asia. Some people also collect spiny softshells for the pet trade.

Conservation status: This species is not listed as endangered or threatened, although many of its nests are destroyed each year by raccoons and other animals that eat the eggs. ■

FOR MORE INFORMATION

Books

Behler, John L., and F. Wayne King. *The Audubon Society Field Guide to North American Reptiles and Amphibians.* New York: Knopf, 1979.

Conant, Roger, and Joseph T. Collins. *A Field Guide to Reptiles and Amphibians of Eastern and Central North America, Third Edition Expanded.* Boston: Houghton Mifflin Co., 1998.

Harding, J. H., and J. A. Holman. *Michigan Turtles and Lizards.* East Lansing: Michigan State University Press, 1990.

Stebbins, Robert C. *A Field Guide to Western Reptiles and Amphibians.* Boston: Houghton Mifflin Co., 1985.

Class: Reptilia

Order: Crocodylia

Number of families: 3 families

order

CHAPTER

PHYSICAL CHARACTERISTICS

The order Crocodylia, also known as the crocodilians, includes 23 species of the most feared and most fascinating animals on the planet. They include 14 species of crocodiles and false gharials in the family Crocodylidae; eight species of alligators and caimans in the family Alligatoridae; and one species of gharial (GUR-ee-ul) in the family Gavialidae.

The crocodilians look somewhat like large lizards, but with thick and scaly skin, exceptionally strong tails, and large teeth-filled jaws. The scales on the upper surface, including the back and top of the tail, are large and rectangular in shape and have bony plates, called osteoderms (OSS-tee-oh-durms), just under the surface. Rows of these scales, which often have knobs or ridges, run from the rear of the head to the tail. On the legs and the sides of the body, the scales are smaller. Belly scales, which may also contain osteoderms, are large and smooth. Crocodilian tails are usually about as long as or a bit longer than the body, and in some species, like the Nile crocodile, the tails have a tall ridge of scales down the center.

The jaws contain large teeth, many of which show outside the mouth even when it is closed. People often describe the "grin" of a crocodilian. Of course, the animals are not actually smiling, but a slight upturn in the back of the jaw line of most species makes them look as if they are. Most, but not all, crocodilians have wide jaws. The Indian gharial is one species without a wide jaw. Instead, it has a very long and exceptionally thin pair of jaws filled with razor-sharp teeth. The false gharial, which looks much like an Indian gharial, has jaws that are only slightly wider and shorter than those of the Indian gharial.

The crocodilian body comes in shades of brown or gray, sometimes with a greenish or reddish tint. The upper surface is typically much darker than the belly, which is usually white to yellow. Bellies of dwarf caimans and dwarf crocodiles, however, are almost black. Many species have patterns of dark brown to black bands or blotches on the back and tail, and often these are most noticeable in youngsters.

The crocodilians are medium- to large-sized species. Cuvier's dwarf caiman is the smallest, with male adults reaching 5 feet (1.5 meters) long and females growing to 4 feet (1.2 meters) long. The largest species include the Indian gharial and the saltwater crocodile. Males of each species commonly grow to 16 feet (4.9 meters) and sometimes, although very rarely, reach 20 feet (6.1 meters). As with other crocodilians, the females are smaller overall than the males.

GEOGRAPHIC RANGE

Most members of the family Alligatoridae live in Central America, Mexico, the southeastern United States, and South America. One species, the Chinese alligator, makes its home in eastern China. The Indian gharial, the lone species in the family Gavialidae, lives in scattered places within India, Nepal, and Pakistan and rarely Bangladesh and Bhutan. The crocodiles and false gharials in the family Crocodylidae live over the largest area of the three families. At least one species lives in Africa, Asia, Australia, North America, and South America.

HABITAT

Most crocodilians live in tropical or subtropical regions. The American alligator, which can be found in the United States as far north as North Carolina, and the Chinese alligator live in the coolest climates of all the crocodilians and sometimes have to survive freezing temperatures. These two species spend the coldest parts of the year in underground burrows, in deep water, or lying in shallow water with just the nose poking above the sometimes ice-covered water surface.

Alligators, caimans, and gharials need freshwater habitat, but crocodiles and false gharials can survive in freshwater or saltwater. Crocodiles usually stay out of the open oceans, however, and instead make their homes in saltwater marshes or creeks.

None of the crocodilians stray very far from the water. The gharials are perhaps most tied to the water. They spend their entire lives either in or within a few feet of the water.

DIET

Crocodilians are meat-eaters, or carnivores (KAR-nih-voars), and most are not picky about their prey. Youngsters usually eat insects, spiders, and other invertebrates (in-VER-teh-brehts), or animals without backbones, as well fishes and other small vertebrates (VER-teh-brehts), which are animals with backbones. As they grow older, they begin taking larger and larger prey. The typical adult crocodilian eats everything from clams to frogs, and birds to mammals. Some, such as the Indian gharial, have jaws that are well-suited to catching fish, and they stick to a mainly fish diet. At the end of its thin jaw, the gharial has a number of very sharp teeth that jut out almost sideways in a pincushion fashion. To catch a fish, the gharial lies still, waits for a fish to come close, and then swishes its jaw sideways to skewer the fish on its teeth. With a flick of its head, the gharial tosses the fish off its teeth and down its throat.

Other crocodiles also use the sit-and-wait style of hunting, which is known as ambush hunting. Alligators and caimans also often stalk (stawk) their prey by swimming up ever so slowly, and then chomping on the surprised animal. Many crocodilians kill especially large prey by clamping on the animal and dragging it underwater to drown. They then bite off pieces to swallow. Sometimes, crocodilians work together when eating. Nile crocodiles, for example, will take turns holding onto a large prey animal while others wrap their jaws around part of the body and twist around to tear off pieces of flesh. For smaller prey, however, a crocodilian will simply swallow it whole. Crocodilian stomachs can digest almost anything, except items like hair, nails or claws, and turtle shells. Just as a cat coughs up hairballs, the crocodilian coughs up balls of this undigested material and spits them out.

A FOSSIL GIANT

About 110 million years ago, a massive beast roamed the waters of Earth. The head of this creature, an ancient relative of modern-day crocodilians, was 5 feet (1.5 meters) long, and its body grew to a whopping 39 feet (12 meters). A team of scientists found the remains of five of the animals, named *Sarcosuchus imperator* or "emperor of the flesh-eating crocodiles," in 2000. From the fossil skulls, they determined that its diet consisted of large animals, which it hunted by ambush.

A SENSITIVE SIDE

Scientists in 2002 discovered that crocodilians use tiny dots on the skin of their faces to feel even the slightest of ripples in the water. These dots, called pressure receptors, can even feel the ripple made by a single raindrop. This ability helps to make them exceptional night hunters. They can feel even small waves made by prey animals as they move through the water.

BEHAVIOR AND REPRODUCTION

Crocodilians are often night hunters and rest or sunbathe during the day. Unlike mammals that use their own energy to keep their bodies warm, crocodilians and other reptiles get their heat from their environment. One of the best ways to warm up is by sunbathing, also known as basking. Crocodilians may bask on dry land or along or just below the surface of the water. Some crocodilians, like gharials, are very careful when they bask on shore and will quickly retreat to the water if they feel the least bit nervous. Others, such as some large American alligators, will continue to bask even if approached quite closely. At a moment's notice, however, this peaceful-looking reptile can spring into action with a swipe of its powerful tail or a snap of its dangerous jaws. Most crocodilians are also quite fast and are actually able to outrun a person over a short distance.

Crocodilians move in several ways. All are excellent swimmers, usually gliding through the water by simply swaying the tail from side to side. Their tails are even strong enough to shoot their bodies several feet straight up and out of the water. On land, they often walk slowly, dragging the belly and tail on the ground. If they want, however, most can do a "high walk," in which they lift up the body to walk much as a lizard does.

Many species live together in groups and get along well for most of the year. During breeding season, however, the males get into arguments, wrestling matches, and sometimes more violent fights. They may bellow back and forth, push one another with their snouts, or bite each other. In some species, males try to attract the females by bellowing, or by rippling their back muscles so that water ripples over their scales. After mating, which occurs in the water, the females of all species lay their eggs out of the water. Some scrape leaves and often mud into a pile and lay their eggs in the pile, and others dig a hole as their nest. Depending on the species, a female may lay fewer than a dozen or many dozen eggs. As in some other reptiles, the temperature of the nest may control the sex of the young. In crocodilians, for example, a nest that is between 87.8 to 89.6°F (31 to 32°C) during a critical time not long before hatching produces mainly males, while an especially high or particularly low temperature during this period produces mainly females. The mother typically remains close by as the eggs develop, often chasing off raccoons or other animals that would dig up her nest and eat her eggs if given the chance.

When the eggs hatch, the mother helps her babies out of the nest and often to the water. Despite her toothy jaws, the mother can safely carry her babies either one or several at a time in her mouth. The young usually stay with their mother, and occasionally both parents, for a while. In most species, the young remain with the family for a few weeks or months, but in the American alligator, they may stay together for as long as two years. During this time, the female may provide protection to her young, may call to them when she finds food, or in some species, may actually chew a prey animal a bit, which helps her young tear off pieces to eat.

CROCODILIANS AND PEOPLE

Crocodilians, which are sometimes hunted for their meat or skin, are perhaps best known as human killers. Death by this reptile, however, is very rare among people who act carefully and responsibly when they are in crocodilian habitat. As people move closer and closer to their habitat, crocodilians may make their presence known by plopping into a swimming pool or eating a family pet.

CONSERVATION STATUS

According to the World Conservation Union (IUCN), almost one-third of the 23 crocodilian species are either Critically Endangered or Endangered. Critically Endangered species are those that face an extremely high risk of extinction in the wild, while Endangered species face a very high risk. The other 16 species are currently doing quite well, thanks to numerous recovery efforts and anti-hunting regulations that have saved them from the brink of extinction.

FOR MORE INFORMATION

Books:

Alderton, D. *Crocodiles and Alligators of the World.* New York: Facts on File, 1991.

Behler, J. L., and D. A. Behler. *Alligators and Crocodiles.* Stillwater, MN: Voyager Press, 1998.

Cleaver, Andrew. *Snakes and Reptiles: A Portrait of the Animal World.* Wigston, Leicester: Magna Books, 1994.

Irwin, Steve, and Terri Irwin. *The Crocodile Hunter.* New York: Penguin Putnam, 1997.

Lamar, William. *The World's Most Spectacular Reptiles and Amphibians.* Tampa, FL: World Publications, 1997.

Ross, C. A., ed. *Crocodiles and Alligators.* New York: Facts on File, 1989.

Rue, Leonard Lee. *Alligators and Crocodiles.* Wigston, Leicester: Magna Books, 1994.

Periodicals:

Barr, Alice. "Supercroc." *National Geographic World.* January–February 2001, page 8.

Grant, Phoebe. "A Peep at the Alligator's Mound." *Monkeyshines on America.* June 1990, page 19.

Perkins, Sid. "Fossils Indicate . . . Wow, What a Croc!" *Science News.* October 27, 2001, volume 160, page 260.

Zackowitz, Margaret. "Dangerous Business: Photographing Crocodiles and Hippos is a Creative Challenge." *National Geographic for Kids.* November 2001, page 26.

Web sites:

"All About Alligators." Enchanted Learning. http://www.enchantedlearning.com/subjects/Alligator.shtml (accessed on September 21, 2004).

"Alligator." Everglades National Park. http://www.nps.gov/ever/eco/gator.htm (accessed on September 21, 2004).

"Alligator." World Almanac for Kids. http://www.worldalmanacforkids.com/explore/animals/alligator.html (accessed on September 21, 2004).

"Alligators and Crocodiles." San Diego Zoo. http://www.sandiegozoo.org/animalbytes/t-crocodile.html (accessed on September 21, 2004).

"American Crocodile." Kids' Planet, Defenders of Wildlife. http://www.kidsplanet.org/factsheets/american_crocodile.html (accessed on September 21, 2004).

"Fathers and Sons." Florida Museum of Natural History. http://www.flmnh.ufl.edu/cnhc/potm-oct00.html (accessed on September 21, 2004).

"Gharial." Smithsonian National Zoological Park. http://nationalzoo.si.edu/Animals/ReptilesAmphibians/Facts/FactSheets/ Gharial.cfm (accessed on September 21, 2004).

"Nile Crocodiles." National Geographic. http://www.nationalgeographic.com/kids/creature_feature/0107/crocodiles2.html (accessed on September 21, 2004).

"Saltwater Crocodile." Australian Museum. http://www.amonline.net
.au/wild_kids/reptiles/crocodile.htm (accessed on September 21, 2004).

"Spectacled Caiman." Enchanted Learning. http://www.enchantedlearn-
ing.com/subjects/reptiles/caiman/Speccaiman.shtml (accessed on
September 21, 2004).

"Wild Things: The Not-So-Friendly Caiman." Kidzworld. http://www
.kidzworld.com/site/p483.htm (accessed on September 21, 2004).

CHAPTER

PHYSICAL CHARACTERISTICS

The lone species of gharial (GAR-ee-ul), also sometimes known as a gavial, looks much like a crocodile or alligator except that a gharial has an extremely long and thin snout. The narrow jaws in both males and females are lined with more than 100 pinpoint-sharp teeth. The back of a gharial is covered with tough scales, but these scales are not lumpy as they are in many alligator and crocodile species. Gharial scales are very smooth. Adults are dark brown or greenish brown on top and yellowish white to white below. Young gharials have dark bands on the body and tail. Adults also have bands, but they fade and become less noticeable as the animal gets older. The name gharial comes from the round knob that forms on the tip of the adult male's snout above the nostrils. This knob is called a ghara, because it looks somewhat like an Indian pot of the same name.

Gharials are large reptiles. Males usually grow to 13 to 15 feet (4 to 4.5 meters) long and 350 to 400 pounds (181 kilograms), although some can reach nearly 20 feet (6.1 meters). Females are a bit smaller, usually reaching 11.5 to 13 feet (3.5 to 4 meters) in length. They have long and powerful tails. They are so strong that the gharial need only sway its tail side to side to glide through the water. While swimming, it usually holds its legs back and alongside the body and does not move them.

People sometimes confuse the gharial with the false gharial. Both are large animals with a similar shape. The false gharial, also known as the Malayan gharial, has a long and thin snout, but it is not quite as long and thin as that of the true gharial.

The false gharial also has a heavier-set body. The false gharial is usually placed in the crocodile family, but a 2003 comparison of its DNA now suggests that it should be considered part of the gharial family. Every cell in the body contains DNA, which provides the instructions for making a specific species of animal. Scientists compare the DNA in different species, such as the false gharial and the gharial, to help them decide which animals are most closely related.

GEOGRAPHIC RANGE

Gharial populations are scattered here and there in India, Nepal, and Pakistan, and individuals are sometimes spotted in Bangladesh and Bhutan.

HABITAT

Gharials live in clear, freshwater rivers with swift currents but prefer river bends and other areas where the water is flowing more slowly and is quite deep. They also seek out sandbars in the middle of the river and use them for sunbathing, or basking, to warm their bodies. Strangely, this freshwater animal has salt glands, which are found in animals that live in saltwater. The glands are small organs that get rid of extra salt. Scientists suspect that the gharial once—perhaps millions of years ago—could survive in saltwater and may have traveled across the oceans.

DIET

As youngsters, gharials eat tadpoles, shrimp, insects, and fish they find in the water. As they get older, they become more selective and will eat almost nothing but fish. They usually hunt by ambush, which means that they remain completely still and wait for a fish to swim close. At that point, their unusual teeth become useful. At the front of the lower jaw, a gharial's teeth face outward at such an angle that the tip of the mouth when it is closed looks like a pin cushion. As the fish nears, the gharial snaps its jaws sideways at the prey and stabs it with these very sharp teeth. With a upward jerk of its head, the reptile flings the fish off of its teeth and into the back of its mouth.

MORE THAN A LUMPY NOSE

Scientists have long wondered about the round growth that appears on the nose of male gharials when they become adults. Many suspect that the growth, called a ghara, may do more than allow the animal to make its unusual buzzing sounds. Some researchers believe that the ghara helps the male to produce bubbles. Both the buzzing and the bubbles may help the males attract females during the mating season. Other scientists guess that the gharials look for the ghara to tell quickly which individuals are males and which are females.

BEHAVIOR AND REPRODUCTION

Like some of the other alligators and crocodiles, gharials usually get along quite well and live together in groups. They stay in the water most of the time, coming out occasionally to bask on shore. While they are excellent swimmers, they are slow on land and must drag their bellies and tails on the ground when they walk. They rarely wander too far from the water's edge and, at the slightest threat, will dive back into the safety of the river. On especially warm days, they may open their mouths wide to cool off. This serves the same purpose as panting does for a dog.

When mating season arrives in December and January, the adult males begin fighting one another to set up and defend territories in shallow water. Their fights look something like wrestling matches. Two males lie side by side, lift their heads out of the water, and begin pushing each other with their snouts. The winner is the one that can topple over the other. Sometimes, the wrestling matches become more violent, and the two males hit each other with their snouts or bite each other. A male with a good territory may be able to attract several large females to mate with him. Scientists also believe that the size of the male's ghara may also be important during the mating season. The males can use the ghara to produce a loud buzz, which may be attractive to females. Males also will buzz to warn other males to stay away.

After mating, a female will lay her eggs sometime from March to May. She crawls up a steep bank at the riverside and begins looking for a spot for her nest. She digs her nest in dry ground at least 5 feet (1.5 meters) above water level. A female gharial is very fussy about her nest and may change her mind several times, even after starting to dig, before settling on the perfect place to lay her eggs. The female becomes territorial and guards her specific nest sites from other females, although she will share the beach with many other females and their nests. After digging a hole in the sand, she lays her eggs inside and carefully covers them. The smallest females lay as few as a dozen eggs, and many first-time mothers lay eggs that never hatch at all. The largest females, on the other hand, may lay almost 100 eggs. A typical gharial egg is 2.2 inches (5.5 centimeters) wide, 3.4 inches (8.6 centimeters) long, and weighs 5.5 ounces (156 grams). Females remain near their nests and will defend them from predators, if necessary. The eggs hatch 53 to 92 days later, with nests in warmest climates hatching out earliest and babies

Scientists suspect that the gharial once — perhaps millions of years ago — could survive in saltwater and may have traveled across the oceans. (Derek Hall/FLPA/Bruce Coleman Inc. Reproduced by permission.)

in the coolest areas breaking out of their eggs last. The temperature of the nest also controls the number of males and females. Especially warm nests produce more males, and cooler ones produce more females.

The mother gharial helps her young out of the nest, and then she and possibly the father watch over them. Despite this care, many of a female's young do not survive. Numerous animals, including pigs, hyenas, monitor lizards, and some humans, are fond of gharial eggs, while some birds and turtles often gobble up babies. In addition, the babies are born during the monsoon season and often drown in the floods that are common at this time of year. Of those that do survive, the females are ready to mate when they reach about 10 feet (3 meters) long and are at least 8 years old. The males can mate once they are 15 years old and about 11.5 feet (3.5 meters) long.

GHARIALS AND PEOPLE

Local people sometimes gather gharial eggs for food or hunt the males for the ghara, which they use to make potions. Some people fear gharials, but they do not attack or eat humans. This reptile does, however, hold a place in Hindu legends of a river goddess, named Ma Ganga, who rides on a gharial's back.

CONSERVATION STATUS

The World Conservation Union (IUCN) and the U.S. Fish and Wildlife Service consider this species to be Endangered,

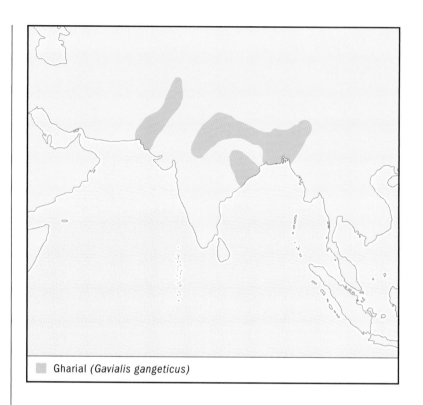

Gharial (*Gavialis gangeticus*)

which means that it faces a very high risk of extinction in the wild and throughout all or a significant portion of its range. In some areas, the gharial has already disappeared or is nearly gone. The greatest threat to this species is habitat loss, often caused when people clear land for farming or for firewood. Conservationists have raised and attempted to release young gharials into the wild. Some of these efforts have been successful, and others have not, but the work to save this unusual species is continuing.

FOR MORE INFORMATION

Books:

Daniel, J. C. *The Book of Indian Reptiles and Amphibians*. New Delhi, India: Oxford University Press, 2002.

Ross, C. A., ed. *Crocodiles and Alligators*. New York: Facts on File Inc., 1989.

Rue, Leonard Lee. *Alligators and Crocodiles*. Wigston, Leicester: Magna Books, 1994.

Web sites:

"Alligators and Crocodiles." San Diego Zoo. http://www.sandiegozoo.org/animalbytes/t-crocodile.html (accessed on September 21, 2004).

"At the Zoo: Gharials Star in the Reptile Discovery Center and on Gharial Cam." Smithsonian National Zoological Park. http://nationalzoo.si.edu/Publications/ZooGoer/2002/6/gharials.cfm (accessed on December 19, 2004).

"*Gavialis gangeticus* (GMELIN, 1789)." Florida Museum of Natural History. http://www.flmnh.ufl.edu/natsci/herpetology/brittoncrocs/csp_ggan.htm (accessed on December 19, 2004).

"Gharial." Smithsonian National Zoological Park. http://nationalzoo.si.edu/Animals/ReptilesAmphibians/Facts/FactSheets/Gharial.cfm (accessed on September 21, 2004).

"The Gharial and the Monkey." The Crocodile Files. http://www.oneworldmagazine.org/tales/crocs/gharial.html (accessed on December 19, 2004).

**ALLIGATORS
AND CAIMANS**

Alligatoridae

Class: Reptilia

Order: Crocodylia

Suborder: Eusuchia

Family: Alligatoridae

Number of species: 8 species

CHAPTER

phylum

class

subclass

order

monotypic order

suborder

▲ **family**

PHYSICAL CHARACTERISTICS

Like crocodiles, the alligators and caimans have a heavy body, with the back and tail covered by armor-like scales. Crocodiles, alligators, and caimans have a strong tail, which is at least as long as the rest of the body, and the back half of the tail often has a row of tall, ridged scales along the top. They also have a long snout, hind limbs larger than the front legs, and large, powerful jaws filled with teeth. Alligators and crocodiles are, however, different. All of an alligator's or caiman's lower teeth are hidden when its mouth is closed. In crocodiles, one lower tooth remains outside the jaw, even when it is clamped shut.

When alligators are young, they often have dark bands on their bodies, but these disappear as they get older. Adults may be dark gray, brown, black, or a bit yellowish. The smallest species is Cuvier's dwarf caiman, which grows to about 4 feet (1.2 meters). The largest is the American alligator, which can reach 13 feet (4 meters) long.

GEOGRAPHIC RANGE

Depending on the species, alligators and caimans may live in Central America, Mexico, the southeastern United States, South America, and/or eastern China.

HABITAT

Alligators and caimans are freshwater species that prefer still or slow-moving water, even if it is muddy or murky. Besides lakes, rivers, and streams, they are often found in swamps, marshes, and roadside ditches. Seven of the eight species live in the New World, which includes Central, South, and North America, but only one lives in the United States. The eighth species makes its home in a small area of eastern China, which is part of the Old World.

DIET

Alligators are meat-eaters, though they are anything but fussy about their prey. Youngsters will dine on snails and other invertebrates (in-VER-teh-brehts), which are animals without backbones. As they grow, they switch to the adult diet, which includes fishes, birds, small mammals, and other vertebrates (VER-teh-brehts), which are animals with backbones. They will also sometimes attack and devour smaller alligators and caimans. The larger species in this family are strong enough to kill a cow or deer for dinner.

Alligators hunt by ambush or by stalking. In ambush hunting, they remain still and wait for a prey animal to wander by. Stalking is usually done in the water. The alligator slowly and carefully swims closer and closer to a prey animal, perhaps a deer drinking at a watering hole, and then lunges forward to snap its jaws shut around the animal.

BEHAVIOR AND REPRODUCTION

A favorite daytime activity for alligators and caimans is sunbathing, or basking, on shore. They can also heat up their bodies by floating in the warm, upper surface of the water. When they need to cool off, they simply sink to colder, deeper water. Some live where the weather is especially cold at times during the year, but none of them actually hibernate (HIGH-bur-nayt), or become inactive and enter a state of deep sleep. Instead, these species either lie still in shallow water and breathe through the nose, the only part of the body not underwater, or they retreat into winter burrows to wait for spring.

A LONG WINTER

The Chinese alligator has only a short time to mate, have babies, and eat enough to survive the year. The reason is the climate in which it lives. Chinese alligators make their home in the Yangtze River basin along China's central Atlantic coastline, an area that is cold much of the year. When temperatures drop in the late fall, the alligators slide into their winter burrows and stay there until the following April. They then crawl out to soak up the sun and warm their bodies. About a month later, the males begin to bellow, which starts the mating season. Females lay their eggs, which usually hatch in September, not long before the temperatures again cool and announce the coming of another long winter period in their burrows.

Alligators and caimans appear very restful when they are basking, but they are actually quite alert. With a quick swipe of the tail, a swift turn of the head with jaws open, or a speedy charge on their powerful legs, they can change from a quiet, peaceful-looking reptile to a dangerous predator. Alligators and caimans can move in several ways. In the water, they usually swim by slowly swaying the tail from side to side. On land, they may crawl along with the belly and tail dragging on the ground, or they can do a "high walk" and run as a lizard does with the body held above the ground.

Alligators and caimans often live in groups. They get along well during most of the year, but during the spring breeding season, the rules change. Adults begin slapping their heads on the water surface or charging one another with their mouths wide open, although they do not normally bite. By summer, the females begin to scrape together piles of leaves on which they lay their 12 to 60 eggs. The mother remains nearby, and when the babies hatch one or two months later, she helps them out of the nest and to the water. In some species, the temperature of the nest decides the sex of the babies. Cool temperatures produce all females, and warm temperatures produce all males. Temperatures in the middle turn out males and females.

ALLIGATORS, CAIMANS, AND PEOPLE

People sometimes hunt alligators and caimans for their skin, their meat, and sometimes for their organs, which are used to make perfume. In Florida, Louisiana, and other places, they are an important tourist attraction and help bring in money to the local community.

CONSERVATION STATUS

The World Conservation Union (IUCN) considers the Chinese alligator to be Critically Endangered, which means that it faces an extremely high risk of extinction in the wild. It also lists the black caiman as Conservation Dependent, which means it still requires attention to make sure it survives. The U.S. Fish and Wildlife Service lists the American alligator, a U.S. species, as Threatened, or likely to become endangered in the foreseeable future. These and other alligators and caimans often suffer from habitat loss and overhunting, and numerous conservation efforts are under way to protect them.

American alligator (*Alligator mississippiensis*)

AMERICAN ALLIGATOR
Alligator mississippiensis

Physical characteristics: A large reptile, the American alligator has a black or dark grayish green back and tail with a white belly. Young alligators have numerous yellow markings on the back and tail. American alligators are sometimes confused with American crocodiles, but the crocodile has a snout that becomes thinner at the tip. The alligator's snout remains wide. Adult American alligators usually grow to 8 to 13 feet (2.4 to 4 meters) long, but some giants may reach 19 feet (5.8 meters) or more.

Geographic range: American alligators live in the United States from North Carolina down to Florida and west to Texas.

Habitat: American alligators make their homes in still or slow-moving freshwater areas, including marshes and swamps, rivers, and lakes.

American alligators are sometimes confused with American crocodiles, but the crocodile has a snout that becomes thinner at the tip. The alligator's snout remains wide. (Illustration by Brian Cressman. Reproduced by permission.)

Occasionally, they make their way into the swimming pools of people who live near their natural habitat.

Diet: Meat-eaters, they will dine on almost any animal they come across, including turtles, fishes, mammals, and sometimes smaller alligators. They swallow most smaller prey whole. For larger animals, however, the alligators first drown the victim, then chomp off mouthfuls of flesh.

Behavior and reproduction: American alligators live in groups, with great grandparents, grandparents, parents, and children often sharing the same area. During the spring breeding season, the males try to interest the females by bumping softly against them and calling out with loud bellows. The females bellow, too, but much less often and not quite as loudly. After mating, the female lays 36 to 48 eggs, which hatch about two months later. She helps the young out of the nest and to the water. The family stays together for two or three months, and sometimes up to three years. The young alligators are ready to become parents themselves when they reach about 10 years old. American alligators live to be 50 years old or older.

American alligators and people: In many areas, people like alligators because they bring money to the community through tourism, but at the same time dislike them because the reptiles sometimes eat pets or have to be removed from golf courses and swimming pools. Now that people have begun to move farther and farther into the alligators' habitat, attacks on humans have also become much more common. According to the Florida Fish and Wildlife Conservation Commission, alligator attacks on humans in that state from 1948 to 2003 numbered 326 and resulted in 13 deaths.

Conservation status: The World Conservation Union (IUCN) does not consider this species to be at risk, but the U.S. Fish and Wildlife Service lists it as Threatened or likely to become endangered in the foreseeable future.   ■

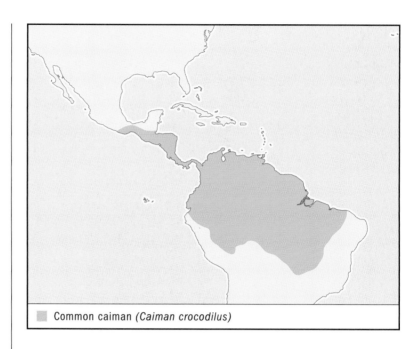

Common caiman *(Caiman crocodilus)*

COMMON CAIMAN
Caiman crocodilus

Physical characteristics: Also known as the spectacled caiman, the common caiman has a bony ridge and slightly lighter color around each eye. Its body is greenish to brownish gray, sometimes with noticeable dark bands on its tail and patches on its back. Adults usually grow to 4 to 6 feet (1.2 to 1.8 meters) long, but some can reach up to 10 feet (3 meters) from the tip of the snout to the end of the tail.

Geographic range: The common caiman lives from southern Mexico to northern Argentina, on the islands of Trinidad and Tobago, and in southern Florida. Cuba and Puerto Rico also have introduced populations.

Habitat: It is found in calm freshwater lakes, rivers, and swamps, as well as man-made roadside ditches.

Diet: From youngsters to adults, common caimans tend to eat animals they find in the water. Although the youngest ones will eat insects and other invertebrates they find on land, juveniles are fond of snails, and adults mainly eat different types of fishes.

Common caimans live in groups quite peacefully for most of the year, but during the mating season, the males begin bellowing and set up territories. (©Kevin Schafer/Photo Researchers, Inc. Reproduced by permission.)

Behavior and reproduction: Common caimans live in groups quite peacefully for most of the year, but during the mating season, the males begin bellowing and set up territories. One male may mate with several females. The female lays 12 to 36 eggs in a leafy nest she makes on land. The male guards the nest until the babies hatch. The mother then carries them to the water. The family stays together for about a year.

Common caimans and people: People sometimes hunt this reptile for its meat and its skin.

Conservation status: This species is not considered endangered or threatened. ∎

FOR MORE INFORMATION

Books:

Lamar, William. *The World's Most Spectacular Reptiles and Amphibians.* Tampa, FL: World Publications, 1997.

Cleaver, Andrew. *Snakes and Reptiles: A Portrait of the Animal World.* Wigston, Leicester: Magna Books, 1994.

Lockwood, C. C. *The Alligator Book.* Baton Rouge: Louisiana State University Press, 2002.

Ross, C. A., ed. *Crocodiles and Alligators.* New York: Facts on File, Inc., 1989.

Rue, Leonard Lee. *Alligators and Crocodiles.* Wigston, Leicester: Magna Books, 1994.

Web sites:

"All About Alligators." Enchanted Learning. http://www.enchantedlearning.com/subjects/Alligator.shtml (accessed on September 21, 2004).

"Alligator." Everglades National Park. http://www.nps.gov/ever/eco/gator.htm (accessed on September 21, 2004).

"Alligator." World Almanac for Kids. http://www.worldalmanacforkids.com/explore/animals/alligator.html (accessed on September 21, 2004).

"*Alligator mississippiensis* (DAUDIN, 1801)." Florida Museum of Natural History. http://www.flmnh.ufl.edu/cnhc/csp_amis.htm (accessed on December 15, 2004).

"Alligators and Crocodiles." San Diego Zoo. http://www.sandiegozoo.org/animalbytes/t-crocodile.html (accessed on September 21, 2004).

"Crocodilian Species List." Florida Museum of Natural History. http://www.flmnh.ufl.edu/cnhc/csl.html (accessed on December 15, 2004).

"The Reptiles: Alligators and Crocodiles." Nature. http://www.pbs.org/wnet/nature/reptiles/ (accessed on December 15, 2004).

"Spectacled Caiman." Enchanted Learning. http://www.enchantedlearning.com/subjects/reptiles/caiman/Speccaiman.shtml (accessed on September 21, 2004).

"Wild Things: The Not-So-Friendly Caiman." Kidzworld. http://www.kidzworld.com/site/p483.htm (accessed on September 21, 2004).

Class: Reptilia

Order: Crocodylia

Family: Crocodylidae

Number of species: 14 species

family

CHAPTER

PHYSICAL CHARACTERISTICS

Fourteen species of crocodiles make up this family, including one called a false gharial. (An Indian gharial also exists, but it is not a crocodile and is instead listed in its own separate family.) The crocodiles are medium to large reptiles, with adults ranging from about 5 feet (1.5 meters) long in the smallest species to 20 feet (6.1 meters) long in the largest. Within species, females are smaller overall. For example, female Johnstone's crocodiles typically grow to 5 feet (1.5 meters), while the average male is about 6.5 feet (2 meters) long. In all species, the tail is about as long as the rest of the body.

Crocodiles, alligators, and caimans are often confused because they all have armor-like scales on the back and tail, a powerful tail, a pair of back legs that are stronger and larger than the front pair, and toes that are webbed on the back pair of feet and unwebbed on the front pair. Perhaps most noticeably, they also all share a long snout filled with teeth. Crocodiles, however, have something the others lack. Counting from the front of the mouth, the large fourth tooth on each side of a crocodile's lower jaw shows outside of the mouth when the jaw is closed. In other species, this large tooth is hidden, although many other teeth on the upper jaw may be visible when the mouth is clamped shut.

GEOGRAPHIC RANGE

At least one species of crocodiles lives in each of these continents: Africa, Asia, Australia, North America, and South America.

HABITAT

Crocodiles spend their time in or near the water. Unlike alligators and caimans that only live in freshwater habitats, crocodiles can survive in freshwater or saltwater. Crocodiles do not, however, swim around in the open ocean. Instead, they live in saltwater marshes or creeks. They have special organs, called salt glands, that get rid of this extra salt so they can survive. Without these organs, they could not live in saltwater. Crocodiles make their homes in warm, tropical areas, although the mugger crocodile and the American crocodile can survive in subtropical regions that are slightly less warm. Those that live in areas with periods of extremely dry weather sometimes find that their watering holes disappear, and they must spend the next few weeks buried deep underground until the rains return.

DIET

Crocodiles are meat-eaters that shift from eating insects and spiders as youngsters to larger and larger animals as they grow. Adults of the largest crocodiles, like the Nile crocodile, eat animals as big as warthogs, cows, and sometimes humans. They are skilled hunters that sneak up on prey by ever so slowly swimming closer and closer, and then lunging out with mouth open to clamp down on the surprised animal. This method of sneaking up on prey is called stalking. Once the jaw snaps shut, the prey has little chance of escaping. With a captured mammal, the crocodile typically pulls it underwater, and when the animal drowns, tears off chunks to swallow. Crocodiles also hunt for prey by ambush, which means that they stay still in the water and wait for a prey animal to happen by. Besides live meals, crocodiles will also eat the dead animals they find.

BEHAVIOR AND REPRODUCTION

Crocodiles are most active at night, which is when they usually look for food. In the morning and evening, they frequently crawl out of the water and lay quietly in an open area to sunbathe, or bask. This helps warm their bodies. Crocodiles are excellent swimmers. By slowly swishing the strong tail from side to side, they can push their bodies through the water without having to paddle with their legs. They can also move well on land. Usually, they walk slowly, dragging the tail behind them, but when they are in a hurry, they run quite quickly while swinging the tail back and forth in the same motion they use when swimming.

Crocodiles usually get along fairly well with one another, but during the mating season, males can become bad-tempered. Usually, a large male need only sound a loud bellow or slap his head against the surface of the water to scare off a smaller male, but sometimes they fight by biting one another. The bites are hard enough to cause wounds that leave noticeable scars. Besides their bellows, crocodiles make other sounds, such as growls and hisses, when they feel threatened.

Male crocodiles may fight each other over the females during mating season, and one male may have babies with several females in a single year. All female crocodiles lay eggs rather than giving birth to babies. The females in some species use their back legs to dig a hole on land, and they bury their eggs there. These females lay their eggs in the dry season, and the eggs hatch when the rains come. In other species, the females lay their eggs in a pile of rotting leaves and dirt that they scrape together. The females lay their eggs at the beginning of the rainy season, and the eggs hatch during the wettest time of year. Depending on the species, females may lay 40 to 70 eggs at a time, with hatching occurring two to three months later. If the nest is especially warm, the eggs all hatch into males. If the nest is particularly cool, the eggs all hatch into females. A mother crocodile stays close to her nest until the eggs are ready to hatch. The baby crocodiles begin to make soft quacking noises when they are ready to break out of their eggs, and the mother rushes to the nest to pick up and carry each of her babies to the water. The mother, and sometimes the father, watches over the young for several weeks, but despite this care, fewer than one out of 10 babies escapes the many predators in their habitat. Those that do survive to adulthood can look forward to a long life. Crocodiles often live for 70 to 80 years in the wild.

CROCODILES, FALSE GHARIALS, AND PEOPLE

People have long been fascinated by crocodiles, which are often mentioned in legends. Some people hunt these animals

ONE TON BEAST

The saltwater crocodile is a huge animal. The largest species of all crocodiles and alligators, it can grow to more than 20 feet (6.1 meters) long and weigh 2,200 pounds (1 metric ton). Occasionally, humans tangle with these beasts and lose. One of the most often-told tales of human versus crocodile dates back to World War II, when hundreds of Japanese soldiers hid in a swamp near Myanmar. A large group of saltwater crocodiles set upon the men that night, killing all but 20 by morning.

for their meat or skin, and some collect and eat their eggs. Crocodiles are perhaps most known, however, as killers of humans. Although death by crocodile is very rare, it does happen occasionally, especially when humans who visit their habitat are careless.

CONSERVATION STATUS

According to the World Conservation Union (IUCN), nine of the 14 species are at risk. This includes three listed as Critically Endangered, which means they face an extremely high risk of extinction in the wild; two as Endangered and facing a very high risk of extinction in the wild; three species as Vulnerable and under a high risk of extinction in the wild; and one as Conservation Dependent, which means it could be at risk if conservation efforts ceased. In addition, the IUCN describes one species as Data Deficient, which means that scientists have too little information to make a judgment about its threat of extinction. The U.S. Fish and Wildlife Service lists 12 of the 14 species as Threatened, or likely to become endangered in the foreseeable future, or Endangered, which means they are in danger of extinction throughout all or a significant portion of their range. Most of the species are at risk because of habitat loss and overhunting. Several efforts are now under way to help protect these animals.

American crocodile (*Crocodylus acutus*)

AMERICAN CROCODILE
Crocodylus acutus

Physical characteristics: The American crocodile is large, with the males averaging 10 to 11 feet (3 to 3.5 meters) long and females usually 8 to 10 feet (2.5 to 3 meters) in length. The largest males, however, can reach a full 20 feet (6 meters), but such giants are extremely rare. Its body is a bit thinner than most crocodiles, and its snout becomes narrower toward the tip. It also has a noticeable lump on its snout in front of its eyes. Adults are usually dark brown to light brownish gray with a white belly. Youngsters are yellow to greenish gray with dark markings.

Geographic range: American crocodiles live in large groups in southern Florida, southern Mexico, Central America, numerous Caribbean islands, and northern South America.

Habitat: Also known as the American saltwater crocodile, this species can survive in various habitats from freshwater canals to somewhat salty marshes near the ocean coast.

Diet: Young American crocodiles catch and eat insects, tadpoles and frogs, crabs, and fish, and then switch to larger prey as they grow. Adults are able to feed on animals as large as cows and, in very rare cases, humans.

Behavior and reproduction: American crocodiles usually hunt at night and spend most of their days resting in the water or basking or sunbathing on shore, especially in the mornings and evenings. During very dry periods, they will dig a tunnel and remain inside until the rains return. Males and females mate from March to May, and each female lays 30 to 60 eggs in a hole that she digs. Sometimes, the mother may lay her eggs in a pile of rotting leaves and dirt instead. She stays nearby until the eggs hatch 80 to 90 days later. She then helps her babies out of the nest and watches over them for a few more days.

American crocodiles and people: This species very rarely attacks humans. Some humans, however, raid the crocodiles' nests to collect their eggs for food.

Conservation status: The World Conservation Union (IUCN) considers this species to be Vulnerable, or facing a high risk of extinction in the wild. The U.S. Fish and Wildlife Service designates it as Endangered, or in danger of extinction throughout all or a significant portion of its range. The primary threat to this animal comes from habitat loss. ∎

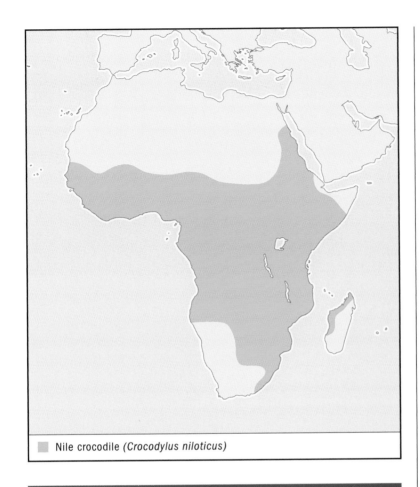

Nile crocodile (*Crocodylus niloticus*)

NILE CROCODILE
Crocodylus niloticus

Physical characteristics: A large and bulky-bodied species, the Nile crocodile has a very lumpy, dark brown to gray back and a light yellow, white, or gray belly. Youngsters are greenish brown to brown with dark markings. Females usually reach about 8 feet (2.5 meters) long, and males typically grow to about 11.5 feet (3.5 meters).

Geographic range: Nile crocodiles live in Africa south of the Sahara Desert and on Madasgascar off Africa's southeast coast.

Habitat: Nile crocodiles mainly live in freshwater habitats, including marshes, lakes, and rivers.

Nile crocodiles spend much of their time in the water, either stalking prey or lying in wait for an animal to come close enough to attack. (©Charles V. Angelo/The National Audubon Society Collection/Photo Researchers, Inc. Reproduced by permission.)

Diet: The adult diet is mostly fish, although Nile crocodiles will also eat large mammals, such as warthogs and antelopes.

Behavior and reproduction: Nile crocodiles spend much of their time in the water, either stalking prey or lying in wait for an animal to come close enough to attack. With their powerful jaws, they can clamp onto even large animals and drag them underwater. After the animal drowns, the crocodile may twirl the animal in the water in an attempt to tear off a chunk of flesh to eat. Nile crocodiles often live in large groups and often bask together on the shoreline. During the August-to-January mating season, however, males will fight one another. After a male and female mate, the female goes off to dig a hole high on shore and lay her 50 to 80 eggs inside. The mother remains nearby, and 80 to 90 days later, she helps her now-hatched young out of the nest and to the water. The young stay under their mother's watchful eye for another month or so, and then go off on their own.

Nile crocodiles and people: These animals occasionally attack and kill ranchers' cattle and other livestock, and very rarely, a person. Some people hunt this reptile for its meat and skin.

Conservation status: Although it was once overhunted, the World Conservation Union (IUCN) no longer considers this species to be at risk. The U.S. Fish and Wildlife Service, however, lists it as Threatened, or likely to become endangered in the foreseeable future. Numerous guidelines are in place to help make sure the crocodile survives into the future. ■

FOR MORE INFORMATION

Books:

Cleaver, Andrew. *Snakes and Reptiles: A Portrait of the Animal World.* Wigston, Leicester: Magna Books, 1994.

Daniel, J. C. *The Book of Indian Reptiles and Amphibians.* New Delhi, India: Oxford University Press, 2002.

Irwin, Steve, and Terri Irwin. *The Crocodile Hunter.* New York: Penguin Putnam, 1997.

Lamar, William. *The World's Most Spectacular Reptiles and Amphibians.* Tampa, FL: World Publications, 1997.

Ross, C. A., ed. *Crocodiles and Alligators.* New York: Facts on File, Inc., 1989.

Rue, Leonard Lee. *Alligators and Crocodiles.* Wigston, Leicester: Magna Books, 1994.

Schmidt, K. P. *A Check List of North American Amphibians and Reptiles.* Chicago: University of Chicago Press, 1953.

Smith, H. M., and E. H. Taylor. *An Annotated Checklist and Key to the Reptiles of Mexico Exclusive of Snakes.* Washington, DC: Bulletin of the U.S. National Museum, 1950.

Webb, G. J. W., and S. C. Manolis. *Crocodiles of Australia.* New South Wales, Australia: Reed Books Pty, Ltd., 1989.

Web sites:

"Crocodilian Species List." Florida Museum of Natural History. http://www.flmnh.ufl.edu/cnhc/csl.html (accessed on December 15, 2004).

"*Crocodylus niloticus* (LAURENTI, 1768)." Florida Museum of Natural History. http://www.flmnh.ufl.edu/cnhc/csp_cnil.htm (accessed on December 15, 2004).

"The Reptiles: Alligators and Crocodiles." Nature. http://www.pbs.org/wnet/nature/reptiles/ (accessed on December 15, 2004).

Class: Reptilia

Order: Sphenodontia

Family: Sphenodontidae

Number of species: 2 species

monotypic order
CHAPTER

PHYSICAL CHARACTERISTICS

At a glance, each of the two species of tuatara could be mistaken for a lizard. A closer look, however, reveals how different they really are. One difference is in their teeth. Tuataras have not one, but two rows of teeth lying side by side in the upper jaw. When the mouth closes, the single row of teeth in the lower jaw fits between the two upper rows. Tuataras have ears as lizards do, but lizards have an ear opening on each side of the head and tuataras do not. Baby tuataras have another unusual feature. They have a pale patch on the top of the head, which some people have called a "third eye." The patch becomes covered with scales as the animal grows up. Scientists are unsure of the patch's purpose but believe it may allow the reptile to see light from the sun. Such information about the sun's location may help the animal find its way.

A tuatara has a large head on a sturdy body that ends in a thick tail. Its skin is wrinkly and covered with noticeable beady scales. A white crest runs along the back of the head and down the middle of the back. The tail also has a row of toothy spines down its center. Males are larger and heavier than females, and they also have larger crests on the head and back. The biggest of the two species, the northern tuatara, can grow to more than 24 inches (61 centimeters) long from head to tail and weigh at least 2 pounds (1 kilogram). The smaller females of the species usually reach 16 inches (40.6 centimeters) and 1 pound (0.5 kilograms) at most. The other species, known as Brother Islands tuatara, is slightly smaller.

The Brother Islands tuatara is often a bit greener in color than the greenish brown northern tuatara, but both are sometimes reddish to almost black in color. The two species have white and black blotches and spots, but the Brother Islands tuatara usually has more white spots. Young tuataras of both species are commonly light grayish brown with light V-shaped patterns running along the back and dark markings by the eyes.

GEOGRAPHIC RANGE

Tuataras have a small range, living on about 30 tiny and hard-to-reach islands off New Zealand's shore.

HABITAT

Although neither species is widespread, the northern tuataras make their homes over a bigger area than the Brother Islands tuataras. The northern tuataras live on 26 islands off northeastern North Island and on four islands of Cook Strait off the northern coast of South Island. The Brother Islands tuatara lives only on North Brother Island in Cook Strait. Both species are burrowers and live in shady forests where the trees grow thick enough to block the sun almost completely from reaching the ground.

DIET

Usually active at night, the tuataras often hunt by ambush, which means that they sit still and wait for a prey animal to come to them. They also forage (FOR-ej), which means that they wander about looking for food. They use their sticky fat tongues to catch and eat mainly non-flying grasshoppers, beetles, and other crawling invertebrates (in-VER-teh-brehts), which are animals without backbones. The unusual arrangement of their teeth is not only excellent for crushing invertebrates but is also well-suited to the occasional meal of a seabird, lizard, or perhaps a smaller tuatara. The younger tuataras are more likely than the adults to hunt during the daytime. This practice may help them avoid being eaten by adult tuataras.

BEHAVIOR AND REPRODUCTION

Tuataras are most active at night, which is when they do the majority of their hunting. During the daytime, each one lives alone in its underground burrow, occasionally coming to the burrow entrance to sunbathe, or bask, and warm their bodies. Tuataras live on very small islands that may become rather

A VERY OLD REPTILE

The tuatara is the only descendant of an ancient group of reptiles that were common in the late Triassic and Jurassic periods about 180 to 220 million years ago. At that time, they were spread out over Europe, Africa, and North America. They started to disappear during the dinosaurs' reign, and almost all of them were completely gone by the early Cretaceous Period, which followed the Jurassic. A tiny group, however, survived on a piece of land that broke off the mainland and eventually formed the islands of New Zealand. This group of animals, called a lineage (LIN-ee-ej) because it connects species through time to their ancestors, gave rise to the two current-day tuatara species.

crowded, sometimes with tuatara burrows less than 3 feet (0.9 meters) apart. In some cases, 810 tuataras may share a single acre of land (2,000 per hectare). They get along quite well, but males will fight one another for small territories, where they hope to attract females for mating. The battles begin with two males lining up next to each other, with each facing in the opposite direction. They then puff up the throat, stiffen the crest spines on the back so they stand on end, open wide the mouth, and snap the jaws shut tight. Usually this display is enough for one of the two males to surrender and leave the area. Occasionally, however, neither one retreats, and the two males engage in biting matches.

Females mate once every two to five years, but males mate every year. Males set up their territories in summer and fall and begin doing what is called a "proud walk" to catch a female's eye. Doing some of the displays he does when battling males, he tries to attract a female by slowly strutting around her while stiffening his back crest and puffing up his throat. If she is interested, she stays. If not, she simply walks away. After mating, a female must wait until the following spring to lay her eggs. Most lay four to 13 eggs, but the larger northern tuataras from Cook Strait often lay eight to 15. Each female makes a hole that may be very shallow or up to 20 inches (50 centimeters) deep, lays her eggs, and covers them loosely with dirt. The eggs do not hatch until 12 to 15 months later. As in many other reptiles, the temperature of the nest controls whether the eggs hatch into males or females. In the case of the Brother Islands tuatara, warmer nests produce mostly males, and cooler ones produce mostly females. Tuataras cannot mate until they are up to 13 years old. They live to be at least 60 and possibly much longer.

TUATARAS AND PEOPLE

The people of New Zealand hold the tuatara in high regard and consider them to be living treasures. Tuataras have also caught the eye of the science community. In the 1800s, for example, so many scientific institutions wanted their own tuataras to study that the local government in 1895 was forced to protect the reptile before its population dropped too low.

CONSERVATION STATUS

The World Conservation Union (IUCN) considers the Brother Islands tuatara to be Vulnerable, which means that it faces a high risk of extinction in the wild. The U.S. Fish and Wildlife Service lists both species as Endangered or in danger of extinction throughout all or a significant portion of their range. One of the greatest threats to the tuataras comes from introduced species, especially rats, which attack and kill the reptiles. Several programs are under way to remove the rats and to prevent any other predators from reaching the islands; these efforts are helping the tuataras to make a comeback. In addition, other programs are helping to return tuataras to those places where they once lived but had disappeared.

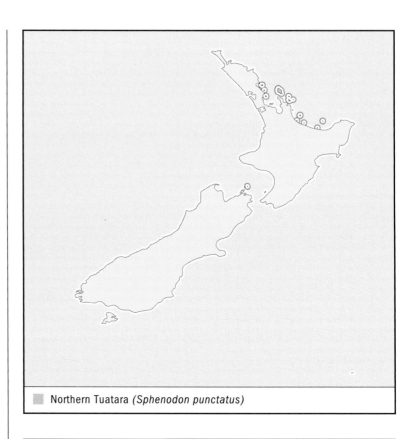

Northern Tuatara (*Sphenodon punctatus*)

NORTHERN TUATARA
Sphenodon punctatus

Physical characteristics: The northern tuatara is a beady-skinned, lizard-looking animal with a crest on the back of its head and on its back. Its color may be gray, greenish gray, red, or black. Males can reach more than 24 inches (61 centimeters) long and 2 pounds (1 kilogram). Females are smaller, usually growing to no more than 16 inches (40.6 centimeters) and 1 pound (0.5 kilograms).

Geographic range: The northern tuatara lives on about 30 islands off New Zealand's coast.

Habitat: Northern tuataras spend much of their lives in or around their underground burrows.

Diet: Their diet is about 75 percent invertebrates, especially beetles and grasshoppers. They occasionally eat lizards, small birds, and other vertebrates (VER-teh-brehts), which are animals with backbones.

Behavior and reproduction: During the day, northern tuataras remain in their burrows, occasionally coming to the entrance to bask in the sun. They do most of their hunting at night. Although they get along quite well, considering that they may sometimes live less than 3 feet apart, the males do fight, especially during the breeding season. Males mate every year, but females mate only once every 2 to 5 years.

The people of New Zealand hold the tuatara in high regard and consider them to be living treasures. (Illustration by Brian Cressman. Reproduced by permission.)

Northern Tuataras and people: Local people respect this reptile. The New Zealand government is very strict in its protection of the tuataras, even limiting travel to the islands where the reptiles live.

Conservation status: The World Conservation Union (IUCN) does not consider this species to be at risk, but the U.S. Fish and Wildlife Service considers it to be Endangered or in danger of extinction throughout all or a significant portion of its range. Efforts are under way to remove introduced predators, especially rats, from the tuatara's islands. ■

FOR MORE INFORMATION

Books:

Tesar, Jenny. *What on Earth is a Tuatara?* Woodbridge, CT: Blackbirch Press, 1994.

Periodicals:

"Quick Bits: Tuatara." *Ranger Rick.* August 1999, vol. 33, page 12.

"Tuataras 'The Living Fossil' Explained." *Monkeyshines on Health & Science.* Spring 1998, page 14.

Web sites:

Musico, B. "*Sphenodon punctatus.*" Animal Diversity Web. http://animaldiversity.ummz.umich.edu/site/accounts/information/Sphenodon_punctatus.html (accessed on December 20, 2004).

"The Tuatara." Kiwi Conservation Club. http://www.kcc.org.nz/animals/tuatara.asp (accessed on December 20, 2004).

"Tuatara." San Diego Zoo. http://www.sandiegozoo.org/animalbytes/t-tuatara.html (accessed on December 20, 2004).

"What Can You Tell Me About Tuatara?" Museum of New Zealand Te Papa Tongarewa. http://www.tepapa.govt.nz/TePapa/English/CollectionsAnd Research/FAQs/FAQs_NaturalEnvironment.htm#tuatara (accessed on December 20, 2004).

SNAKES AND LIZARDS
Squamata

Class: Reptilia
Order: Squamata
Number of families: About 42
families

PHYSICAL CHARACTERISTICS

The 7,200 species of snakes, lizards, and wormlizards all fall under the order Squamata and are therefore known as squamates (SKWAH-mates). Perhaps the most noticeable difference between the snakes and the lizards are the legs, or the lack of them. Most lizards, except for a few species, have working legs. Snakes are legless. The most noticeable feature of the worm lizards is their earthworm-like body. While they have scales and earthworms do not, worm lizards' scales are arranged in rings and separated with grooves to give them the appearance of an earthworm's ringed body. Most of the worm lizards are legless, although a few have two front legs just behind the head.

Besides smelling with their noses and tasting with their tongues, most squamates also smell with a special organ on the roof of their mouths. They use it by first flicking or otherwise picking up chemicals on the tongue. They then place the tongue on the roof of the mouth at what is called the Jacobson's organ, which smells the chemicals. For hearing, many lizards have ears that are visible as a hole on either side of the head. Neither the snakes nor the wormlizards have the openings for their ears. Scientists believe that snakes can probably only hear very low-pitched sounds, including ground vibrations that they sense in the jaw and send to the ear.

In addition to the presence or absence of ear holes, known as external ears, snakes and lizards have another obvious difference. The majority of lizards have eyelids that close and open. Snakes, on the other hand, have a spectacle over their

phylum

class

subclass

● **order**

monotypic order

suborder

family

eyes. A spectacle is a clear scale, which looks much like a contact lens. In other words, a lizard noticeably blinks, but a snake always appears to have its eyes open. Although most squamates have obvious eyes, those species that spend most of their lives underground often have very small eyes, which are sometimes invisible under their scales.

The size of the squamate depends on the species. Among the lizards, the heaviest is the Indonesian Komodo dragon, which can grow to be at least 9.9 feet (3 meters) long and 330 pounds (150 kilograms). Many people consider the crocodile monitor to be the world's longest lizard. It can reach 12 feet (nearly 3.7 meters) long, although some reports claim that the lizards can reach 15 to 19 feet (4.6 to 5.8 meters) long. The smallest lizard, on the other hand, is the jaragua lizard, also known as the dwarf gecko. From one end to the other, adults of this recently discovered species only reach about 1.2 inches (3.2 centimeters) long. Snakes also come in different sizes. Some of the smallest are in the blind snake and slender blind snake families, which include species that only grow to 4 inches (10 centimeters) long and weigh just 0.05 ounces (1.4 grams). This compares to the reticulated python, which often reaches 20 feet (6.1 meters) or more. The largest reticulated python ever discovered was killed in 1912 in Indonesia. This beast measured 33 feet (10.1 meters) in length. The South American green anaconda is another enormous species, often reaching 25 feet (7.7 meters) long and 300 pounds (136 kilograms). Wormlizard adults range from 3.1 inches (8 centimeters) to more than 32 inches (81 centimeters) long.

GEOGRAPHIC RANGE

Besides the Arctic, Antarctic, and other very cold places, squamates live almost the world over.

HABITAT

Squamates can live in many habitats, from the dry conditions in the desert to the wet and warm rainforests. Many of them, including numerous lizards and snakes, live above ground on land. Some, such as the wormlizards, are fossorial (foss-OR-ee-ul), which means that they remain underground most of the time. Others, including many snakes, are arboreal (ar-BOR-ee-ul), which means that they often live above the ground among tree branches. Some, like the water snakes, rarely leave their freshwater streams or ponds, while the sea kraits are snakes that spend their lives in salt water.

DIET

Most of the squamates eat other animals. Many of the lizards and the smaller snake species eat insects or other invertebrates (in-VER-teh-brehts), which are animals without backbones. Even some of the medium-sized snakes eat invertebrates. Eastern garter snakes, for example, like to dine on earthworms. A large number of the medium- to large-sized snakes, however, eat other snakes, lizards, frogs and tadpoles, mammals and other vertebrates (VER-teh-brehts), which are animals with backbones. Boa constrictors, pythons, and other very large snakes sometimes eat calves, deer, and other big mammals. Monitor lizards, which can grow to 12 feet (3.7 meters) or longer, can also capture, kill, and eat large mammals, such as deer, monkeys, wild pigs, and even buffalo. They are also known to eat dead animals, or carrion (CARE-ee-yun), that they come across. Some species of squamates eat plants either in addition to or instead of meat. Many of the iguanas, for instance, eat flowers, fruits, and leaves.

All squamates shed their skin—actually just the outer layer—once a year. If a snake eats well and grows quickly, it may shed additional times. The lizards typically shed in small pieces, while the snakes usually shed in one piece that peels off inside out. Often, a shed snake skin still shows enough of the animal's patterns for a careful observer to identify the species that left it.

SHOWING OFF OR BLENDING IN?

The beautiful stripes, bands, and blotches on many snakes and lizards may be helping the animal to blend into the background or to show off to predators or to mates. Most of the time, the patterns camouflage the snake or lizard by breaking up its outline and making it difficult for predators to see where the animal's body begins and ends. A striped snake, for example, may look quite noticeable on the pavement but almost disappear when placed on the many-colored forest floor where it lives. Some species, however, benefit from advertising themselves. The bright colors of numerous snakes warn potential predators to stay away, and the brilliant hues in some male lizards attract females during the mating season.

BEHAVIOR AND REPRODUCTION

Because they are ectothermic (ek-toe-THERM-ik), which means that their body temperature changes based on the outside temperature, many squamates sunbathe, or bask, to warm up. Others, however, stay out of sight during the day. Some of the fossorial species rarely come out of the ground at all. These species will sometimes increase their body temperatures by moving to a warmer underground spot. For hunting, many of the squamates actively walk or slither about looking for prey. Others, however, hunt by ambush, which means that they sit still,

THE SHELL GAME

When it comes to living on dry land, the snakes, lizards, and worm lizards, known as squamates, have a big advantage over the frogs and salamanders. Most squamates lay eggs, just like the frogs and salamanders do, but the squamate eggs have shells. Even though the shells may be quite thin and often even flimsy, they help protect the eggs from drying out before they hatch. Without the shell, squamates would have to follow the pattern of the frogs and salamanders and lay their eggs in the water or some other wet spot. With the shell, however, the snakes, lizards, and worm lizards can make their homes well away from the water. This has allowed squamates to exist in nearly every habitat around the world.

wait for a prey animal to come along, then spring out to grab and eat it. Some snakes, including the pit vipers and the boas, have a special method of hunting. They can sense heat through small holes, called pit organs, on the face. Using these pit organs, they are able actually to see the heat given off by an animal in 3-D. These pit organs come in especially handy when hunting for food at night or in places where the snake has a limited view.

Compared to mammals and birds, squamates must have meals much less frequently. Because they are ectothermic and do not have to use their energy to keep up a constant body temperature, as the mammals and birds do, they can get by on much less food. Some of the large snakes can survive many months —even a full year—on one big meal.

Depending on the species, a squamate female may lay eggs or give birth to live young. Many species lay their eggs in nests, which are little more than holes dug in moist ground. A few, like the wormlizards, lay their eggs inside ant or termite nests. Most squamate mothers provide no care for their young and leave almost immediately after they lay their eggs or give birth. Some lizards and snakes are exceptions. Many female skinks, for example, stay with the eggs until they hatch.

While most species reproduce only after the male and female mate, some species are parthenogenic (parth-enn-oh-GEN-ik), which means that a female can produce young by herself. In many of these species, such as the lizard known as the desert grassland whiptail, only females exist. The female's young are all identical copies of herself. Besides this species in the whiptail family of lizards, seven other families of lizards and snakes have some all-female species.

SQUAMATES AND PEOPLE

For the most part, squamates either freeze or flee when humans approach. If a person comes too close, however, many will bite. Fortunately, most species are not venomous, and the bite only serves to surprise the person rather than hurt him or her. Some snakes, and two species of lizards, are venomous. The lizards are the Gila monster and the Mexican beaded lizard. Usually, quick medical attention can treat squamate bites.

CONSERVATION STATUS

The World Conservation Union (IUCN) lists 265 species as being at risk or as already extinct, which means they are no longer in existence. Of these, 14 are Extinct, 36 are Critically Endangered, and 31 are Endangered. Critically Endangered means the species faces an extremely high risk of extinction in the wild. Endangered means the species faces a very high risk of extinction in the wild. Many of these species have been hurt by habitat loss or by the introduction of new species, especially predators, to their habitat.

FOR MORE INFORMATION

Books:

Badger. D. *Lizards: A Natural History of Some Uncommon Creatures — Extraordinary Chameleons, Iguanas, Geckos, and More* Stillwater, MN: Voyageur Press, 2002.

Cleaver, Andrew. *Snakes and Reptiles: A Portrait of the Animal World.* Wigston, Leicester: Magna Books, 1994.

Greene, Harry W. *Snakes: The Evolution of Mystery in Nature.* Berkeley: University of California Press, 1997.

Lamar, William. *The World's Most Spectacular Reptiles and Amphibians.* Tampa, FL: World Publications, 1997.

Mattison, Chris. *Lizards of the World.* New York: Facts on File, 1989.

Mattison, Chris. *The Encyclopedia of Snakes.* New York: DK Publishing, 1997.

McCarthy, Colin. *Eyewitness: Reptile.* New York: DK Publishing, 2000.

Montgomery, Sy. *The Snake Scientist (Scientists in the Field).* Boston: Houghton Mifflin, 2001.

O'Shea, Mark, and Tim Halliday. *Smithsonian Handbooks: Reptiles and Amphibians (Smithsonian Handbooks).* New York: DK Publishing, 2002.

Pianka, E. R. *Ecology and Natural History of Desert Lizards: Analyses of the Ecological Niche and Community Structure.* Princeton, NJ: Princeton University Press, 1986.

Pianka, E. R., and L. J. Vitt. *Lizards: Windows to the Evolution of Diversity.* Berkeley: University of California Press, 2003.

Zug, George R., Laurie J. Vitt, and Janalee P. Caldwell. *Herpetology: An Introductory Biology of Amphibians and Reptiles.* 2nd edition. San Diego: Academic Press, 2001.

Web sites:

"About Snakes." Ohio Public Library Information Network. http://www.oplin.lib.oh.us/snake/about/snakes.html (accessed on December 13, 2004).

"Herpetology Program." Savannah River Ecology Laboratory. http://www.uga.edu/srelherp/ (accessed on December 13, 2004).

Myers, P. 2001. "Reptilia." *Animal Diversity Web.* http://animaldiversity.ummz.umich.edu/site/accounts/information/Reptilia.html (accessed on December 13, 2004).

"Reptiles." San Diego Natural History Museum. http://www.sdnhm.org/exhibits/reptiles/reptiles.html (accessed on December 13, 2004).

ANGLEHEADS, CALOTES,
DRAGON LIZARDS,
AND RELATIVES

Agamidae

Class: Reptilia

Order: Squamata

Family: Agamidae

Number of species: About 420
species

family
CHAPTER

phylum

class

subclass

order

monotypic order

suborder

▲ **family**

PHYSICAL DESCRIPTION

Agamids can be rather plain, or they can look quite strange and unusual. Their bodies may have crests, or ridges of large spines, on the back and tail. They may have neck frills and folds and body decorations, such as lumps and spines on the head. Some agamids have dewlaps, or throat fans.

Agamids come in many colors. Some are gray, brown, or black, but they may also have more showy colors. The Thai water dragon is bright green with golden eyes. The rainbow lizard is yellow or orange on top and blue on the bottom. Some species, or types, can change color rapidly, depending on their mood. Their lengths range from 10 inches (25.4 centimeters) to 36 inches (91.4 centimeters). In many species, males look different from females. They often have brighter colors, especially during the mating season, and bigger body parts, such as heads. All agamids have four well-developed limbs, or legs. There are usually five toes on each foot.

The head of an agamid is large and triangular, with a visible neck area. They all have movable eyelids and a circular pupil. In most agamids the ear opening is on the side of the head. Body scales are rough or spiny in most species. Some agaminds have a small or large crest, like a fin of scales, along their backs. Unlike some other lizards, agamids never lose their long tails when chased by a predator (PREH-duh-ter), or an animal that hunts the agamid for food.

GEOGRAPHIC RANGE

Agamids are found in Europe and Africa and throughout Southeast Asia, including Indonesia and the Philippines. They also inhabit New Guinea, the Solomon Islands, and Australia.

HABITAT

Agamids prefer to live in sandy and rocky deserts. They also may be found in dry forest habitats and dry scrub areas, which are flat areas with small bushes. Flying lizards are found in rainforests, areas with a great deal of rain and warm temperatures throughout the year. The Asian water dragon lives part of the time in trees near streams.

DIET

An agamid does not chase insects for food. Instead, it sits and waits in hiding until an insect comes by. Then out darts its sticky tongue to capture the insect and eat it. A few agamids, such as the Dabb spiny-tailed lizard, prefer plants for food.

BEHAVIOR AND REPRODUCTION

Agamids are diurnal (die-UR-nuhl), or active during the day. They spend a lot of time basking, or resting, in the sun. Some species prefer to sun themselves on flat rocky areas, while others like to climb onto tree trunks or shrubs to sunbathe. If the desert species get too hot, they go into cooler underground burrows, or holes, to rest.

Agamids have different ways of protecting themselves against predators. The bearded dragon lizard, for example, has spiny body scales. Some agamids run underground or into a rock crevice (KREH-vuhs), or crack. The Dabb spiny-tailed lizard runs into its burrow and lets the spiny part of its long, thick tail hang out. If the predator keeps pestering it, the lizard swishes its tail from side to side, which discourages most predators.

Agamid males typically are very territorial, meaning that they are protective of their living areas. A male agamid mates with females inside his territory, where several females may live.

When challenging other males for a mate, an agamid may bob its head, push up on rocks to make it look bigger, open and close its mouth, and enlarge its dewlap, the expandable flap under the chin. Some males become brightly colored during courtship. The Indian bloodsucker agamid expands the dewlap during courtship, and its head and throat turn bright red. That color gives the "bloodsucker" its name.

Most agamid females lay soft-shelled eggs after mating. The smaller agamid species lay a small number of eggs. The larger species may lay up to two dozen eggs. There may be one egg clutch, or group, per season or several throughout the year. Eggs are usually buried in damp soil or in leaf litter. There are some agamid species, such as the toad-headed lizards, that give birth to live young.

AGAMIDS AND PEOPLE

Agamids do not normally interact with people. They eat many insects, and so they are considered useful animals. A few species are captured for the legal and illegal pet trade, and some larger species are exhibited in zoos. A few larger species are caught for food.

CONSERVATION STATUS

Most agamids are not threatened. The World Conservation Union (IUCN) labels two species as Endangered, meaning that they face a very high risk of extinction in the wild. One species is listed as Near Threatened, meaning that it might soon face serious threats. Habitat loss, or loss of their preferred living area, is a major problem for agamids. The introduction of new predators, such as cats and rats, to their living areas has also harmed them.

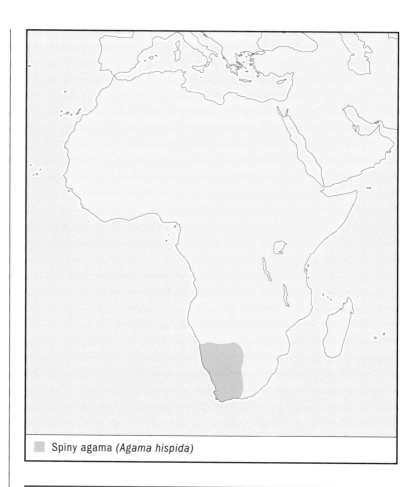

Spiny agama (*Agama hispida*)

SPINY AGAMA
Agama hispida

Physical characteristics: Spiny agamas are medium-size lizards, about 12 inches (30.5 centimeters) long. They are usually gray-brown or bright green, but these colors can change. During the mating season, males have a blue head with a red throat and yellow shoulders. Females are plainer, with orange, brown, and cream-colored blotches. Spiny agamas have spines along their backs and two fanglike teeth in the front of their mouths. These teeth are strong enough to pierce tough insect shells and can give a painful bite.

Geographic range: The spiny agama lives in southern Africa.

Habitat: Spiny agamas live in and between sand dunes, or hills of sand piled up by the wind, in coastal areas and in dry semidesert areas, where some water is available.

Diet: Spiny agamas eat ants, beetles, and termites.

Behavior and reproduction: Spiny agamas live alone. They usually stay close to the ground, digging short tunnels at the base of bushes. They also climb small upright items, such as fence posts. Spiny agamas are sit-and-wait predators, meaning that they do not chase after their insect food. They wait until the insect wanders by and then catch and eat it.

Spiny agamas live in and between sand dunes. (Clem Haager/Bruce Coleman Inc. Reproduced by permission.)

During the mating season, spiny agama males become quite colorful. Males fight to defend their living and mating territories. They will mate with several females within this area. Each female will lay about forty-five groups of eggs, each containing about thirteen eggs.

Spiny agamas and people: Spiny agamas do not interact with people. There is a popular belief that these lizards climb trees to look skyward to see if it will rain.

Conservation status: The spiny agama is not threatened. ■

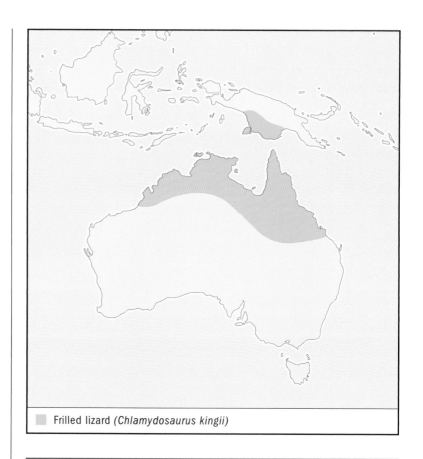

Frilled lizard (*Chlamydosaurus kingii*)

FRILLED LIZARD
Chlamydosaurus kingii

Physical characteristics: The frilled lizard is large, with gray-brown coloring. Its length ranges from 2 to 3 feet (61 to 91.4 centimeters). Adult males weigh about 30 ounces (850 grams) and females about 14 ounces (397 grams). A frilled lizard has long legs and a medium-long tail. It has a large neck frill, or neck folds, made of thin skin. Most of the time, the frill is kept folded like a cape over the lizard's shoulders and back. The tongue and mouth lining are pink or yellow.

Geographic range: Frilled lizards are found in northern Australia and southern New Guinea.

Habitat: Frilled lizards inhabit grassy woodlands and dry forests. These tree-living lizards are seldom found very far away from trees.

Diet: Frilled lizards eat cicadas (suh-KAY-duhs), ants, spiders, and small lizards.

Behavior and reproduction: The frilled lizard spends most of its time on tree trunks and low branches. It is active during the day and comes down to the ground after it rains and to search for food. When it is threatened or alarmed, the frilled lizard quickly enlarges the big, reddish-orange, fanlike frill around its neck. This frill can enlarge to a size of 8 to 12 inches across (20.3 to 30.5 centimeters). The frill has zigzag edges and red, blue, and brown spots. At rest, the folded frill helps keep the lizard cool. It also acts as camouflage (KA-mah-flahzh), a sort of disguise, allowing the lizard to look like a branch or bark.

If a predator threatens, at first the frilled lizard may hide, become absolutely still, or run to the nearest tree. If cornered, the frilled lizard faces the predator. It enlarges its frill and opens it brightly colored mouth. Sometimes it hisses, stands up on its hind legs, or leaps at the predator. If these actions do not work, frilled lizards can run on their hind legs for short distances.

Frilled lizards mate during the wet season. Males are territorial, protecting their living area. They may use their frills to attract mates. Females lay a clutch or group of eight to fourteen eggs twice a year, in spring and summer. Nests are made in flat, sandy soil, surrounded by thin grass and leaf litter. They are not covered.

Frilled lizards and people: Frilled lizards are the reptile emblem of Australia. They are shown on the Australian two-cent coin. There are books for children about frilled lizards, and a frilled lizard was featured on one automobile commercial on television. Fire-prevention road signs in Australia say, "We like our lizards frilled, not grilled." The frilled lizard is protected by law in Australia.

Conservation status: The frilled lizard is not threatened, but problems are expected. Toxic, or poisonous, cane toads have been introduced to the areas in which they live. Thought to be helpful, these toads instead have become pests, eating lizards and other small animals. In some areas, land clearing and the introduction of cats have caused frilled lizard numbers to decline. ■

Flying lizard (*Draco volans*)

FLYING LIZARD
Draco volans

Physical characteristics: The flying lizard is a slender, long-legged, small lizard. It measures 8 inches (20.3 centimeters) from head to tail tip. It has winglike body parts formed from thin skin stretched over extra-long ribs. When the lizard leaps from a tree, these body parts are stretched out at right angles to the body, forming a pair of gliding wings. At rest, these skin "sails" are folded along the body, keeping the lizard's appearance slim. The lizard's body color is gray or brown, but the wings are brightly colored. Male and female wing colors differ.

Geographic range: The flying lizard lives in Indonesia, Thailand, Malaysia, and the Philippines.

These long-tailed, lightly built lizards glide gracefully, sometimes as far as 55 yards (50.3 meters). (©Stephen Dalton/Photo Researchers, Inc. Reproduced by permission.)

Biomes: Coniferous forest, deciduous forest, rainforest

Habitat: Flying lizards live in open forests and rainforests.

Diet: Flying lizards eat ants and other insects.

Behavior and reproduction: These small lizards live in trees. On land they are clumsy and easy victims for predators. When scared, they run up a tree. When threatened, they leap off the tree. With their "wings" stretched out, these long-tailed, lightly built agamid lizards glide gracefully. The wings act like parachutes. When gliding, these delicate, slender lizards use their tails to steer and sometimes can travel as far as 55 yards (50.3 meters). They gently land on another tree, head up. When they land, they run up the tree, getting ready for their next flight.

During mating season, male flying lizards defend their territories. They court females by displaying their bright yellow throat flap. Females lay one to four eggs.

Flying lizards and people: Flying lizards do not interact with people.

Conservation status: Flying lizards are not threatened. ■

FOR MORE INFORMATION

Books:

Barrett, Norman S. *Dragons and Lizards*. Danbury, CT: Franklin Watts, 1991.

Capula, Massimo. *Guide to Reptiles and Amphibians of the World*. New York: Simon & Schuster, 1989.

Mattison, Chris. *Lizards of the World*. New York: Facts on File, 1989.

Miller, Jake. *The Bearded Dragon* New York: PowerKids Press, 2003.

Robinson, Fay, and Jean Day Zallinger. *Amazing Lizards* New York: Scholastic, 1999.

Uchiyama, Ryu. *Reptiles and Amphibians*. San Francisco: Chronicle Books, 1999.

Zoffer, David. *Agamid Lizards: Keeping and Breeding Them in Captivity*. Neptune City, NJ: T. F. H. Publications, 1996.

Periodicals:

"Australian Lizards: True Blue, Mate." *National Geographic* (January 1998): Earth Almanac.

"Frilled Lizards." *Ranger Rick* (September 1995): 44–45.

"Living Jewels." *National Geographic WORLD Magazine* (June 1979): 30–31.

"Spiny Lizards." *Ranger Rick* (May 1997): 44.

"Thorny Devil." *Ranger Rick* (February 1996): 24–25.

"Tricks to Escape Predators." *Ranger Rick* (September 1995): 40–48.

Web sites:

"Agamids of the Cederberg." Cape Nature Conservation. http://www.capenature.org.za/cederbergproject/html/agamids.html (accessed on August 12, 2004).

"*Chlamydosaurus kingii* (Frillneck Lizard)." Animal Diversity Web. http://animaldiversity.ummz.umich.edu/site/accounts/information/Chlamydosaurus_kingii.html (accessed on August 12, 2004).

"Common Flying Dragon." www.wildherps.com. http:/www.wildherps.com/species/D.volans.html (accessed on August 14, 2004).

"Rainbow Lizard." America Zoo. http://www.americazoo.com/goto/index/reptiles/102.htm (accessed on August 12, 2004).

CHAPTER

PHYSICAL CHARACTERISTICS

Chameleons (kuh-MEEL-yuns) are best known for their ability to change colors easily. Once, color change was thought to serve as camouflage (KA-mah-flahzh), or a sort of disguise, allowing the chameleon to match or blend in to its surroundings. Scientists now believe that colors change in response to differences in temperature, light, and the chameleon's mood. Colors may change in both males and females or only in males, depending on the species, or type, of chameleon. Some species can change color only into shades of brown. Others have a wider color range, turning from pink to blue or green to red. Varieties of color may be displayed on different body parts, such as the throat, head, or legs. When the chameleon is excited, stripes or patterns may appear. Sleeping or ill chameleons tend to be pale.

Chameleons range in length from 1 inch (2.5 centimeters) to 26.8 inches (68 centimeters). Males may be larger or smaller than females. A chameleon's body is flexible (FLEK-suh-buhl), meaning that it can bend easily. It can be rather flat from side to side and shaped somewhat like a leaf. This allows it to blend better with leafy surroundings. A chameleon can also make its body look longer, to seem more a part of a twig. If it is threatened by a predator (PREH-duh-ter), or an animal that hunts it for food, the chameleon can inflate, or puff up, its lungs and make its rib cage expand, to appear larger.

Chameleons have long, slim legs, with four feet. There are five toes on each foot. The toes are fused, or joined, in bundles of two and three toes to form a pincer (PIN-suhr), a kind of claw for grabbing and holding. Sharp claws on each toe aid in climbing. The tail is formed in a way to help the chameleon hold on to twigs and branches.

These animals have large eyes that protrude, or stick out. Each eye can move independently of the other, so the chameleon can look in two directions at once. For this reason, chameleons can look forward, sidewise, or backward without moving their heads, and they can follow moving objects without changing their body position. If they see an insect, they will focus both eyes on it to see how far away it is.

A chameleon's tongue can extend the length of its entire body, or even longer. The sticky tongue can flick out to full length within one-sixteenth of a second, fast enough to catch a fly in midair. The tongue tip is like a wet suction cup that attaches to its prey, or an animal that it hunts for food. A chameleon can capture and pull in prey weighing up to about half of its own body weight. Then the chameleon relaxes its tongue, with prey attached, and draws it slowly back into its mouth. Chameleons also use their long tongues to lap up water from leaves and other surfaces.

A chameleon's head can be covered with many bumps and bulges and other body structures that stick out. Scales on its back can resemble small or large crests, or ridges. Some crests are barely noticeable, but others are quite large. Body scales also can be found on the throat and belly. On the sides of the head there may be movable skin flaps. Bumps and growths of differing sizes may be seen on the snout, or nose area. Depending on the species, chameleons also may have one to six bony "horns," of varying sizes and shapes, on their heads. Although chameleons do not have vocal cords, or body parts used to produce sound, some species can make a hissing or squeaking noise by forcing air from their lungs. Others can vibrate (VIE-brayt), moving back and forth rapidly to create sound.

SUCCESSFUL HAWAIIAN CHAMELEONS

There are no native American chameleons, although there are many pet chameleons. Normally, the survival rate of imported chameleons is very low; they do not often live long in captivity. In 1972, however, thirty-six Jackson's chameleons were sent from Kenya, in Africa, to a pet store owner in Hawaii. Because the chameleons were so stressed from travel, the store owner released them. Some of these chameleons survived and multiplied on the island of Oahu. Jackson's chameleons are quite unusual in that they are the only chameleons in the United States that live and breed in the wild. There are now reports of wild populations in California, Texas, and parts of Florida.

GEOGRAPHIC RANGE

Chameleons are found mainly in Madagascar and Africa, and a few species live in southern Europe, Asia, the Seychelles and the Comoros. No chameleons are native to the Americas, which means that all of them were brought into the Americas. One species is now found there in the wild.

HABITAT

Chameleons live in a variety of habitats, such as dry deserts; tropical, rainy woodlands of evergreens; forests with trees that lose their leaves in winter; thorn forests; grasslands; scrublands, or land with low bushes and trees; and cloud forests, or wet, tropical, mountain forests. They can be found from sea level up to mountainous areas as high as 15,000 feet (4,572 meters).

DIET

Chameleons eat a variety of flying and crawling insects, including butterflies; insect larvae (LAR-vee), or young; and snails. The larger chameleons eat birds, smaller chameleons, lizards, and sometimes snakes. Chameleons also eat plant matter, including leaves, flowers, and fruits. Some chameleons stay within small areas for their food supply, but others travel long distances seeking food. All chameleons need drinking water, which they get from dew or rain.

BEHAVIOR AND REPRODUCTION

Chameleons are cold-blooded animals, meaning that their body temperature varies with the weather. After resting during the night, they warm up in the daytime by basking, or resting, in the sun. If they get too warm, they lower their body temperature by resting in the shade. All their activities take place during daylight hours.

Most chameleons prefer to live alone. Males are very territorial, or protective of their living areas. Males and females tolerate each other only briefly, during the mating season. When males with bony head horns fight over territory, one may lower its head and attempt to ram the other with its horns. Usually no harm is done, unless an eye or lung is damaged.

In the mating season, males try to attract females by bobbing their heads, inflating their throats, puffing up their bodies, and displaying their brightest colors. A female may accept or reject the courting male. If she rejects him, she might run away or she might face the male and hiss at him with an open mouth. She might even attack and bite him. These bites can kill.

Most chameleon species lay eggs. Eggs are placed in tunnels or pits in the ground or under rocks or leaves. This keeps them cool and moist. After laying their eggs, females cover the area with dirt to hide it from predators. Depending on the species, young chameleons hatch one to eighteen months later. They are independent at birth and must find their own food and shelter. A few chameleon species give birth to live young, rather than lay eggs. These species often live in areas where the weather is very cold in winter and where eggs placed directly on the ground might not hatch because of the cold.

CHAMELEONS AND PEOPLE

Chameleons do not normally interact with people. Wild chameleons are sometimes caught and sold to tourists. Chameleons are also taken from their habitats in the illegal pet trade, and many die from stress or improper care. Habitat destruction, forest fires, and air and water pollution, or poison, waste, or other material that makes the environment dirty and harmful to health, are major problems.

CONSERVATION STATUS

The World Conservation Union (IUCN) lists four chameleon species as Vulnerable, meaning that they face a high risk of extinction in the wild. One is Endangered, meaning that it faces a very high risk of extinction in the near future, and one is Critically Endangered, meaning that it faces an extremely high risk of extinction.

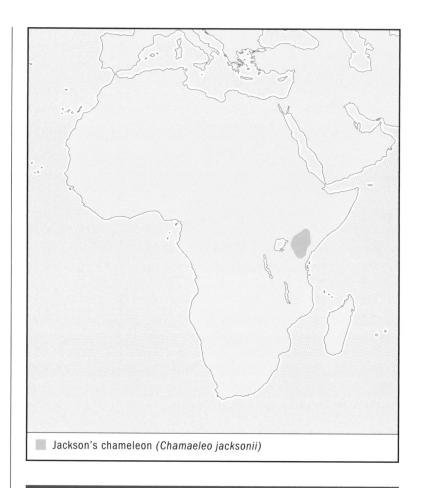

■ Jackson's chameleon (*Chamaeleo jacksonii*)

JACKSON'S CHAMELEON
Chamaeleo jacksonii

Physical characteristics: The body color of Jackson's chameleon can be shades of green or brown, with dark red, yellow, or blue on the head, sides, or tail. Males have three large, pointed, hornlike protrusions on their heads, which are used in fights with other males. Females may or may not have these "horns." Adults grow to 14 inches (35.6 centimeters) in length.

Geographic range: Jackson's chameleon is found mainly in the lower mountain ranges of eastern Africa. There is a wild population in Hawaii.

Habitat: Jackson's chameleon lives in areas with warm days and cool nights, including moist forests, crop plantations, and dense bushes.

Diet: Jackson's chameleons feed on a wide variety of insects.

Behavior and reproduction: Jackson's chameleons live in trees. They are usually calm creatures, but during courtship the male is very territorial and will fight to defend its living area or the female with whom it wants to mate. These fights are shoving contests using the horns. Males court females with their most brilliant colors and with head bobbing. Females give birth to three to fifty live young. Young are ready to reproduce at about six to ten months of age. In the wild these chameleons may live two to four years.

Jackson's chameleons and people: Jackson's chameleons do not interact with people in the wild. They are captured for the illegal and legal pet trade, and they typically do not survive well in captivity. Their living areas are suffering destruction.

Conservation status: Jackson's chameleons are not threatened, but they may become threatened unless their capture for the pet trade is closely controlled. ■

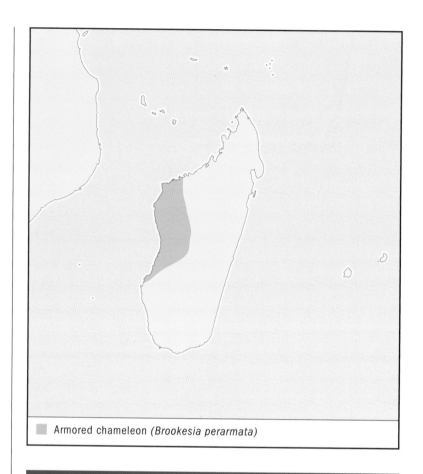

Armored chameleon (*Brookesia perarmata*)

ARMORED CHAMELEON
Brookesia perarmata

Physical characteristics: The armored chameleon is reddish brown, brown, and tan. It has a row of pointed scales projecting from its spine, decreasing in size from the neck to the tail tip. The rest of the body has many thorny scales, giving it an armored appearance. Adults are 6 inches (15.2 centimeters) long.

Geographic range: Armored chameleons are found only in the Tsingy de Bemaraha Nature Reserve in Madagascar.

Habitat: Armored chameleons inhabit bushes, shrubs, and leaf litter in or near dense, dry, deciduous (di-SID-joo-wus) forest, or forests with trees that lose their leaves in cold weather.

Diet: The armored chameleon feeds on insects and insect larvae.

Behavior and reproduction: The armored chameleon is calm and secretive. It spends most of its life on the ground and does not move about much. Little is known about its breeding habits.

Armored chameleons and people: Armored chameleons are rarely seen; they hide and do not interact with people in the wild. They are collected for the illegal pet trade, but few survive once they are captured.

Conservation status: As a result of habitat destruction and collection for the pet trade, the IUCN has listed the armored chameleon as Vulnerable, meaning that it faces a high risk of extinction in the wild. ■

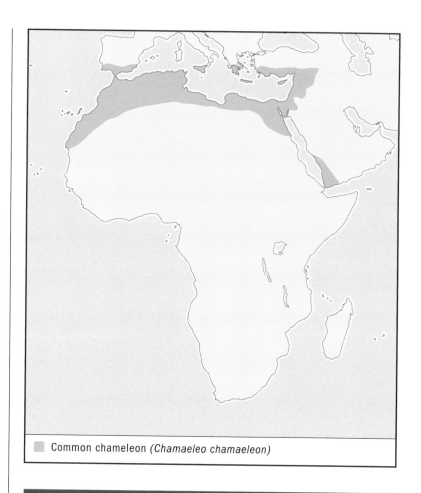

Common chameleon (*Chamaeleo chamaeleon*)

COMMON CHAMELEON
Chamaeleo chamaeleon

Physical characteristics: The colors of the common chameleon vary widely; they include green, yellow, gray, and brown, with many stripes and spots.

Geographic range: Common chameleons inhabit Europe, the Middle East, and northern Africa.

Habitat: Common chameleons are found in many different areas, among them, semidesert scrubland, coastal scrubland, crop plantations, and forested areas as high as 8,500 feet (2,591 meters).

The colors of the common chameleon vary widely; they include green, yellow, gray, and brown, with many stripes and spots. (J.C. Carton/Carto/Bruce Coleman, Inc. Reproduced by permission.)

Diet: Common chameleons eat insects, young birds, and small reptiles.

Behavior and reproduction: Common chameleons living in areas with very cold winters will lie dormant, slowing down or entirely stopping most of their activities until the weather warms up. At the onset of warm weather, mating begins. Females carry their young for two months and then produce about sixty eggs. The young hatch in six to eleven months.

Common chameleons and people: Common chameleons do not interact with people in the wild. They are sometimes killed crossing roadways. They are also captured for the illegal pet trade, but few survive. Habitat destruction is another threat.

Conservation status: The IUCN lists the common chameleon as Vulnerable. Only in Greece are they strictly protected. ■

FOR MORE INFORMATION

Books:

Bartlett, Richard D., and Patricia Bartlett. *Jackson's and Veiled Chameleons.* Hauppauge, NY: Barron's Educational Series, 2001.

Darling, Kathy, and Tara Darling. *Chameleons: On Location.* New York: HarperCollins, 1997.

Mara, W. P. *Chameleons: Exotic Lizards.* Mankato, MN: Capstone Press, 1996.

Miller, Jake. *The Chameleon: Lizard Library.* New York: PowerKids Press, 2003.

Schmidt, W., K. Tamm, and E. Wallikewitz. *Chameleons: Basic Domestic Reptile and Amphibian Library.* Broomall, PA: Chelsea House Publishers, 1998.

Stefoff, Rebecca. *Chameleon.* New York: Benchmark Books, 1996.

Uchiyama, Ryu. *Reptiles and Amphibians.* San Francisco: Chronicle Books, 1999.

Periodicals:

Cooper, Sharon Katz. "Chameleons and Other Quick- Change Artists." *National Geographic Explorer* (October 2002): 4–7.

"Chameleons' Emotional Signals." *National Geographic* (August 1993): Earth Almanac.

"Panther Chameleons." *Ranger Rick* (February 1998): 5–9.

Risley, T. "Chameleon Profile: *Brookesia* and *Rampholeon. Chameleon Information Network* 31 (Spring 1999): 21–23.

Risley, T. "The Fate of Wild-Caught Chameleons Exported for the Pet Trade." *Chameleon Information Network* 42 (Winter 2001): 15–18.

Web sites:

Fry, Michael. "Introduction." *Chameleon Information Network.* http://www.animalarkshelter.org/cin/ (accessed on July 29, 2004).

Heying, Heather. "Family Chamaeleonidae." Animal Diversity Web. http://animaldiversity.ummz.umich.edu/site/accounts/information/Chamaeleonidae.html (accessed on July 28, 2004).

Mayell, Hillary. "Evolutionary Oddities: Duck Sex Organs, Lizard Tongue." *National Geographic News.* http://news.nationalgeographic.com/news/2001/10/1023_corkscrewduck.html (accessed on July 29, 2004).

Raxworthy, Christopher J. "A Truly Bizarre Lizard." Madagascar—A World Apart. http://www.pbs.org/edens/madagascar/creature3.htm (accessed on July 29, 2004).

"Veiled Chameleon." Reptiles & Amphibians: Smithsonian National Zoological Park. http://national http://nationalzoo.si.edu/Animals/ReptilesAmphibians/Facts/FactSheets/Veiledchameleon.cfm (accessed on July 29, 2004).

ANOLES, IGUANAS,
AND RELATIVES
Iguanidae

Class: Reptilia
Order: Squamata
Family: Iguanidae
Number of species: About 900
species

phylum

class

subclass

order

monotypic order

suborder

▲ **family**

PHYSICAL CHARACTERISTICS

Iguanids (ee-GWA-nids) range in size from 4 to 72 inches (10 centimeters to 2 meters). They have many different body types. There are, for example, the squat, toadlike horned lizards small enough to fit in the palm of a hand; the slim, long-tailed anoles (uh-NOH-lees); and the large marine iguanas. A typical iguanid has a long tail and four legs, with five-clawed toes on each leg. Some have body colors or body patterns that match their surroundings. They may display bright colors during the mating season. Some iguanids have scales, throat fans, crests along the back, and fringes on the toes. Certain iguanids have the ability to lose the tail or part of the tail, to distract or fool a predator (PREH-duh-ter), an animal that hunts them for food. Their teeth are placed in grooves within the jaw, rather than in sockets, or holes.

GEOGRAPHIC RANGE

Iguanid lizards are found in North America, Central America, South America, Fiji, the Galápagos Islands, Madagascar, and the West Indies.

HABITAT

Iguanids live in a variety of habitats. They usually are terrestrial, living on land. A few are arboreal, living in trees. Many prefer arid, or dry, areas. These desert dwellers often seek territories, or home areas, with at least some vegetation, rocks, or other cover to provide escape routes from predators, or animals

THIS LIZARD WALKS ON WATER

Brown basilisk lizards are sometimes called "Jesus" lizards. When escaping a predator, they may appear to walk upright on water. These lizards have a fringe of scales on their hind toes. These fringes temporarily trap a bubble of air beneath the lizards' feet, which keeps them from sinking if they run quickly enough across ponds or streams.

that hunt them for food. Other iguanids seek wooded areas, including rainforests. An unusual habitat is that of the marine iguana, which lives by the ocean.

DIET

Iguanids feed on insects, spiders, and smaller lizards. A few species, such as the desert iguana and the chuckwalla, eat leaves, fruits, and flowers. The marine lizard eats (AL-jee), plantlike organisms that live mainly in water.

BEHAVIOR AND REPRODUCTION

Iguanids are cold-blooded, which means that their body temperature varies with the outside weather. At night, when it is cool, many species sleep in burrows. In the morning, iguanids emerge from their burrows and rest in the sun to warm up. They are often seen stretched out on a rock. It is necessary for them to raise their body temperature to prepare for the day's activities of feeding, perhaps breeding, and escaping ever-present predators. All iguanids are diurnal (die-UR-nuhl), meaning that they are active during the daytime. If the temperature grows too warm, these lizards find a shady spot so that they do not become overheated.

Iguanids have many predators, among them, snakes, birds, cats, rats, and wild dogs. When a predator approaches, some species remain still and blend into the surroundings. Others are quick runners and dash off almost immediately. They hide under rocks or between thick leaves and bury themselves in sand. A few species use special tactics to avoid their predators. The common chuckwalla fixes itself into a crack between rocks and then puffs up, making itself nearly impossible to remove. Horned lizards puff up too, which makes their spines stand up even higher. Biting predators will avoid the sharp spines. The zebra-tailed lizard keeps changing direction when it runs, as a way to confuse its pursuer. Other lizards squirm under the sand, so they cannot be seen.

Iguanids have lively mating behavior. Body movements include head bobbing, pushups, and open-mouth displays. Some species inflate their chests and throats and extend their dewlaps, or throat flaps, showing bright colors. They might also curl their tails or even show bright body colors.

After courtship, mating takes place. Most iguanids are oviparous (oh-VIH-puh-rus), meaning that they lay eggs. From one to sixty eggs may be laid at one time, and egg laying may take place once or as many as four times a year. The young hatch from the eggs in one to two months. A few iguanids, such as the blue spiny lizard and the short-horned lizard, give birth to live young. Usually, the parents do not care for them. The young must find their own shelter and food immediately after birth. A few species, such as the rhinoceros iguana, will protect their egg groups for a short while. They may guard the nests with threatening body displays or even physical attacks.

IGUANIDS AND PEOPLE

Iguanids do not interact with people in the wild. Habitat destruction from the clearing of forests and commercial land development can wipe out the places where the lizards hide and breed. Too much collecting for the legal and illegal pet trade causes problems for some species. Certain mammals (such as dogs and cats) that enter their territory along with humans can kill the lizards. In some areas people use larger lizards as food.

CONSERVATION STATUS

The World Conservation Union (IUCN) lists two types of iguanids as Extinct, meaning that none remains alive. Six species are Critically Endangered, which means that they face an extremely high risk of extinction in the wild. Four species are Endangered, which means that they are less endangered but still face a very high risk of extinction. These ten species might soon disappear from Earth. Twelve iguanids are Vulnerable, that is, they face threats that put them at high risk of extinction and they could vanish unless they are protected. One iguanid is Near Threatened, meaning that there is a risk that they will be threatened with extinction. There is not enough information to judge the status of seventeen other species. Attempts are being made to gather the eggs of endangered and threatened iguanids from the wild and raise the young in protected sites, such as zoos.

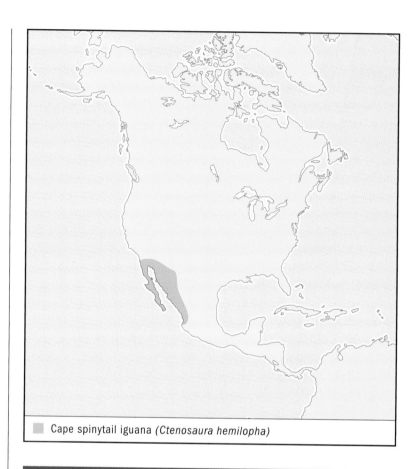

Cape spinytail iguana (*Ctenosaura hemilopha*)

CAPE SPINYTAIL IGUANA
Ctenosaura hemilopha

Physical characteristics: Cape spinytail iguanas are gray-brown, large, stocky, wrinkled lizards. They have a ridged, long tail and a crest of scales along the top of the back. Males have a larger crest than do females. An adult can reach 3 feet (1 meters) in length from the head to the tip of the tail.

Geographic range: Cape spinytail iguanas are found in northwestern Mexico, including the state of Sonora, and the islands of the Gulf of California.

Habitat: Cape spinytail iguanas live in areas with many rocky crevices, or cracks; these areas often also have trees.

Diet: Cape spinytail iguanas eat flowers, fruits, and leaves. They feed only during the day.

Behavior and reproduction: Cape spinytail iguanas are territorial, protecting their dwelling areas. If threatened, they usually run into rocky crevices. If such a hiding place is not available, they can fight with their jaws and legs. These lizards usually live in groups. Each group has a dominant male, one who acts as leader. There are also less-strong males and several females. After mating, females lay twenty-four or more eggs in a group. The eggs hatch in about three months.

Cape spinytail iguanas and people: These iguanas are sold in the pet trade.

Conservation status: Cape spinytail iguanas are not threatened. ■

Common chuckwalla (*Sauromalus obesus*)

COMMON CHUCKWALLA
Sauromalus obesus

Physical characteristics: Chuckwallas are large, big-bellied lizards that can weigh up to 2 pounds (1 kilograms) and can reach a length of 16 inches (40.6 centimeters). They have a thick tail that is as long as the head and body together. The tail narrows to a blunt point at the end. Chuckwalla skin feels like sandpaper. There are folds of loose skin on the sides of the neck and body. Adult males have a black head, shoulders, and legs. The body color is red or gray, with yellow toward tail. Females and young have gray and yellow bands.

Geographic range: Chuckwallas are found in the United States.

Habitat: Chuckwallas live in rocky deserts with plenty of hiding places.

Diet: Chuckwallas feed on leaves, flowers, and fruits.

Behavior and reproduction: The chuckwalla is cold-blooded; their body temperature changes with the environment. Chuckwallas spend cool desert nights in burrows, which tend to remain warm. In the morning, when the sun comes up, they come out of their burrows. To warm up, chuckwallas bask, or stretch out, in the sun. They place their bodies sidewise to the sun, to warm them up more quickly. They bask until they reach a temperature of 100°F (38°C). Then they begin searching for food. If the surrounding temperature becomes too hot, chuckwallas hide under rocks or bushes until the weather cools down.

Chuckwallas are large, big-bellied lizards that can weigh up to 2 pounds (1 kilograms). (Wai Ping Wu/Bruce Coleman Inc. Reproduced by permission.)

When disturbed, the chuckwalla hides in a rock crevice. It begins gulping air. The loose skin folds around its neck and the sides of its body puff up, until the chuckwalla becomes larger. For the moment, it is jammed in the rock crevice, and this makes it almost impossible for a predator to pull it out. If, however, a predator does manage to grab a chuckwalla by the tail, the tail separates from the body and wriggles. This distracts the predator, letting the chuckwalla escape. A new tail grows back.

Chuckwallas make a combination of movements to defend a territory or attract a mate: head bobbing, open-mouth displays, and body pushups. In the summer, females place five to ten eggs in rock crevices. The eggs hatch two months later, in early fall.

Chuckwallas and people: Chuckwallas are sold in the pet trade and sometimes are eaten as food.

Conservation status: Chuckwallas are not threatened with extinction. ■

Green anole (Anolis carolinensis)

GREEN ANOLE
Anolis carolinensis

Physical characteristics: Green anoles are slim lizards with narrow, pointed heads and long, thin tails that can be twice as long as the rest of the animal. Body sizes range in length from 5 to 8 inches (12.7–20.3 centimeters). The body color can vary from shades of brown to shades of green. Males are larger than females. Both males and females have dewlaps, or throat fans, but the male dewlap is much larger. Dewlaps can inflate, or enlarge. An inflated dewlap is reddish-pink. Green anoles are sometimes called "chameleons" (kuh-MEEL-yuns), owing to their ability to change color, but they are not true chameleons.

Geographic range: The green anole is the only anole that inhabits the United States. These anoles are also found in Cuba and on Caribbean islands.

Habitat: The green anole lives on the ground but suns itself in small trees and shrubs, on vines and tall grasses, and within palm fronds. It likes vertical surfaces, or ones that stand upright, such as fence posts and walls.

Diet: The green anole hunts and eats small insects and spiders and laps water from leaves.

Behavior and reproduction: Green anoles are active in the daytime. If they are grabbed or threatened, their tails can fall off. A new tail will grow, but the new tail usually does not match the previous one in color or size.

During the breeding, or mating, season, males court females by facing them. They bob their heads up and down, and expand, or make larger, the bright pink dewlap under the throat. Next, the male may approach the female with a stiff-legged walk. If the female accepts the male, she stays still and arches her neck. If she does not accept him, she runs away. After mating, female lays single eggs every two weeks, for a total of about ten eggs per breeding season. She places the eggs in warm, moist spots, such as leaf litter. Young appear in five to seven weeks.

Green anoles and people: Green anoles are popular pets.

Conservation status: Green anoles are common in the southeastern United States. ■

Green anoles are sometimes called "chameleons" owing to their ability to change color, but they are not true chameleons. (©David M. Schleser/Nature's Images/Photo Researchers, Inc.)

FOR MORE INFORMATION

Books:

Arnosky, Jim. *All about Lizards.* New York: Scholastic, 2004.

Bartlett, Richard D., and Patricia Pope Bartlett. *Lizard Care from A to Z.* Hauppauge, NY: Barron's Educational Series, 1997.

Bartlett, Richard D., and Patricia Bartlett. *Anoles: Facts & Advice on Care and Breeding.* Hauppauge, NY: Barron's Educational Series, 2001.

Behler, John L. *The Audubon Society Field Guide to North American Reptiles and Amphibians.* New York: Alfred A. Knopf, 1979.

Claybourne, Anna. *The Secret World of Lizards.* Chicago: Raintree Publishers, 2003.

Conant, R., J. T. Collins, I. H. Conant, T. R. Johnson, and S. L. Collins. *A Field Guide to Reptiles & Amphibians of Eastern & Central North America.* Boston: Houghton Mifflin, 1998.

Lamar, William. *The World's Most Spectacular Reptiles & Amphibians.* Tampa, FL: World Publications, 1997.

Uchiyama, Ryu. *Reptiles and Amphibians.* San Francisco: Chronicle Books, 1999.

Periodicals:

"Amazing Lizards!" *National Geographic* (March 1978): 8–11.

"Color These Animals before They Change." *National Geographic* (March 1980): 10–15.

Hazen-Hammond, S. "Horny Toads Enjoy a Special Place in Western Hearts." *Smithsonian* 25 (1994): 82–86.

Hughes, Catherine D. "Where Am I?" *National Geographic Kids* (July/August 2004): 32–35.

"Iguanas." *Ranger Rick* (August 1996): 8–9.

"Marine Iguanas." *Ranger Rick* (November 2003): 18–20.

"Shrinking Iguanas." *National Geographic* (September 2000).

Web sites:

"Anoles." Melissa Kaplan's Herp Care Collection. http://www.anapsid .org/anole.html (accessed on July 31, 2004).

"Glossary of Iguana Terms." Green Iguana Society. http://www .greenigsociety.org/glossary.htm (accessed on August 3, 2004).

"Green Anole." Texas Parks and Wildlife. http://www.tpwd.state.tx.us/ nature/wild/reptiles/anole/ (accessed on July 31, 2004).

"Green Anole Care Sheet." AOL Hometown. http://members.aol.com/ Mite37/TPFGA.html (accessed on July 31, 2004).

"Marine Iguanas." Galápagos Geology on the Web. http://www.geo.cornell .edu/geology/GalápagosWWW/MarineIguanas.html (accessed on August 3, 2004).

GECKOS AND PYGOPODS
Gekkonidae

Class: Reptilia

Order: Squamata

Family: Gekkonidae

Number of species: 1,109 species

PHYSICAL CHARACTERISTICS

Geckos range in size from 0.67 inch (17 millimeters) to 14 inches (35.6 centimeters) in length. The smallest gecko weighs about 0.07 ounce (1.98 grams). The largest gecko, which lives in rainforests, can weigh up to 1.5 pounds (680 grams). While most geckos are brown, gray, or black, a few are yellow, red, blue, orange, or green. They may be plain, or they may have stripes or spots. Colors on the head and neck may be different from the colors on the back. The nocturnal geckos, or those that are active at night, are plainer than the diurnal (die-UR-nuhl) geckos, or those active in the daytime, which tend to have brighter colors.

Geckos usually have flattened bodies and four short limbs, or legs. Each limb has five toes. Some species have claws on each foot. Other types of geckoes have widened toe pads. These toe pads are made to allow the gecko to stick to smooth surfaces. Geckos have large eyes that are open all the time. Except for a few species, the eyes do not have movable eyelids. Instead, the eyes are protected by clear, see-through scales, or thin coatings. Geckos clean these scales regularly with their long tongues. Most geckos are nocturnal. These geckos have vertical pupils (PYU-puhls), meaning that they are positioned straight up and down, in the center of their eyes. Diurnal geckos have round pupils in the center of their eyes. Pupils are parts of the eye that allow light to enter.

Gecko skin is soft and loose and typically covered with granular, or grainy, scales that do not overlap. A few species have smooth skin. Gecko tails come in varied shapes. Many geckos have tails shaped like carrots or turnips. Some have rounder tails that are used to store food.

Pygopods (PIE-go-pods) are also called "snake lizards," limbless lizards," and "flap-footed lizards." They range in length from less than 8 inches (20.3 centimeters) to 2 feet (61 centimeters). Their colors range from pale yellow to dark brown, with or without a pattern of spots or stripes.

Pygopods have a narrow face and an almost snakelike appearance. The snout, or nose area, is pointed. The eyes are always open, protected by transparent, or clear, scales. Most pygopods do not have an outside ear opening. They have no front limbs and only flaplike hind limbs. Their long tails break off easily.

GEOGRAPHIC RANGE

Pygopods are found in Australia and New Guinea. Geckos are found in the tropics and subtropics, the warmer areas of the world. These areas include India, Nepal, Burma, the Malaysian peninsula, China, the Philippines, Indonesia, New Zealand, Saudi Arabia, Central America, and South America. Geckos and skinks are often the only land reptiles on remote islands in the ocean. A few gecko species have been found in southern Europe, southern Siberia, and the southwestern United States.

HABITAT

Geckos live in a variety of habitats. Their preferred living areas include coniferous forests, with pine and other evergreen trees, and deciduous forests, where trees, such as maples, lose their leaves each year. They also live in rainforests, tropical forests that get at least 100 inches of rain per year; this type of forest has many very tall evergreen trees that form a thick umbrella of leaves and branches overhead. Geckos also live in deserts and in grassland, or meadows. Pygopods live in desert and in grassland.

DIET

Nearly all geckos eat insects and spiders. A few larger species eat small snakes, small lizards, and baby birds. In some habitats, geckos also eat plant pollen and ripe fruit. Smaller pygopods are insect eaters, and larger ones eat snakes and lizards.

BEHAVIOR AND REPRODUCTION

Most geckos are nocturnal. During the day they typically hide under tree bark or in tree hollows. In the early evening they come out to feed and to look for mates. The diurnal species are most active in the late morning and middle of the afternoon. In tropical areas, which are warm throughout the year, geckos stay active all the time. In other areas, geckos enter burrows or rock cracks and remain there most of the time during the cool season.

Geckos typically live by themselves; only a few types live in groups. Some species are seen around peoples' homes. Males defend their feeding and resting places by using warning sounds, usually many clicks and chirps. Defense methods include running away; squirting a sticky fluid at predators, or animals that hunt them to eat them; biting; and shedding their tails. A gecko's tail will continue to wriggle after it is shed, fooling the predator and allowing the gecko to escape. Some gecko species also can shed body skin if they are grabbed by other animals. This skin regrows, as do the tails.

Geckos are the most vocal lizards, meaning that they make the most sounds. Most geckos make several different sounds, including barking, croaking, squeaking, and chirping. The giant Asian Tokay gecko makes a loud noise that sounds to some people like "geh-oh." It is possibly from this sound that the gecko gets its name.

During mating season, the males of some species have violent fights over females.

After mating, most gecko females lay a nest of two hard-shelled or leathery eggs. Some tropical species lay eggs throughout the year, and others have just one clutch, or nest of eggs. Some lay several egg groups within a mating season. Eggs are placed under loose bark or under a rock, where it is slightly damper than it is in the open air. Hatching occurs in six to ten weeks. A few species give birth to living young instead of laying eggs.

Because pygopods are secretive, not much is known about them. They hide in rocky areas, in tall grass, and in burrows.

WALKING UP WALLS

Scientists have investigated how geckos can walk up shiny walls and across ceilings. They found that geckos have millions of tiny foot hairs, called "setae" (SEE-tee), on each toe pad. The tips of these setae are very sticky. Geckos can hang from a wet or dry ceiling attached by just one toe. How do they get their feet off the ceiling and move? Scientists think that they peel foot hairs off like tape.

Some are active during the day. The desert species move about at night. After mating, females lay two eggs per clutch.

GECKOS, PYGOPODS, AND PEOPLE

Pygopods seldom have anything to do with people. Some gecko species live near human homes. They are valuable in insect control, eating mosquitoes, flies, and cockroaches. In some areas of the world, deforestation, or the cutting down of trees, destroys their habitat. The killing of geckos by rats, cats, and other predators has led to declines in the numbers of geckos in some areas. In parts of Asia, geckos are used in medicines. Geckos, especially the brightly colored ones, are collected for the legal and illegal pet trade. A few species breed, or multiply, readily in captivity and do well.

CONSERVATION STATUS

The conservation status of most species is unknown. Because of illegal pet trade collection, the World Conservation Union (IUCN) lists one brightly colored group of geckos as Endangered and internationally protected.

Western banded gecko (*Coleonyx variegatus*)

WESTERN BANDED GECKO
Coleonyx variegatus

Physical characteristics: The western banded gecko, also known as the banded gecko, is 4.5–6 inches long (11–15 centimeters) from its head to the end of its tail. The skin on its back is made up of small, grainy scales. The skin is delicate, soft, and loose. The gecko's back and tail are cream colored, with wide black or brown stripes that run from side to side. The tail is long, and the head is somewhat large. The eyes have eyelids that move, with pupils that are vertical.

Geographic range: Western banded geckos are found in the south-western United States and northern Mexico.

Habitat: Western banded geckos are found in dry desert dune, or hill, areas; dry juniper-oak woodlands; desert areas with small shrubs; and rocky desert sites.

Diet: Western banded geckos eat insects and spiders. Surplus, or extra, food may be stored as fat in the tail.

Behavior and reproduction: Western banded geckos move about only at night. They rest during the day under rocks or within the burrows, or underground homes, of small animals. During the day these areas are damper than areas above ground. Several of these geckos may rest together in the burrows. If the burrow is disturbed, the western banded gecko may twitch its tail like a cat. If it is attacked, it runs away quickly. It may leave its tail behind to distract the attacker.

During the mating season, western banded gecko males face each other and make threatening movements. After mating, females lay two or more egg groups, with two eggs in each group. Hatching takes place in thirty to forty-five days.

Western banded geckos and people: Western banded geckos are kept as pets, and they have been successfully bred in captivity. They have no other human interaction.

Conservation status: The western banded gecko is not threatened. ∎

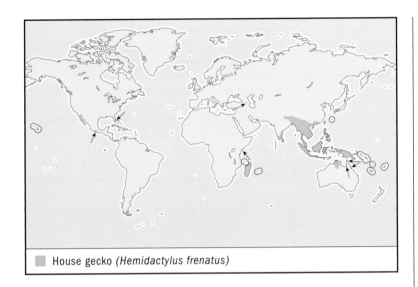

House gecko (*Hemidactylus frenatus*)

HOUSE GECKO
Hemidactylus frenatus

Physical characteristics: The house gecko is grayish, pinkish, or pale brown with darker flecks. The color may vary, depending on the surrounding temperature. It also may vary depending on the surface on which the gecko is resting; this gecko can blend with its background, such as a tree branch or a leafy area. The body is flattened. This gecko grows to 2.6 inches (66 millimeters) in length, from the head to the base of the tail. It has toe pads on each of its toes, and the first toe is smaller than the rest.

Geographic range: House geckos exist in Southeast Asia, the Philippines, Taiwan, and much of Micronesia, Melanesia, and Polynesia. It was introduced, or brought by people, into tropical Australia, eastern Africa, Mexico, and the United States.

Habitat: These geckos live among many types of vegetation, or greenery, including tropical rainforest and dry scrubland, or land covered with low trees and bushes. They are often found around human homes and rubbish dumps.

Diet: House geckos eat insects.

A house gecko can blend with its background, such as a tree branch or a leafy area. (Illustration by Patricia Ferrer. Reproduced by permission.)

Behavior and reproduction: This gecko is active at night, although it may be seen outside on cloudy days. Male house geckos can be unfriendly and mean. This is especially true when there are many of them in one area and plenty of food. They can produce several types of clicking sounds, including "chi-chak."

After mating, females can store sperm (SPUHRM), the male reproductive cells that fertilize the female's eggs. The females lay groups of hard-shelled eggs throughout the year, and the eggs hatch in forty-five to seventy days.

House geckos and people: This species is often found in and around people's homes.

Conservation status: The species itself is not threatened, but it may cause a decrease in native geckos in the areas where it is introduced. House geckos are unfriendly and compete for the food supply of other gecko species. ■

FOR MORE INFORMATION

Books:

Bartlett, Richard D. *Geckos: In Search of Reptiles and Amphibians.* New York: E. J. Brill, 1988.

Bartlett, R. D., and Patricia P. Bartlett. *Geckos: Everything about Selection, Care, Nutrition, Diseases, Breeding, and Behavior.* Hauppauge, NY: Barron's Educational Series, 1995.

Behler, John L. *The Audubon Society Field Guide to North American Reptiles and Amphibians.* New York: Knopf, 1979.

Capula, Massimo. *Guide to Reptiles and Amphibians of the World.* New York: Simon & Schuster, 1989.

Hernandez-Divers, Sonia. *Geckos (Keeping Unusual Pets).* Portsmouth, NH: Heinemann Library, 2002.

Mattison, Chris. *The Care of Reptiles and Amphibians in Captivity.* London: Blandford Press, 1987.

Miller, Jake. *The Leopard Gecko.* New York, NY: PowerKids Press, 2003.

Sprackland, Robert G., Jr. *All about Lizards.* Neptune City, NJ: T. F. H. Publications, 1977.

Uchiyama, Ryu. *Reptiles and Amphibians.* San Francisco: Chronicle Books, 1999.

Periodicals

"At Home in the Rocks, a New Gecko Emerges." *National Geographic* (June 1997): Geographica.

"Barking Gecko." *National Geographic* (October 1989): 26–29.

"Fat-Tailed Gecko." *Ranger Rick* (May 1994): 14–15.

"Leopard Gecko." *Ranger Rick* (November 1994): 4–7.

"Where'd the Gecko Go?" *National Geographic World* (July 1985): 38.

Web sites

Autumn, Kellar. "Gecko Story." http://www.lclark.edu/autumn/dept/geckostory.html (accessed on August 8, 2004).

Muir, Hazel. "Minute Gecko Matches Smallest Living Reptile Record." NewScientist.com. December 3, 2001. http://www.newscientist.com/news/news.jsp?id=ns99991635&lpos;=related_article2 (accessed on August 9, 2004).

Schweitzer, Sophia. "Guardian Geckos." *Coffee Times.* http://www.coffeetimes.com/geckos.htm (accessed on August 9, 2004).

family

CHAPTER

phylum

class

subclass

order

monotypic order

suborder

▲ **family**

PHYSICAL CHARACTERISTICS

Blindskinks (also called "blind lizards," "blind skinks," "legless lizards," and "wormlizards") are small to medium-sized lizards with a slim, snakelike form. They are fewer than 10 inches (25.4 centimeters) long. Their body colors range from pale pink to light brown, with the under area, or belly, sometimes a bit paler. Their bodies are covered with shiny, smooth, and squarish overlapping scales. The scales on the head are large and platelike, especially on the snout, or nose area, and lower jaws.

The heads of these reptiles are blunt, not pointed. The bones of the skull are fused, or firmly joined together. This makes the head area very solid, which helps in burrowing, or digging holes. Their tiny eyes look like dark specks and have no lids. The eyes are hidden under a head scale that does not move. The nostrils, or nose openings, are small and placed at the tip of the snout. These lizards have no ear openings that can be seen. Their ears are covered with scales. There are only a few lower teeth, set in sockets, or hollow openings. The teeth are small and pointed, curving backward. The tongue is short and wide and is not divided at the tip. The tip of the tongue does not retract, or pull back, completely.

The tails of blindskinks are very short and blunt. They are able to break off at various places to deter predators (PREH-duh-ters), or animals that hunt the blindskink for food. Blindskinks do not have any working limbs, or legs. Males have small, flaplike hind limbs, or back legs. These limbs may be used in mating. Females have no limbs or flaps. Pectoral (PECK-ter-uhl), or chest, bones are absent. The hip-bone area is very small. These features give the blindskink its slim shape.

GEOGRAPHIC RANGE

The majority of blindskink species are found in eastern India; southern Thailand; Borneo; Vietnam; Laos; Kampuchea; the Nicobar, Sunda, and Andaman Islands; southern China; Sumatra; Malaysia; most of Indonesia; the Philippines; and westernmost New Guinea. A single species is found in a very small area of northeastern Mexico.

HABITAT

Almost all blindskinks live in rainforests. Most species require damp humus (HYU-mus) or broken up, loose, rotting plant material. During the dry season these species of blindskink burrow beneath rocks or logs. The blindskink of northeastern Mexico has adapted to a wider type of living area. It is found in semiarid deciduous (di-SID-joo-wus) brushland and open scrubland, or areas with bushes and small trees that lose their leaves in dry or cold weather. This lizard also lives in desert areas, often near ant and termite nests. It also inhabits pine-oak forests. It has been found beneath rocks, in or under rotting logs, in loose litter, and in the decayed, or rotting, bases of yuccas, a treelike plant that grows in dry areas.

DIET

Blindskinks feed on tiny insects, such as ants and termites and possibly spiders.

BEHAVIOR AND REPRODUCTION

Very little is known about the living habits of blindskinks. They are secretive lizards, preferring to hide. Blindskinks live on the forest floor, often underneath stones, but sometimes

WHO ARE THE RELATIVES?

Scientists are still trying to find out more about the blindskinks' evolution (eh-vuh-LU-shun), or the changes they have undergone to adapt to their environment over time. These are very unusual lizards, both in appearance and in living habits. Most species are known from fewer than 20 specimens, or examples. Over the years scientists have proposed that blindskinks are related closely to snakes; geckos; skinks; carnivorous (KAR-nih-vuh-rus), or meat-eating, anguid lizards; and worm lizards, which look like earthworms. There is still no definite answer.

underneath leaf litter or moving about underground. They enter the earth through cracks in the soil or by way of tunnels made by other animals. In soft, loose soils or rotting leaf litter their slim body shape and rigid head allow them to dig their own tunnels. Blindskinks may take up residence in tunnels made by other insects or in the underground homes made by insects that live in groups, such as termites.

Nothing is known of the mating or egg-laying habits of the blindskinks living in Mexico. Little is known of the mating habits of the rainforest species. It is believed that after mating, the females lay just one egg. An egg may be laid more than once a year. The eggs are soft and somewhat long. Later they become harder and shaped more like eggs.

BLINDSKINKS AND PEOPLE

Blindskinks do not interact with people. Few people ever see them.

CONSERVATION STATUS

Blindskinks are not threatened. Many species suffer from loss of their habitat, or their preferred living area, as the result of movements of people, farming, tree removal, and pollution, or poison, waste, or other material that makes the environment dirty and harmful to health. There are no conservation efforts under way to protect blindskinks.

Blindskink *(Dibamus bourreti)*

FOR MORE INFORMATION

Books:

Arnosky, Jim. *All about Lizards.* New York: Scholastic, 2004.

Bartlett, Richard D. *In Search of Reptiles and Amphibians.* New York: E. J. Brill, 1988.

Cogger, Harold, and Richard Zweifel, eds. *Reptiles and Amphibians.* San Francisco: Weldon Owens, 1992.

Halliday, Tim, and Kraig Adler, eds. *Encyclopedia of Reptiles and Amphibians.* New York: Facts on File, 1986.

Lamar, William. *The World's Most Spectacular Reptiles and Amphibians.* Tampa, FL: World Publications, 1997.

Mattison, Chris. *Lizards of the World.* New York: Facts on File, 1989.

Pough, F. Harvey, Robin M. Andrews, John E. Cadle, Martha L. Crump, Alan H. Savitzky, and Kentwood D. Wells. *Herpetology.* Upper Saddle River, NJ: Prentice Hall, 1998.

Riccuiti, Edward R. *Reptiles.* Woodbridge, CT: Blackbirch Press, 1993.

Sprackland, Robert G., Jr. *All about Lizards.* Neptune City, NJ: T. F. H. Publications, 1977.

WORMLIZARDS
Amphisbaenidae

Class: Reptilia
Order: Squamata
Suborder: Amphisbaenia
Family: Amphisbaenidae
Number of species: 160 species

family
CHAPTER

phylum
class
subclass
order
monotypic order
suborder
▲ **family**

PHYSICAL CHARACTERISTICS

The members of this family, known simply as wormlizards, are long, thin, legless animals. Their scales are arranged in rings around the body with each ring separated from the next by a shallow groove. This ring and groove pattern makes them look much like earthworms, even though the worms lack scales. In some species of wormlizard, the head is round. In others, it may be shaped like a shovel, or in some cases the snout may come to a point. They have no openings for their ears, as the lizards do, and they have only the smallest of eyes showing below a see-through scale, if they are visible at all. They have no legs, but all species in this family have tiny bits of hip bones inside their bodies. They do not, however, have a sternum (STER-num), which is the bone at the front of the chest that in most animal species connects to the ribs.

Most wormlizards reach about 10 to 16 inches (25 to 40 centimeters) long as adults, but some species are much smaller or much larger. The smallest species lives in Africa and only grows to 4 inches (10 centimeters) long, while the largest, known as the white-bellied wormlizard, can reach more than 32 inches (80 centimeters). A wormlizard's tail, which can look much like the rest of the body, actually starts at the vent, a slit-like opening on the underside of the animal. The tails in these animals are very short, usually less than one-tenth of the overall body length. The tails may be rounded, pointed at the end, or have a flattened shape. Many of the 160 species of wormlizards have about the same color: pale pink or pale orange-pink, sometimes with a whitish belly. Some species, however, are colored brown, yellow, purple, or gray, and a few even have eye-catching black-and-white patterns. The males and females of each species look alike.

The wormlizards in this family have many of the same features of three other families of animals: the mole-limbed wormlizards, the Florida wormlizards, and the spade-headed wormlizards. These four families all fall under the group called amphisbaenians (am-fizz-BAY-nee-ens). Like the wormlizards in this family, many of them look much like earthworms, and all except the mole-limbed wormlizards are legless. Interestingly, all wormlizards have only one lung, or one large lung and one tiny lung, and one larger tooth in the middle of the upper jaw. In those that have eyes, they have no eyelids. They also have a forked tongue and a thick, strong skull. They have an unusual hearing system that allows them to pick up even slight vibrations underground. In this system, a little structure attaches the ear to tissue on the side of the face. When they are slithering about, they can feel vibrations through the ground with the bottom of the face. The vibration then runs up the tissue and to the ear, which hears it. This ability, which lets the wormlizards hear even small movements made by other animals, comes in particularly handy when the wormlizards are looking for ants and other insects to eat.

IS IT A WORM OR A LIZARD?

Is a wormlizard more like a worm that looks like a lizard, or a lizard that looks like a worm? Animals are split into two major groups: vertebrates, which have backbones, and invertebrates, which do not have backbones. Wormlizards and lizards have backbones, but earthworms do not, so wormlizards are more like lizards than earthworms. In fact, both wormlizards and lizards are reptiles, but wormlizards are not true lizards. Instead, wormlizards are a unique group of reptiles that mostly live underground, have rings of scales separated by shallow grooves, and have a number of other characteristics that separate them from the lizards.

GEOGRAPHIC RANGE

Wormlizards live in both the western and eastern hemispheres, including South America, Central America, the West Indies, Africa, Asia, and Europe. They tend to live in tropical areas or in spots with a slightly less warm, subtropical climate.

HABITAT

Wormlizards stay out of sight most of the time, either remaining in their burrows or beneath rocks or leaf litter on the ground. Some of them make themselves at home in the nests of ants or termites, possibly even laying their eggs or having their young there. They will come out on the surface after particularly heavy rains that flood their underground homes.

DIET

Wild wormlizards eat mainly ants, termites, beetles, grubs (young beetles), caterpillars, and cockroaches. In one study, scientists looked inside the stomachs of wormlizards and found that some were filled with fungi. In another study, they found one wormlizard that had eaten a lizard, or at least its leg, and another that had swallowed a burrowing snake—whole. In captivity, wormlizards will eat other large vertebrates (VER-teh-brehts), which are animals with backbones, so some people believe they may do the same in the wild.

BEHAVIOR AND REPRODUCTION

Wormlizards are fossorial (foss-OR-ee-ul), which means that stay underground most of the time. Depending on the shape of the head, they dig their tunnels in different ways. Those with a round head butt their heads straight into the dirt like a battering ram and move forward that way. Other species with heads shaped like shovels, scoop up dirt onto the top of the head and then press it into the roof of the tunnel. Those with sideways-flattened heads, on the other hand, press the head and the body side to side and force an opening through the soil. No matter how they make their tunnels, they all use them to hunt for animals to eat. They mostly hunt by using their excellent hearing and by smelling. Like other amphisbaenians, wormlizards have forked tongues that pick up chemicals left by prey animals. They then touch their tongues to a small opening on the roof of the mouth that opens to a special organ. This organ, called a Jacobson's organ, can smell the chemicals.

Although wormlizards stay underground, which protects them from most predators, they sometimes come under attack. When this happens, most species can drop the tail, which can confuse a predator (PREH-duh-ter) enough to give the wormlizard time to escape. Unlike many of the lizards that also drop their tails, wormlizards cannot regrow theirs.

Scientists know little more about their behavior, courtship, or mating. The females of most species lay eggs, but some give birth to baby wormlizards. The number of eggs in each clutch is typically between one and four, although a few species can lay more than a dozen. Females sometimes lay their eggs inside ant or termite nests.

WORMLIZARDS AND PEOPLE

Wormlizards and people rarely run across one another.

CONSERVATION STATUS

None of these species is considered endangered or threatened.

White-bellied wormlizard (*Amphisbaena alba*)

WHITE-BELLIED WORMLIZARD
Amphisbaena alba

Physical characteristics: Among the largest members of the family, the white-bellied wormlizard can grow to 33.4 inches (85 centimeters) long with a body that can reach up to 2 inches (25 centimeters) wide. Adults can, however, be much smaller, growing to only half that size. Of their total length, only 6 percent is tail. Like other wormlizards, their scales form rings around the body and give the animal an earthworm-like appearance. The scales on their back are small and square. They have a rounded head with one large tooth and six smaller ones in the front of the upper jaw.

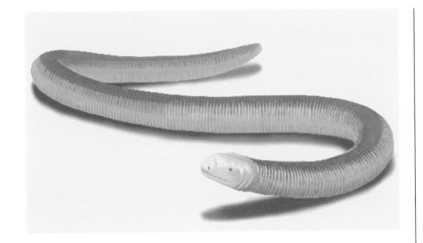

Geographic range: The white-bellied wormlizard lives in Panama, which is in far southern Central America, in the West Indies, and in South America east of the Andes Mountains.

Habitat: This burrowing animal almost always stays in its underground tunnels, buried under dead leaves, or inside the nests of leaf-cutter ants.

Diet: With its strong jaws, the white-bellied wormlizard can eat animals as large as mice and rats in a scientist's laboratory. In the wild, however, they are known only to eat smaller animals, such as ants, termites, crickets, and other insects, as well as spiders and other invertebrates (in-VER-teh-brehts), which are animals without backbones.

Behavior and reproduction: Unlike other wormlizards that drop the tail when they feel threatened, this species cannot. Instead, it curls up its body so the head and tail are next to one another, and then raises its head and opens wide its mouth while lifting up and swaying its tail. This behavior makes the wormlizard almost look as if it has two heads, and, in fact, some people call it a "two-headed snake." Females lay eight to 16 eggs at a time, probably once a year during the dry season.

White-bellied wormlizards and people: White-bellied wormlizards and people rarely run across one another.

Conservation status: This species is not considered endangered or threatened. ◼

FOR MORE INFORMATION

Books:

Gans, C. *Biomechanics: An Approach to Vertebrate Biology.* Philadelphia: J. B. Lippincott Company, 1974.

Halliday, Tim, and Kraig Adler, eds. *The Encyclopedia of Reptiles and Amphibians.* New York: Facts on File, 1986.

Mattison, Chris. *Lizards of the World.* New York: Facts on File, 1989.

Schwenk, K. "Feeding in Lepidosaurs." In *Feeding: Form, Function, and Evolution in Tetrapod Vertebrates.* San Diego: Academic Press, 2000.

Vanzolini, P. E. *Evolution, Adaptation and Distribution of the Amphisbaenid Lizards (Sauria: Amphisbaenidae).* Ph.D. diss. Harvard University, 1951.

Web sites:

"Amphisbaenidae." Innvista. http://www.innvista.com/science/zoology/reptiles/amphisba.htm (accessed on December 9, 2004).

"Family Amphisbaenidae." Animal Diversity Web. University of Michigan Museum of Zoology. http://animaldiversity.ummz.umich.edu/site/accounts/classification/Amphisbaenidae.html (accessed on December 1, 2004).

"The Keeping and Maintenance of Amphisbaenians." Cyberlizard (UK). http://www.nafcon.dircon.co.uk/amphisb1.html (accessed on December 1, 2004).

"The ReptiPage: Amphisbaenia." The ReptiPage. http://reptilis.net/amphisbaenia/overview.html html (accessed on December 9, 2004).

MOLE-LIMBED WORMLIZARDS

Bipedidae

Class: Reptilia

Order: Squamata

Suborder: Amphisbaenia

Family: Bipedidae

Number of species: 3 species

PHYSICAL CHARACTERISTICS

The three species of mole-limbed wormlizards in this family are sometimes confused with earthworms, but they have scales and front legs. They are one of four families that fall into the group known as wormlizards or amphisbaenians (am-fizz-BAY-nee-ens). In all amphisbaenians, small rectangular scales form circular rings around their long thin bodies. A worm has rings around its body, too, but it has no scales and lacks most of the other features of wormlizards. Mole-limbed wormlizards, like other amphisbaenians, have one large tooth in the middle of the upper jaw, a thick and strong skull, small and sometimes invisible eyes, and a forked tongue. They do not, however, have ear holes or eyelids, like most lizards do. The mole-limbed wormlizards are different from other wormlizards, because they have a pair of small but strong front legs right behind the short rounded head. In addition, one of their clawed fingers has an extra bony piece, compared to the fingers of other reptiles. Mole-limbed wormlizards use their strong front legs, and probably this extra finger bone, to help them dig. Some scientists believe that, because the mole-limbed wormlizards have front legs, they are probably the most primitive of all the amphisbaenians. Other scientists disagree. These questions will no doubt continue, since no one has yet found a single fossil of any member of this family. Although mole-limbed wormlizards do not have hind legs, the skeleton still has some bits of hip bone and a tiny nub of thigh bone.

Mole-limbed wormlizards grow to 4.5 to 9.4 inches (11.5 to 24 centimeters) long and at the middle of the body are about

phylum

class

subclass

order

monotypic order

suborder

▲ **family**

0.27 to 0.39 inches (7 to 10 millimeters) across. Only one-tenth to one-fifth of the body length is tail. The body is very bland-looking with no pattern and is colored pale pink, sometimes with a slightly orange tint. Individuals occasionally have a whiter belly. This animal sheds its skin (actually just the outer layer of skin) once in a while. When it sheds, the skin layer comes off in a single piece, just like it does in most snakes.

GEOGRAPHIC RANGE

The three species of mole-limbed worm-lizard, or ajolote (ah-joe-LOW-tay) as they are often called, live in western Mexico. Depending on the species, they may make their homes in Baja California, Guerro, or Michoacán.

HABITAT

Mole-limbed wormlizards are found along the coast in deserts and dry shrubby areas, in dried streambeds, or in the shoreline soils of streams and rivers. They usually remain in their underground burrows but sometimes crawl above ground, especially at night.

DIET

Mole-limbed wormlizards are like many other underground-living, or fossorial (foss-OR-ee-ul), animals in that their diet is something of a mystery. Scientists have not watched them feed but have occasionally caught them and looked at what was in their stomachs. From these scraps of partially digested food, they have learned that the mole-limbed wormlizards will eat ants, termites, grubs, and other invertebrates (in-VER-teh-brehts), which are animals without backbones. These species find their food underground or beneath logs, rotting leaves, and other things that cover the ground by following chemicals trails that the invertebrates leave behind. Mole-limbed wormlizards pick up these chemicals with the tongue. The tongue then places the chemical odors on a little opening, or duct, on the roof of the mouth that connects to a special organ. This organ, called a Jacobson's organ, helps them smell the chemicals.

BEHAVIOR AND REPRODUCTION

These three species spend most of their time in the underground tunnels that they dig. They dig their tunnels with their front legs and with their heads, typically starting new tunnels with their legs and then switching to their heads to make them longer and deeper. When they are digging with their heads, they lay the front legs along the sides of the body. Their tunnels can wander through the soil, sometimes opening underneath rocks or logs at the surface, scooting along less than an inch (2.5 centimeters) underground, or dropping down to almost 8 inches (20 centimeters) deep. At night, they may leave their tunnels and crawl about above ground, but they rarely venture out during the daytime. By living underground, they avoid most predators. If a predator (PREH-duh-ter) does manage to capture one, the mole-limbed wormlizard is able to drop its tail. Unlike many other lizards, however, it does not regrow its tail.

Females of all three species lay eggs, usually one to four at a time. Some may only have young every other year. Females in two of the three species lay their eggs in January, and the eggs hatch three months later. Females of the third species lay their eggs in July, and the eggs hatch two months later.

MOLE-LIMBED WORMLIZARDS AND PEOPLE

People rarely see these animals. Occasionally, a person may turn over a rock or log and see a mole-limbed wormlizard for a few seconds until it quickly slinks back into its tunnel and disappears. Although people rarely think about them, the wormlizards may be helpful to humans because they eat termites and other so-called pest animals.

CONSERVATION STATUS

Scientists still have much to learn about these animals; however, they are not now considered endangered or threatened.

Two-legged wormlizard (*Bipes biporus*)

TWO-LEGGED WORMLIZARD
Bipes biporus

Physical characteristics: Colored very pale pink or orangish-pink, and sometimes with a whitish belly, the two-legged wormlizard has two front legs, each with five claws. Adults can reach 7.5 to 8.3 inches (19 to 21 centimeters) long, including a short tail. The tail looks much like the rest of the body but actually begins at the vent, a slit-like opening on the underside of the animal. In this species, the tail is about one-tenth as long as the rest of the body. In other words, a 7.5-inch-long (19-centimeter-long) wormlizard has a tail about 0.75 inches (1.9 centimeters) long. It is a thin animal, and at the middle of its body, it only measures about one-quarter of an inch (6 to 7 millimeters) across.

Geographic range: It makes its home along the western side of the Baja California peninsula in Mexico.

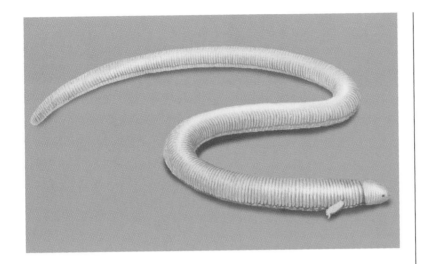

People rarely see these wormlizards, unless they happen to turn over a rock, a pile of leaves, or some other hiding spot where one is lying. (Illustration by John Megahan. Reproduced by permission.)

Habitat: The two-legged wormlizard lives underground in sandy soils usually around the roots of certain shrubs called mesquite (mess-KEET). Their tunnels are usually very shallow—less than an inch (2.5 centimeters) deep—but they sometimes drop to about 6 inches (15 centimeters) under the surface.

Diet: They search underground for ants, termites, and the larvae (LAR-vee) of insects to eat. Larvae are newly hatched insects that usually have soft bodies. Grubs, for example, are the larvae of beetles. At night, they also look for food, including insects and spiders, above ground.

Behavior and reproduction: These animals stay in their shallow tunnels most of the time. In the mornings, they tend to move up to shallower tunnels, then go deeper as the day warms up. Scientists believe that they also search for warm or cool spots underground by moving into the open where the sun beats down to heat up the sand, or under chillier shady areas beneath shrubs or trees. They will leave their tunnels and come up to the surface sometimes, especially at night, to hunt for invertebrates. They are not speedy, graceful animals. Rather, they move slowly and clumsily, sometimes swinging around their front legs in an overhand swimming type of motion. Like other members of this family, the two-legged wormlizard can drop its tail if it is attacked. They squeeze muscles around a weak spot in the tail bone, and the tail drops off. The wound heals, but the worm lizard cannot grow a new tail.

The females lay one to four eggs in July, which is a very dry time in their habitat. The eggs hatch about two months later, just as the rainy season starts and food for the young becomes more plentiful. In the summer after the females reach their fourth birthday, they are old enough to have young of their own. Some scientists think that females may only have young once every other year. Only more research will say for sure.

Two-legged wormlizards and people: People rarely see one of these wormlizards, unless they happen to turn over a rock, a pile of leaves, or some other hiding spot where one is lying. The wormlizard usually responds by quickly slipping into a nearby tunnel and disappearing.

Conservation status: This species is not considered endangered or threatened.   ■

FOR MORE INFORMATION

Books:

Burnie, David, and Don Wilson, eds. *The Definitive Visual Guide to the World's Wildlife.* New York: DK Publishing, 2001.

Gans, C. *Biomechanics: An Approach to Vertebrate Biology.* Philadelphia: J. B. Lippincott Company, 1974.

Halliday, Tim, and Kraig Adler, eds. *The Encyclopedia of Reptiles and Amphibians.* New York: Facts on File, 1986.

Mattison, Chris. *Lizards of the World.* New York: Facts on File, 1989.

Schwenk, K. *Feeding: Form, Function, and Evolution in Tetrapod Vertebrates.* San Diego: Academic Press, 2000.

Vanzolini, P. E. *Evolution, Adaptation and Distribution of the Amphisbaenid Lizards (Sauria: Amphisbaenidae).* Ph.D. diss. Harvard University, 1951.

Web sites:

"Family Bipedidae (two-legged worm lizards)." Animal Diversity Web. University of Michigan Museum of Zoology. http://animaldiversity.ummz .umich.edu/site/accounts/classification/Bipedidae.html (accessed on December 1, 2004).

FLORIDA WORMLIZARD

Rhineuridae

Class: Reptilia

Order: Squamata

Suborder: Amphisbaenia

Family: Rhineuridae

One species: Florida worm lizard
(*Rhineura floridana*)

family
CHAPTER

PHYSICAL CHARACTERISTICS

Florida wormlizards, the only living species in this family, are long and thin creatures without legs. They have thin rings circling their round bodies, no ear openings, and usually no visible eyes. This combination of features makes many people confuse them with earthworms. Florida wormlizards, however, have scales, and worms do not. In fact, it is the scales on the wormlizard's head that cover its eyes. The head is hard and somewhat flattened with a bladelike front edge, which helps the lizard to dig into the soil. The upper jaw sticks out farther than the lower jaw, so the animal has an overbite of sorts. The shape of the head has caused some people to call them shovelnose wormlizards. They are usually a pearly pinkish white color, but some individuals may be tinted slightly orange-pink. Their heads and tail tips are sometimes a bit darker. Like most snakes, they shed their skin—actually just the top layer of skin—in one piece.

Adults can grow to about one-half inch (1.2 centimeters) around at the middle of the body and reach 9.5 to 11 inches (24 to 28 centimeters) long, including a short tail. The tail begins at the vent, a slit-like opening on the underside of the animal, and is only about one-tenth of the total length of the wormlizard. The tail, which is slightly flattened, is covered on top with little cone-shaped bumps called tubercles (TOO-ber-kuls).

Inside the body, Florida wormlizards look much like other types of wormlizards, which are all grouped together under the name amphisbaenians (am-fizz-BAY-nee-ens). The

phylum

class

subclass

order

monotypic order

suborder

▲ **family**

A GREATER PAST

The only species of the family Rhineuridae makes its home in parts of Florida and in southern Georgia, but this family once lived over a much larger area. Scientists have identified fossils from wormlizards in the central and western United States. These fossils, which date back as much as 60 million years ago, tell scientists that the wormlizards of the past looked quite similar to the Florida wormlizard alive today. They also were a little different. For example, while they had the same flattened and somewhat pointy skull that the current species has, the fossil worm lizards also had at least one bony feature that Florida wormlizards lack. In their skulls, the fossil wormlizards have orbit and jugal (JEW-gul) bones, that form a complete ring around the eye.

amphisbaenians include four different families of wormlizards: the Rhineuridae, or Florida wormlizards; the Bipedidae, or mole-limbed wormlizards; the Trogonophidae, or spade-headed wormlizards; and Amphisbaenidae, which are known simply as worm lizards. The Florida wormlizard is the only amphisbaenian that naturally lives in the United States. The others live in Africa, Central and South America, and a few places in Europe and Asia. All amphisbanians are long, thin reptiles that look much like worms, but with scales. They have an odd ear set-up in which parts of the ear attach to tissue on the sides of the face. When the ground vibrates, the tissue senses the vibrations and sends them on to the ear, so the animal can actually hear the ground move. In addition, amphisbaenians have two lungs like almost all other vertebrates (pronounced VER-teh-brehts), which are animals with backbones, but one of their lungs is either extremely small or missing altogether. This arrangement works well in these species, and indeed in many snakes, that have very thin bodies without room for two side-by-side lungs. They also have a forked tongue, no visible ear holes, and one center tooth in the front of the upper jaw that is bigger than the other teeth. The Florida wormlizards sometimes have one little tooth on either side of the center tooth. Florida wormlizards also have their nostrils toward the bottom of the head rather than on the top as many other reptiles do.

GEOGRAPHIC RANGE

Once thought to live only in north-central and northeastern Florida, scientists now know that it also exists in southern Georgia.

HABITAT

Florida wormlizards make their homes in the sandy and loose but rich soil of usually dry pine and broad-leaved forests. They are burrowing animals and therefore spend most of their time underground. When heavy rains drench the forests, these worms often leave their tunnels and venture out above ground. Because people usually only see them after a downpour, they sometimes call the animals thunderworms.

DIET

Scientists are unsure exactly what Florida wormlizards eat, but they believe they probably eat the same things that other amphisbaenians eat. Most amphisbaenians travel through their underground burrows looking for and dining on the ants, termites, and grubs that they find there. The Florida wormlizards flick their forked tongues to pick up chemicals in the air and on the ground. They then press the tongue on the roof of the mouth, where a special organ, called a Jacobson's organ, lies. This organ "tastes" the chemicals to tell the wormlizard about the prey animals that might be nearby. They also use their special ear set-ups to "hear" even very faint vibrations in the ground. This super-hearing ability probably helps the wormlizards to hear movements made by even very small insects and therefore makes them especially good hunters.

BEHAVIOR AND REPRODUCTION

Florida wormlizards stay underground most of the time, although they sometimes—and just for a moment—poke their heads up and out of piles of leaves. Scientists call such underground-living animals fossorial (faw-SOR-ee-ul). Florida wormlizards dig through the soil with their hard, shovel-shaped heads. The snout is also very hard and forms a sharp edge for tunneling. Although its tail is short, the Florida wormlizard uses it well. As the wormlizard begins digging, its tail is often exposed on top of the ground. Fortunately, dirt fits between the cone-shaped bump on the top of the tail and helps to hides it from the sight of passing predators (PREH-duh-ters), or animals that might hunt it for food. If a predator comes too close, the wormlizard quickly digs further into the soil and uses its tail like a cork to plug the tunnel entrance. Unlike many lizards, the Florida wormlizard cannot drop its tail.

Florida wormlizards stay underground most of the time. (©Dave Norris/Photo Researchers, Inc. Reproduced by permission.)

Florida wormlizard *(Rhineura floridana)*

Female Florida wormlizards lay eggs, usually two at a time, in their underground burrows. The eggs hatch into babies about 4 inches (10 centimeters) long. Scientists know little else about their courtship, mating, or reproduction.

FLORIDA WORM LIZARDS AND PEOPLE

People rarely see these shy animals, but they may get some benefits from the wormlizards. If they eat ants, termites, and beetle grubs, the wormlizards may be helping to rid gardens and parks of some of humankind's pests.

CONSERVATION STATUS

This species is not considered endangered or threatened.

FOR MORE INFORMATION

Books:

Behler, John, and F. Wayne King. "Worm Lizard *(Rhineura floridana)*." *National Audubon Society Field Guide to Reptiles and Amphibians*. New York: Alfred A. Knopf, 1979.

Burnie, David, and Don Wilson, eds. *The Definitive Visual Guide to the World's Wildlife* New York: DK Publishing, 2001.

Conant, Roger. *A Field Guide to Reptiles and Amphibians of Eastern/ Central North America.* Boston: Houghton Mifflin Company, 1975.

Gans, C. *Biomechanics: An Approach to Vertebrate Biology.* Philadelphia: J. B. Lippincott Company, 1974.

Halliday, Tim, and Kraig Adler, eds. *The Encyclopedia of Reptiles and Amphibians.* New York: Facts on File, 1986.

Schwenk, K. In *Feeding: Form, Function, and Evolution in Tetrapod Vertebrates.* San Diego: Academic Press, 2000.

Vanzolini, P. E. *Evolution, Adaptation and Distribution of the Amphisbaenid Lizards (Sauria: Amphisbaenidae).* Ph.D. diss. Harvard University, 1951.

Web sites:

"Animals of the Florida Scrub: Florida Worm Lizard." Flori-Data. http://www.floridata.com/tracks/scrub/animals/rhi_flor.htm (accessed on November 23, 2004).

"Suborder: Amphisbaenia." Georgia Wildlife Web. http://museum.nhm.uga.edu/gawildlife/reptiles/squamata/amphisbaenia.html (accessed on November 23, 2004).

"Wildlife: Florida Worm lizard." Native Florida. http://www.nsis.org/gallery/wl-fl_worm_lizard.html (accessed on November 23, 2004).

"Worm lizard." Fact Monster. http://www.factmonster.com/ce6/sci/A0852748.html (accessed on November 23, 2004).

SPADE-HEADED WORMLIZARDS
Trogonophidae

Class: Reptilia

Order: Squamata

Suborder: Amphisbaenia

Family: Trogonophidae

Number of species: 8 species

PHYSICAL CHARACTERISTICS

At first glance, the spade-headed wormlizards look like big earthworms. Just as earthworms have rings around their bodies, these wormlizards have thin rings from the back of the head to the tip of the tail. Such rings are called annuli (ANN-you-lie). In the spade-headed wormlizards, the rings are made of tiny square-shaped scales that are the same size and shape from the belly to the back. Also like earthworms, the wormlizards have no legs. Wormlizards, however, do still have tiny leftover hip and shoulder bones inside their bodies.

The heads of spade-headed wormlizards are shaped like shovels, or spades, which gives them their name. Sometimes, people also call them by another common name, short-headed wormlizards, because their heads are quite small and end quickly after the neck. The edges of the face are quite sharp, providing an excellent digging tool for these burrowing animals. The body is flattened into an upside down "U" shape, so that the wormlizard has a rounded back and an inward-curved belly side. It has a very short, sometimes ridged, or keeled, tail. The tail begins at the vent, a slit-like opening on the underside of the animal.

Some spade-headed wormlizards are patterned with checks and spots. They are rather small animals, with adults ranging from 3.1 to 9.4 inches (8 to 24 centimeters) in length.

GEOGRAPHIC RANGE

They live in northern Africa, in eastern Somalia, and in the Middle East from western Iran to the island of Socotra, which lies east of Somalia and south of Saudi Arabia.

HABITAT

Spade-headed wormlizards tunnel in loose soils, which may be sandy or loamy. A loamy soil is one that is not quite as grainy as sand but still is quite loose.

DIET

Most of the spade-headed wormlizards eat termites, grubs, and ants. Grubs are actually young beetles, which are also known as beetle larvae (LAR-vee). When the grubs are old enough, they go through another life stage called pupae (PYU-pee) and then turn into the adult crawling beetles familiar to most people. Wormlizards in captivity will also eat larger animals by biting off chunks and chewing them up. Scientists are unsure if they eat larger animals in the wild because they have never seen a wild wormlizard eating a larger animal. On the rare occasions when they have been able to catch and cut open a wild wormlizard to check its stomach and see what it had been eating, scientists have not found pieces of large animals inside. Until more studies on wormlizards are done, scientists cannot say for sure whether they eat larger animals in the wild.

LIZARD EARS

On a person, a dog, or a cat, the ears are obvious. They are called "external" ears because external means something that is on the outside. Some animals, including many reptiles, have no external ears. Instead, their ears are often little more than holes on the sides of the head. Some species do not even have the holes. They are covered with scales. Spade-headed wormlizards are an example of reptiles without external ear openings. They can, however, still hear and are especially good at hearing vibrations in the soil. Such vibrations could be made by a predator walking overhead or a prey animal moving about.

BEHAVIOR AND REPRODUCTION

These wormlizards move oddly when they are tunneling. Instead of forcing their heads forward into the soil, they turn their heads up on one side and then up on the other, scraping the sharp sides of the face in this back-and-forth swiveling motion, and scrape away dirt. Just as twisting an apple corer will cause the corer to cut into and through an apple, swiveling the head of one of these wormlizards slices into the soil to make a tunnel. This swiveling motion is known as oscillation (AH-sih-LAY-shun). Besides cutting through the soil, the oscillation packs the dirt against the sides of the tunnel to make it smooth and rather strong. Although the head turns back and forth, the rest of the wormlizard's body does not. Its body's upside down

"U" shape helps the wormlizard grab hold of the soil with its belly side and keep its body still. In addition, its very short tail digs in to the bottom of the tunnel to hold the body in place while the head swivels.

Because they have tiny eyes, if they have them at all, these wormlizards do not rely on vision to find their prey. Instead, they have excellent senses of hearing and smell. Although their ears are hidden by scales, they can hear even small movements, like a termite taking a few steps somewhere else in the soil. They also stick out their forked tongues to pick up chemical odors, then draw the tongue back inside the mouth to touch a special organ on the roof of the mouth. This organ, called the Jacobson's organ, smells the chemical odor.

Their underground homes provide considerable protection against predators (PREH-duh-ters), or animals that hunt other animals for food. Sometimes, when they are on the surface, however, they may face a predator. Unlike wormlizards in other families, the spade-headed wormlizard cannot drop the tail, a tactic that other species use to escape attackers. Instead, wormlizards roll over to be belly-up, and they stop moving. Predators may be surprised by the color or the belly or may lose interest because the wormlizard is so still. Either way, this behavior apparently helps the wormlizard to live another day.

The females of some species of these wormlizards give birth to about five baby wormlizards at a time. Scientists believe that some other species lay eggs. Little else is known about the courtship, mating, or reproduction of these animals.

SPADE-HEADED WORM LIZARDS AND PEOPLE

Although people rarely see these wormlizards, they may be helpful to people because they eat pest insects such as ants and termites that might damage the wood in buildings or cause other problems for people.

CONSERVATION STATUS

These species are not considered endangered or threatened, but scientists know little about them in the wild.

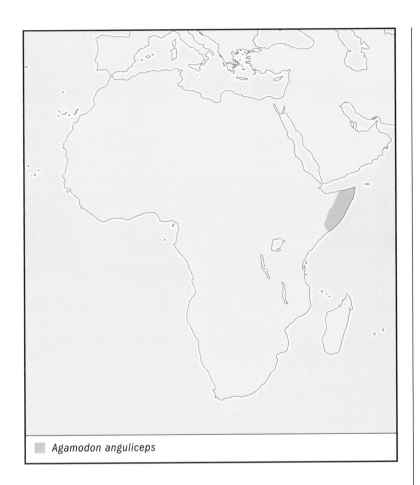

Agamodon anguliceps

NO COMMON NAME
Agamodon anguliceps

Physical characteristics: *Agamodon anguliceps* has a short shovel-shaped head and a sharp-sided face. Its back is mottled with yellow and dark brown to brownish purple blotches, and its underside is pink to purplish pink. Its tiny squarish scales form rings around its body. It grows to about 4 to 8 inches (10 to 18 centimeters) in length.

Geographic range: This species lives in eastern Ethiopia and Somalia along the eastern edge of central Africa.

Habitat: They tunnel in loose and sandy soils.

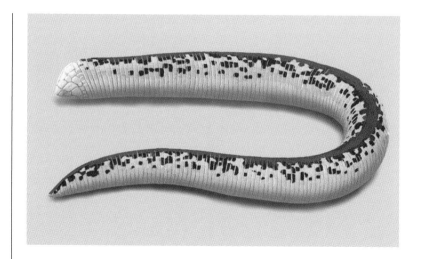

Agamodon anguliceps lives in eastern Ethiopia and Somalia along the eastern edge of central Africa. (Illustration by John Megahan. Reproduced by permission.)

Diet: Scientists have not studied this animal in the wild, but they suspect that it eats termites, grubs, and other invertebrates (in-VER-teh-brehts), which are animals without backbones. In captivity, however, this wormlizard can also attack and kill larger vertebrate prey, which they then eat by biting off and chewing up the pieces. Vertebrates (VER-teh-brehts) are mammals and other animals that have backbones.

Behavior and reproduction: Like other members of this family, this species digs its tunnels by swiveling its head and using the sharp sides of its face to slice through the soil. It appears to stay closer to the surface of the ground during the night and move deeper into the soil in the daytime. When it feels threatened, it flips onto its back to show off its pink underside and then plays dead. Scientists know almost nothing about its reproduction, but they believe that the females probably lay eggs.

***Agamodon anguliceps* and people:** People and this wormlizard rarely see one another.

Conservation status: This species is not considered endangered or threatened, but scientists know little about them in the wild.

FOR MORE INFORMATION

Books:

Burnie, David, and Don Wilson eds. "Amphisbaenians." *The Definitive Visual Guide to the World's Wildlife* New York: DK Publishing, 2001.

Gans, C. *Biomechanics: An Approach to Vertebrate Biology.* Philadelphia: J. B. Lippincott Company, 1974.

Schwenk, K. *Feeding: Form, Function, and Evolution in Tetrapod Vertebrates.* San Diego: Academic Press, 2000.

Vanzolini, P. E. *Evolution, Adaptation and Distribution of the Amphisbaenid Lizards (Sauria: Amphisbaenidae).* Ph.D. diss. Harvard University, 1951.

Web sites:

"Amphisbaenia." Virtual Museum of Natural History. http://www.curator.org/LegacyVMNH/WebOfLife/Kingdom/P_Chordata/ClassReptilia/O_Squamata/InfraAmphisbaenia/amphisbaenia.htm (accessed on November 15, 2004).

"Family Trogonophidae (Shorthead Worm Lizards)." EMBL Reptile Database. http://www.embl-heidelberg.de/uetz/families/Trogonophidae.html (accessed on November 15, 2004).

"The Keeping and Maintenance of Amphisbaenians." Cyberlizard. http://www.nafcon.dircon.co.uk/amphisb1.html (accessed on November 15, 2004).

"Order Squamata, Suborder Amphisbaenia (worm-lizards)." San Francisco State University. http://online.sfsu.edu/uy/AnimDiv/lab/lab8/Biol171Lab8.html. (accessed November on 15, 2004).

Species List by Biome

CONIFEROUS FOREST
Blind lizard
Boomslang
Common chameleon
Common garter snake
Eastern box turtle
Eastern hog-nosed snake
Florida wormlizard
Flying lizard
Frilled lizard
Green anole
Green python
House gecko
Indigo snake
Milksnake
Neotropical sunbeam snake
North American coral snake
Reticulated python
Texas blind snake
Timber rattlesnake

CONTINENTAL MARGIN
Green seaturtle
Loggerhead turtle

DECIDUOUS FOREST
Agamodon anguliceps
Armored chameleon
Black-headed python

Blackish blind snake
Blind lizard
Boa constrictor
Boomslang
Broad-headed skink
Common chameleon
Common garter snake
Common sunbeam snake
Crocodile tegu
Eastern box turtle
Eastern hog-nosed snake
Florida wormlizard
Flying lizard
Galápagos tortoise
Gila monster
Green python
Indigo snake
Knob-scaled lizard
Komodo dragon
Lesser blind snake
Milksnake
Neotropical sunbeam snake
North American coral snake
Northern Tuatara
Prehensile-tailed skink
Red-tailed pipe snake
Reticulated python
Sand lizard
Southern bromeliad
  woodsnake

Texas alligator lizard
Texas blind snake
Timber rattlesnake
Yellow-margined box turtle

DESERT
Agamodon anguliceps
Boa constrictor
Cape flat lizard
Cape spiny-tailed iguana
Common chameleon
Common chuckwalla
Death adder
Desert night lizard
Desert tortoise
Gila monster
Horned viper
House gecko
Jackson's chameleon
North American coral snake
Sandfish
Southern burrowing asp
Spiny agama
Texas alligator lizard
Texas blind snake
Western banded gecko

GRASSLAND
Bachia bresslaui

Black-headed python
Blackish blind snake
Black-necked spitting cobra
Boa constrictor
Boomslang
Common garter snake
Common sunbeam snake
Death adder
Desert tortoise
Eastern box turtle
Eastern hog-nosed snake
Galápagos tortoise
Gila monster
Indigo snake
Komodo dragon
Lesser blind snake
Milksnake
Nilgiri burrowing snake
Sand lizard
Six-lined racerunner
Southern burrowing asp
Texas alligator lizard
Texas blind snake
Two-legged wormlizard
Western banded gecko

LAKE AND POND
American alligator
American crocodile
Central American river turtle
Common caiman
Common garter snake
Cottonmouth
False coral snake
Green anaconda
Helmeted turtle
Little file snake
Matamata
Nile crocodile
North American coral snake
Painted turtle
Pig-nose turtle
Reticulated python

Snapping turtle
Spiny softshell
Stinkpot
Yellow-margined box turtle

OCEAN
Green seaturtle
Leatherback seaturtle
Little file snake
Loggerhead turtle
Sea krait

RAINFOREST
Black-headed bushmaster
Black-headed python
Blind lizard
Boa constrictor
Crocodile monitor
Emerald tree boa
False coral snake
Flying lizard
Green python
House gecko
Jackson's chameleon
King cobra
Lesser blind snake
Neotropical sunbeam snake
Southern bromeliad
  woodsnake
Splitjaw snakes
White-bellied wormlizard
Yellow-margined box turtle

RIVER AND STREAM
American alligator
American crocodile
Big-headed turtle
Central American river turtle
Common caiman
Common garter snake
Cottonmouth
Crocodile tegu

False coral snake
Gharial
Green anaconda
Helmeted turtle
Little file snake
Matamata
Nile crocodile
Painted turtle
Pig-nose turtle
Reticulated python
Snapping turtle
South American river turtle
Spiny softshell
Stinkpot
Yellow-margined box turtle

SEASHORE
Green seaturtle
Loggerhead turtle
Sea krait

UNKNOWN
False blind snake

WETLAND
American alligator
American crocodile
Broad-headed skink
Common caiman
Common garter snake
Cottonmouth
Green anaconda
Helmeted turtle
Komodo dragon
Little file snake
Nile crocodile
Pig-nose turtle
Red-tailed pipe snake
Reticulated python
Sea krait
Snapping turtle

Species List by Geographic Range

AFGHANISTAN
Gharial

ALGERIA
Common chameleon
Horned viper
Sandfish

ANGOLA
Black-necked spitting cobra
Boomslang
Helmeted turtle
Nile crocodile
Southern burrowing asp

ARCTIC OCEAN
Leatherback seaturtle

ARMENIA
White-bellied wormlizard

ATLANTIC OCEAN
Green seaturtle
Leatherback seaturtle
Loggerhead turtle

AUSTRALIA
Black-headed python
Blackish blind snake

Death adder
Frilled lizard
Green python
House gecko
Little file snake
Pig-nose turtle

AUSTRIA
Sand lizard

BANGLADESH
House gecko
King cobra
Little file snake
Reticulated python

BELARUS
Sand lizard

BELGIUM
Sand lizard

BELIZE
American crocodile
Boa constrictor
Central American river turtle
Common caiman
Indigo snake

Milksnake
Snapping turtle

BENIN
Boomslang
Helmeted turtle
Nile crocodile

BHUTAN
Gharial
Reticulated python

BOLIVIA
Boa constrictor
False coral snake
South American river turtle
White-bellied wormlizard

BOTSWANA
Boomslang
Helmeted turtle
Spiny agama

BRAZIL
Bachia bresslaui
Boa constrictor
Common caiman
Crocodile tegu

Early blind snake
Emerald tree boa
False coral snake
Green anaconda
Indigo snake
Matamata
South American river turtle
White-bellied wormlizard

BRUNEI
House gecko
King cobra
Little file snake
Red-tailed pipesnake
Reticulated python

BULGARIA
Sand lizard

BURKINA FASO
Black-necked spitting cobra
Boomslang
Helmeted turtle
Nile crocodile

BURUNDI
Black-necked spitting cobra
Boomslang
Helmeted turtle
Nile crocodile

CAMBODIA
Common sunbeam snake
House gecko
King cobra
Little file snake
Red-tailed pipesnake
Reticulated python

CAMEROON
Black-necked spitting cobra
Boomslang
Helmeted turtle
Nile crocodile

CANADA
Common garter snake
Eastern hog-nosed snake
Milksnake
Painted turtle
Snapping turtle
Spiny softshell
Stinkpot
Timber rattlesnake

CENTRAL AFRICAN REPUBLIC
Black-necked spitting cobra
Boomslang
Nile crocodile

CHAD
Boomslang
Sandfish

CHINA
Big-headed turtle
Common sunbeam snake
King cobra
Red-tailed pipesnake
Sand lizard
Yellow-margined box turtle

COLOMBIA
American crocodile
Boa constrictor
Common caiman
Crocodile tegu
Emerald tree boa
False coral snake
Green anaconda
Indigo snake
Matamata
Milksnake
Snapping turtle
South American river turtle
Southern bromeliad
  woodsnake
White-bellied wormlizard

COMOROS
Helmeted turtle

COSTA RICA
American crocodile
Black-headed bushmaster
Common caiman
Indigo snake
Milksnake
Neotropical sunbeam snake
Snapping turtle
Southern bromeliad woodsnake

CUBA
American crocodile
Milksnake
White-bellied wormlizard

CYPRUS
Common chameleon

CZECH REPUBLIC
Sand lizard

DEMOCRATIC REPUBLIC OF THE CONGO
Black-necked spitting cobra
Boomslang
Helmeted turtle
Nile crocodile
Southern burrowing asp

DENMARK
Sand lizard

DJIBOUTI
Boomslang
Helmeted turtle
Horned viper

DOMINICAN REPUBLIC
American crocodile
Milksnake
White-bellied wormlizard

ECUADOR
American crocodile
Common caiman
False coral snake
Galápagos tortoise
Matamata
Milksnake
Snapping turtle

EGYPT
Common chameleon
Horned viper
Sandfish

EL SALVADOR
American crocodile
Boa constrictor
Common caiman
Indigo snake
Milksnake
Neotropical sunbeam snake

EQUATORIAL GUINEA
Boomslang
Helmeted turtle
Nile crocodile

ERITREA
Boomslang
Helmeted turtle
Horned viper
Nile crocodile

ESTONIA
Sand lizard

ETHIOPIA
Agamodon anguliceps
Black-necked spitting cobra
Boomslang
Helmeted turtle
Nile crocodile

FIJI
House gecko

FRANCE
Sand lizard

FRENCH GUIANA
American crocodile
Boa constrictor
Common caiman
Emerald tree boa
False coral snake
Green anaconda
Indigo snake
Matamata
Milksnake
White-bellied wormlizard

GABON
Black-necked spitting cobra
Boomslang
Helmeted turtle
Nile crocodile

GAMBIA
Black-necked spitting cobra
Helmeted turtle
Nile crocodile

GERMANY
Sand lizard

GHANA
Boomslang
Helmeted turtle
Nile crocodile

GREECE
Common chameleon

GUATEMALA
American crocodile
Boa constrictor

Central American river turtle
Common caiman
Indigo snake
Knob-scaled lizard
Milksnake
Neotropical sunbeam snake
Snapping turtle

GUINEA
Black-necked spitting cobra
Boomslang
Helmeted turtle
Nile crocodile

GUINEA-BISSAU
Black-necked spitting cobra
Boomslang
Helmeted turtle
Nile crocodile

GUYANA
American crocodile
Boa constrictor
Common caiman
Emerald tree boa
False coral snake
Green anaconda
Indigo snake
Matamata
Milksnake
White-bellied wormlizard

HAITI
American crocodile
Milksnake
White-bellied wormlizard

HONDURAS
American crocodile
Boa constrictor
Common caiman
Indigo snake
Milksnake

Neotropical sunbeam snake
Snapping turtle

HUNGARY
Sand lizard

INDIA
Gharial
House gecko
King cobra
Little file snake
Nilgiri burrowing snake

INDIAN OCEAN
Green seaturtle
Leatherback seaturtle
Loggerhead turtle
Sea krait

INDONESIA
Blind lizard
Common sunbeam snake
Flying lizard
House gecko
King cobra
Komodo dragon
Little file snake
Red-tailed pipesnake
Reticulated python

IRAQ
Sandfish

ISRAEL
Common chameleon
Horned viper
Sandfish

IVORY COAST
Boomslang
Helmeted turtle
Nile crocodile

JAMAICA
American crocodile
Milksnake

JORDAN
Common chameleon
Horned viper
Sandfish

KENYA
Black-necked spitting cobra
Boomslang
Helmeted turtle
Jackson's chameleon
Nile crocodile

LAOS
Big-headed turtle
Common sunbeam snake
House gecko
King cobra
Red-tailed pipesnake
Reticulated python

LATVIA
Sand lizard

LEBANON
Common chameleon
Sandfish

LESOTHO
Boomslang
Helmeted turtle

LIBERIA
Boomslang
Helmeted turtle
Nile crocodile

LIBYA
Common chameleon
Horned viper
Sandfish

LITHUANIA
Sand lizard

LUXEMBOURG
Sand lizard

MACEDONIA
Sand lizard

MADAGASCAR
Armored chameleon
Helmeted turtle
House gecko
Nile crocodile

MALAWI
Boomslang
Helmeted turtle
Nile crocodile

MALAYSIA
Blind lizard
Common sunbeam snake
False blind snake
House gecko
King cobra
Little file snake
Red-tailed pipesnake
Reticulated python

MALI
Boomslang
Nile crocodile
Sandfish

MALTA
Common chameleon

MAURITANIA
Horned viper
Sandfish

MAURITIUS
Splitjaw snake

MEXICO
American crocodile
Boa constrictor
Cape spinytail iguana
Central American river turtle
Common caiman
Common chuckwalla
Desert night lizard
Desert tortoise
Eastern box turtle
Gila monster
Green anole
House gecko
Indigo snake
Knob-scaled lizard
Milksnake
Neotropical sunbeam snake
North American coral snake
Six-lined racerunner
Snapping turtle
Spiny softshell
Texas alligator lizard
Texas blind snake
Two-legged wormlizard
Western banded gecko

MOLDOVA
Sand lizard

MOROCCO
Common chameleon
Horned viper

MOZAMBIQUE
Boomslang
Helmeted turtle
Nile crocodile
Southern burrowing asp

MYANMAR
Big-headed turtle
Common sunbeam snake

House gecko
King cobra
Little file snake
Red-tailed pipesnake
Reticulated python

NAMIBIA
Black-necked spitting cobra
Boomslang
Helmeted turtle
Southern burrowing asp
Spiny agama

NEPAL
Gharial
King cobra

NETHERLANDS
Sand lizard

NEW ZEALAND
Tuatara

NICARAGUA
American crocodile
Boa constrictor
Common caiman
Indigo snake
Milksnake
Neotropical sunbeam snake
Snapping turtle
Southern bromeliad
  woodsnake

NIGER
Black-necked spitting cobra
Boomslang
Sandfish

NIGERIA
Black-necked spitting cobra
Boomslang
Helmeted turtle
Nile crocodile

PACIFIC OCEAN
Green seaturtle
Leatherback seaturtle
Loggerhead turtle
Sea krait

PAKISTAN
Gharial

PANAMA
American crocodile
Black-headed bushmaster
Boa constrictor
Common caiman
Indigo snake
Snapping turtle
Southern bromeliad
  woodsnake

PAPUA NEW GUINEA
Blind lizard
Crocodile monitor
Frilled lizard
Green python
House gecko
Little file snake
Pig-nose turtle

PARAGUAY
Bachia bresslaui
Boa constrictor
Early blind snake
White-bellied wormlizard

PERU
Boa constrictor
Common caiman
False coral snake
South American river turtle

PHILIPPINES
Blind lizard
House gecko
Little file snake
Reticulated python

POLAND
Sand lizard

REPUBLIC OF THE CONGO
Black-necked spitting cobra
Boomslang
Helmeted turtle
Nile crocodile

ROMANIA
Sand lizard

RUSSIA
Sand lizard

RWANDA
Black-necked spitting cobra
Boomslang
Helmeted turtle
Nile crocodile

SAMOA
House gecko

SÃO TOMÉ AND PRÍNCIPE
Helmeted turtle
Nile crocodile

SENEGAL
Black-necked spitting cobra
Helmeted turtle
Nile crocodile
Sandfish

SERBIA AND MONTENEGRO
Sand lizard

SIERRA LEONE
Boomslang
Helmeted turtle
Nile crocodile

SINGAPORE
Common sunbeam snake
False blind snake
House gecko
King cobra
Little file snake
Red-tailed pipesnake
Reticulated python

SLOVAKIA
Sand lizard

SLOVENIA
Sand lizard

SOLOMON ISLANDS
House gecko
Prehensile-tailed skink

SOMALIA
Agamodon anguliceps
Boomslang
Helmeted turtle

SOUTH AFRICA
Black-necked spitting cobra
Boomslang
Cape flat lizard
Helmeted turtle
Southern burrowing asp
Spiny agama

SPAIN
Common chameleon

SRI LANKA
House gecko
Little file snake

SUDAN
Black-necked spitting cobra
Boomslang

Helmeted turtle
Horned viper
Nile crocodile

SURINAME
American crocodile
Boa constrictor
Common caiman
Emerald tree boa
False coral snake
Green anaconda
Indigo snake
Matamata
Milksnake
White-bellied wormlizard

SWAZILAND
Boomslang
Helmeted turtle
Southern burrowing asp

SWEDEN
Sand lizard

SYRIA
Common chameleon
Horned viper
Sandfish

TAIWAN
Yellow-margined box turtle

TANZANIA
Black-necked spitting cobra
Boomslang
Helmeted turtle
Jackson's chameleon
Nile crocodile
Southern burrowing asp

THAILAND
Big-headed turtle

Blind lizard
Common sunbeam snake
House gecko
King cobra
Little file snake
Red-tailed pipesnake
Reticulated python

TIMOR-LESTE
House gecko
Little file snake
Red-tailed pipesnake

TOGO
Boomslang
Helmeted turtle
Nile crocodile

TUNISIA
Common chameleon
Horned viper

TURKEY
Common chameleon

TUVALU
House gecko

UGANDA
Black-necked spitting cobra
Boomslang
Helmeted turtle
Nile crocodile

UKRAINE
Sand lizard

UNITED KINGDOM
Sand lizard

UNITED STATES
American alligator
Broad-headed skink
Common chuckwalla
Common garter snake
Cottonmouth
Desert night lizard
Desert tortoise
Eastern box turtle
Eastern hog-nosed snake
Florida wormlizard
Gila monster
Green anole
House gecko
Indigo snake
Milksnake
North American coral snake
Painted turtle
Six-lined racerunner
Snapping turtle
Spiny softshell
Stinkpot
Texas alligator lizard
Texas blind snake
Timber rattlesnake
Western banded gecko

URUGUAY
Boa constrictor
White-bellied wormlizard

VANUATU
House gecko

VENEZUELA
American crocodile

Boa constrictor
Common caiman
Crocodile tegu
Emerald tree boa
False coral snake
Green anaconda
Indigo snake
Matamata
Milksnake
South American river turtle
White-bellied wormlizard

VIETNAM
Blind lizard
Common sunbeam snake
House gecko
King cobra
Little file snake
Red-tailed pipesnake
Reticulated python

YEMEN
Common chameleon
Helmeted turtle
Horned viper

ZAMBIA
Boomslang
Helmeted turtle
Nile crocodile
Southern burrowing asp

ZIMBABWE
Boomslang
Helmeted turtle
Nile crocodile
Southern burrowing asp

Index

Italic type indicates volume number; **boldface** type indicates entries and their pages; (ill.) indicates illustrations.

Argentinosaurus species, *1*: 2

Armadillo lizards, *2*: 244

Armored chameleons, *1*: 162–63, 162 (ill.), 163 (ill.)

Arrau. *See* South American river turtles

Asian giant softshells, *1*: 95–96

Asian giant tortoises, *1*: 11

Asian grass lizards, *2*: 222

Asian pipe snakes. *See* Pipe snakes

Asian river turtles, *1*: 11

Asian sunbeam snakes. *See* Sunbeam snakes

Asian water dragons, *1*: 146

Asiatic rock pythons, *2*: 355

Aspidites melanocephalus. See Blackheaded pythons

Atlantic Ridley seaturtles, *1*: 26

Atractaspididae. See African burrowing snakes

Atractaspis bibronii. See Southern burrowing asps

Australian pygmy monitors, *2*: 279

AustraloAmerican sidenecked turtles, *1*: **18–23**

B

Bachia bresslaui, *2*: 231–33, 231 (ill.), 232 (ill.)

Bachia species, *2*: 228

Ball pythons, *2*: 354

Banana boas. *See* Southern bromeliad woodsnakes

Banded geckos, western, *1*: 181–82, 181 (ill.), 182 (ill.)

Bearded dragon lizards, *1*: 146

Bibron's burrowing asps. *See* Southern burrowing asps

Bigheaded turtles, *1*: **72**, **76–80**, 78 (ill.), 79 (ill.), **82–83**

Bipedidae. See Molelimbed wormlizards

Bipes biporus. See Twolegged wormlizards

Bites, snake, *2*: 382

Black and white dwarf boas, *2*: 369

Black caimans, *1*: 116

Blackheaded bushmasters, *2*: 390–91, 390 (ill.), 391 (ill.)

Blackheaded pythons, *2*: 356–57, 356 (ill.), 357 (ill.)

Blackish blind snakes, *2*: 306–7, 306 (ill.), 307 (ill.)

Blacknecked spitting cobras, *2*: 419–20, 419 (ill.), 420 (ill.)

Blind lizards. *See* Blindskinks

Blind skinks. *See* Blindskinks

Blind snakes, *1*: **140**; *2*: **288–89**, **295**, **302–8**, **337**
   early, *2*: **288–94**, **295**
   false, *2*: **309–13**, 312 (ill.), 313 (ill.), **320**
   slender, *1*: **140**; *2*: **288–89**, **295–301**, **402**

Blindskinks, *1*: **186–89**, 188 (ill.), 189 (ill.); *2*: 260, 262

Bloodsucker agamids, Indian, *1*: 147

Blue spiny lizards, *1*: 169

Bluetail mole skinks, *2*: 252

Boa constrictors, *1*: 141, 142; *2*: 342–43, 346–47, 346 (ill.), 347 (ill.)

Boas, *2*: **342–52**, 353, 369, 370
   See also Neotropical sunbeam snakes; Splitjaw snakes

Bobtail skinks, *2*: 250–51

Bog turtles, small, *1*: 50

Boidae. See Boas

Bolyeriidae. See Splitjaw snakes

Boomslangs, *2*: 402, 403–4, 403 (ill.), 404 (ill.)

Bougainville's skinks, *2*: 251

Box turtles
   eastern, *1*: 55–57, 55 (ill.), 56 (ill.)
   yellowmargined, *1*: 61–63, 61 (ill.), 62 (ill.)

Brachiosaurus species, *1*: 1, 2

Brahminy blind snakes, *2*: 303

Broadheaded skinks, *2*: 255–56, 255 (ill.), 256 (ill.)

Broadley's mud turtles, *1*: 72

Bromeliad boas. *See* Southern bromeliad woodsnakes

Bromeliad dwarf boas. *See* Southern bromeliad woodsnakes

Bromeliad woodsnakes, *2*: 370, 372–73, 372 (ill.), 373 (ill.)

Brookesia perarmata. See Armored chameleons

Brother Islands tuataras, *1*: 132–35

Brown basilisk lizards, *1*: 168

Brown snakes, *2*: 416

Brown tree snakes, *2*: 402

Burrowing asps, *2*: 394–95, 396–97, 396 (ill.), 397 (ill.)

Burrowing boas. *See* Neotropical sunbeam snakes

Burrowing snakes
   African, *2*: **393–98**
   shieldtail, *2*: **315**

C

Caiman crocodilus. See Common caimans

Caiman lizards, Paraguayan, *2*: 236

Caimans, *1*: **114–22**

Calabar ground boas, *2*: 344

Calotes, *1*: **145–55**

Calyptommatus species, *2*: 228

Camouflage, by snakes and lizards, *1*: 141

Cape flat lizards, *2*: 246–47, 246 (ill.), 247 (ill.)

Cape spinytail iguanas, *1*: 170–71, 170 (ill.), 171 (ill.)

Carcharodontosaurus species, *1*: 2

Caretta caretta. See Loggerhead turtles

Water moccasins. *See* Cottonmouths
Water monitors, Merten's, *2:* 280
Water skinks, *2:* 250
Water snakes, *1:* 140; *2:* 400, 402
Western banded geckos, *1:* 181–82, 181 (ill.), 182 (ill.)
Western blind snakes, *2:* 295
Western sand lizards, *2:* 225
Western sandveld lizards, *2:* 222
Western slender blind snakes, *2:* 296
Western swamp turtles, *1:* 20
Western thread snakes, *2:* 295
Whiptail lizards, *1:* 142; *2:* **235–42**
Whitebellied wormlizards, *1:* 190, 191, 194–95, 194 (ill.), 195 (ill.)
Wood turtles, neotropical, *1:* 51, **58–63,** 77
Woodsnakes, *2:* **369–74**
World Conservation Union (IUCN) Red List of Threatened Species
    on African sidenecked turtles, *1:* 72
    on AfroAmerican river turtles, *1:* 83
    on Agamidae, *1:* 147
    on alligators, *1:* 116
    on American crocodiles, *1:* 128
    on American mud and musk turtles, *1:* 66
    on Anguidae, *2:* 262–63
    on armored chameleons, *1:* 163
    on AustraloAmerican sidenecked turtles, *1:* 20
    on bigheaded turtles, *1:* 80
    on blind snakes, *2:* 305
    on boas, *2:* 344
    on caimans, *1:* 116
    on Central American river turtles, *1:* 42
    on chameleons, *1:* 159, 163, 165
    on colubrids, *2:* 402
    on common chameleons, *1:* 165
    on crocodiles, *1:* 126, 128, 130–31
    on crocodillians, *1:* 105
    on desert tortoises, *1:* 93–94
    on eastern box turtles, *1:* 57
    on Elapidae, *2:* 416
    on Eurasian pond and river turtles, *1:* 60
    on false blind snakes, *2:* 311, 313
    on false coral snakes, *2:* 329
    on false gharials, *1:* 126
    on Galápagos tortoises, *1:* 91
    on geckos, *1:* 180
    on gharials, *1:* 111–12
    on gila monsters, *2:* 275, 277–78
    on girdled lizards, *2:* 245
    on goannas, *2:* 281–82
    on iguanidae, *1:* 169
    on Komodo dragons, *2:* 281–82, 284
    on Lacertidae, *2:* 223–24
    on leatherback seaturtles, *1:* 48
    on lizards, *1:* 143
    on Mexican beaded lizards, *2:* 275
    on monitors, *2:* 281–82
    on neotropical wood turtles, *1:* 60
    on New World pond turtles, *1:* 52
    on night lizards, *2:* 217
    on Nile crocodiles, *1:* 130–31
    on northern tuataras, *1:* 137
    on pignose turtles, *1:* 17
    on pitvipers, *2:* 382
    on plate lizards, *2:* 245
    on pygopods, *1:* 180
    on pythons, *2:* 355
    on seaturtles, *1:* 26, 31
    on skinks, *2:* 251–52
    on snakes, *1:* 143
    on snapping turtles, *1:* 34
    on softshell turtles, *1:* 97
    on South American river turtles, *1:* 86
    on splitjaw snakes, *2:* 366–67
    on Teiidae, *2:* 237
    on tortoises, *1:* 11, 88–89
    on tuataras, *1:* 135, 137
    on turtles, *1:* 11
    on vipers, *2:* 382
    on yellowmargined box turtles, *1:* 63
Worm snakes. *See* Slender blind snakes
Wormlizards, *1:* **139–44, 190–96**
    Florida, *1:* 191, **203–7,** 205 (ill.), 206 (ill.)
    molelimbed, *1:* 191, **197–202,** 204
    spadeheaded, *1:* 191, 204, **208–13**
    See also Blindskinks

X

Xantusia vigilis. See Desert night lizards
Xantusiidae. *See* Night lizards
Xenopeltidae. *See* Sunbeam snakes
Xenopeltis unicolor. See Common sunbeam snakes
Xenosauridae. *See* Knobscaled lizards
Xenosaurus grandis. See Knobscaled lizards